CONTE ...

1. Introducing Kenya 5
The Land 6
History in Brief 16
Government and Economy 25
The People 28

2. Central Kenya 33
Nairobi 34
Aberdare National Park 41
Mount Kenya National Park 43

3. Western Kenya 49
Masai Mara National Reserve 50
Lake Victoria 54

4. Great Rift Valley 61
Lake Turkana 62
Lake Baringo and Lake Bogoria 66
Lake Nakuru and Lake Naivasha 69

5. Northern and Eastern Kenya 79
Samburu and Buffalo Springs 80
Shaba National Reserve 82
Meru National Park 84

6. Southern Kenya 91
Amboseli National Park 92
Tsavo National Park 94

7. The Coral Coast 103
Old Mombasa Town 104
South and North Coasts 108
Lamu Archipelago 117

Travel Tips 122

Index 128

1
Introducing Kenya

Kenya covers an area slightly larger than France, and roughly the size of Texas in the United States. The equator almost exactly divides the country in half. With the Indian Ocean washing its eastern shores and the immense **Lake Victoria** on its western border, Kenya is truly a land of contrasts. From the snow-covered peaks of **Mount Kenya** astride the equator, to the warm sun-kissed beaches, the scenery embraces mountains, forests, deserts and lakes, plus a staggering diversity of wildlife.

Just as diverse is the proliferation of tribes and other peoples who have settled in this country, and the contrasts within Kenya's towns and cities: a good illustration is the contradiction between **Nairobi** and its modern high-rise buildings and traffic congestion, and **Lamu,** on the Indian Ocean, which still resembles an old Arab town and boasts only one motor car! Nairobi's infrastructure and its accessibility to many parts of the world make it an obvious first choice as a conference centre for many international organizations.

Most visitors are attracted to the country's coast, followed by its wonderful wildlife areas. Many come to climb **Mount Kenya**, and a smaller number is attracted by the deep-sea game-fishing, mainly around **Watamu** near **Malindi** on the north coast, and at **Shimoni** on the south coast near the Tanzanian border. Kenya also has many fine golf courses, with golfing safaris becoming a new tourist attraction. Visits to some of the national parks and reserves, as well as to the beaches, can easily be combined with a golfing vacation.

TOP ATTRACTIONS

*** **Masai Mara National Reserve**: Africa's finest wildlife area.
*** **Coral Coast**: unspoilt, sandy beaches, snorkelling and deep-sea fishing, ruins.
** **Mount Kenya**: climbing, walking, bird-watching and photographic opportunities.
** **Tsavo West National Park**: scenic, wildlife.
** **Amboseli National Park**: best place to see elephant herds, views of Kilimanjaro.
** **Lake Nakuru**: flocks of pink flamingo.

Opposite: *Diani Beach, on the south coast.*

FACTS AND FIGURES

Highest mountain is Mount
Kenya at 5199m (17,058ft);
although it lies on the equator, its summit and upper
slopes are covered in snow
and ice all year round.
Longest river is the Tana; it
flows for almost 605km
(376 miles) from the Mount
Kenya and Aberdare slopes
eastwards to the Indian
Ocean, north of Malindi.
Largest waterfall is Gura
Falls, around 457m (1500ft)
high, in the Aberdare
National Park.

Opposite: *the Mara River
makes its serpentine way
through the Masai Mara
National Reserve.*
Below: *an unusual view
of Lake Magadi at the end
of the long rains.*

THE LAND

Kenya has several very distinct geographic regions.
Two-thirds of the country, in the north and east, is
mainly arid semidesert composed of acacia and commi-
phora bush, while the south and southwest comprise
predominantly tree-dotted savanna at an altitude of
between 900 and 1525m (3000 to 5000ft). In the east is a
narrow fertile strip of land bordered by the Indian
Ocean. Inland from this coastal stretch, the land quickly
rises in altitude and soon becomes dry, inhospitable
thorn-bush country. **Lake Victoria**, the world's second
largest freshwater lake, lies to the west bordered by
richly arable agricultural land.

Cutting through the country in a north–south direction is the **Great Rift Valley**, containing a string of lakes
(most of which are strongly alkaline) and a number of
mostly dormant volcanos. To the centre of Kenya, on the
eastern edge of the Rift, an area of high plateau rises
above 1829m (6000ft) and is dominated by **Mount
Kenya**, the **Aberdare mountain range** and the Rift
Valley. This area, aptly named the Highlands, is one of
the world's richest agricultural areas. West of the Rift
Valley in central Kenya lies the **Mau Escarpment**, another

high-lying rich farming area, which slowly falls away westwards down to Lake Victoria. To the north of the lake, on the border with Uganda, the second highest mountain within Kenya's boundary – one of the peaks of Mount Elgon's volcanic cone – rises to 4321m (14,177ft).

Mountains and Rivers

The upper slopes of the country's highest mountain, **Mount Kenya**, and its two adjacent salients make up the Mount Kenya National Park. The **Aberdare** mountain range, also a national park (the official new name of this park is Nyandarua but is hardly used), actually consists of two peaks, namely Ol Doinyo Satima and Kinangop. These are approximately 40km (25 miles) apart. Between these two peaks is a

moorland plateau covered in coarse, tussocky grasses and giant heaths interspersed with forest patches.

To the west, the Kenya-Uganda border bisects **Mount Elgon**. The mountain slopes protruding into Kenya form a national park whose principal attractions are game-viewing, climbing and walking. There is also trout fishing. In the northeast of the country, the forested mountain of **Marsabit** rises out of a low, arid plain; it was made famous in the 1920s by the early game photographers, Martin and Osa Johnson, and more recently by Ahmed, an elephant sporting a spectacular pair of tusks and given presidential protection in 1970.

A number of mountain streams flowing from the slopes of Mount Kenya and the Aberdares converge to form the source of the **Tana**, Kenya's longest river. Most of the river's length traverses dry bush country, and

KENYA'S VISITORS	
Visitors recorded in Kenya's national parks and reserves (1997):	
Amboseli N.P.	117,200
Lake Nakuru N.P.	132,100
Masai Mara N.R.	118,300
Nairobi N.P.	149,600
Tsavo West N.P.	88,600
Tsavo East N.P.	123,200
Aberdares N.P.	59,000
Malindi Marine N.R.	27,000
Mount Kenya N.P.	14,800
Most tourists are from Germany, Britain, Canada and the USA.	

eventually discharges into the Indian Ocean south of Lamu. Both Meru and Kora national parks have their borders along the Tana. This river is also a major producer of hydroelectric power, supplying approximately 80% of Kenya's power; five hydroelectric dams exist along the Tana's banks.

The **Athi River** rises near Nairobi, and flows through the Tsavo East National Park and along the base of the **Yatta Plateau** on its way to the Indian Ocean. The 306km-long (190 miles) Yatta Plateau is one of the world's longest lava flows. After passing through Lugard's Falls (named after Lord Lugard who travelled up the river on his way to Uganda in 1890 where he was to become governor) in the Tsavo East National Park, the Athi changes its name to the **Galana** and turns eastwards, flowing through the park's arid thorn-bush country. As the Galana leaves Tsavo its name changes to **Sabaki**, which slowly meanders through riverine forest before meeting the Indian Ocean just north of the resort town of Malindi.

The **Mara River** rises in the Mau forest, flowing westwards through the Masai Mara National Reserve and on into the Serengeti National Park in Tanzania, from where it runs into Lake Victoria – source of the Nile. The **Saum-Turkwel** River has its source on Mount Elgon and heads northwards to Lake Turkana where Kenya's latest hydroelectric power plant in the Turkwel gorge has been completed. When operating to full capacity, it is expected to be Kenya's biggest producer of electrical power.

Seas and Shores

Lapped by the warm Indian Ocean, Kenya's coastline, from just north of Kiwaiyu on the Somalian border to Lunga Lunga on the Tanzanian border, boasts miles and miles of beautiful white beaches, interspersed with tidal creeks and mangrove swamps.

COMPARATIVE CLIMATE CHART	NAIROBI				LAKE NAKURU				MOMBASA			
	SUM **JAN**	**AUT** **APR**	**WIN** **JULY**	**SPR** **OCT**	**SUM** **JAN**	**AUT** **APR**	**WIN** **JULY**	**SPR** **OCT**	**SUM** **JAN**	**AUT** **APR**	**WIN** **JULY**	**SPR** **OCT**
MAX TEMP. °C	27	26	23	27	27	26	24	25	32	31	28	30
MIN TEMP. °C	13	15	11	13	8	11	10	9	23	24	21	22
MAX TEMP. °F	80	79	73	80	80	79	75	77	90	88	82	86
MIN TEMP. °F	55	59	52	55	46	52	50	48	73	75	70	72
HOURS SUN	9	6	4	7	9	6	7	6	8	7	7	9
RAINFALL in	2	6	.5	2	1	6	4	2	.5	4	1	2
RAINFALL mm	50	154	14	49	34	160	95	59	18	109	35	62

Opposite: running south from Mombasa is a string of enchanting lagoons, creeks and beaches and, here and there, relics of ancient Arab settlement.

Most of the tourist hotels are to be found to the north and south of Mombasa, Kenya's second largest city. Malindi, on the north coast, is also a major tourist centre. A wide variety of beach hotels line the shore from the pristinely modern to Arab-styled architecture blending perfectly into the local surroundings. Along the coast there are many remnants of old Arab civilizations that flourished 500 years ago, the best examples of which are the 15th-century ruins of the town of **Gedi**, just south of Malindi. Near to Gedi is **Mida Creek**, world famous in ornithological circles for its huge concentrations and variety of shore birds. The **Lamu Archipelago**, too, is steeped in history: tumbling ruins reflect the rich cultural influences from centuries of Arab-African civilization. On Manda Island the ruins of **Takwa** dating back to the 16th or 17th centuries, are as archaeologically significant as Gedi.

The coast's marine national reserves offer a rainbow-coloured array of fish and wonderful coral – a haven for snorkellers and scuba divers. Watamu and Malindi to the north are renowned for their exhilarating deep-sea fishing (sailfish, marlin, tunny).

Climate

As most of Kenya is high-plateau country it enjoys a pleasant climate: warm days and cool nights are the norm for most of the year. In the Highlands and Rift Valley it is not unusual to experience temperatures of around 30°C (86°F) during the day, while at night one can happily sit in front of a log fire, as the temperature drops below 10°C (50°F). Around Lake Victoria and at the coast, however, it can be very hot and humid, although the sea breezes off the Indian Ocean make a stay at the coast very pleasant.

For most of Kenya, the main rains normally occur during the period March to May, followed by a short rainy period towards the end of October, lasting until early December. However, there are local variations. Along the coastal strip the rains are mainly from May until July and again in November. In the areas around Lake Victoria, the lake itself has a strong influence on the weather and it can rain, usually at night, during every month of the year.

Above: *the pale pink springtime blooms of a Cape chestnut grace the Aberdare uplands. The species belongs to the citrus family.*

Above right: *a shy bushbuck, relative of the much larger kudu and invariably seen near water, pauses in the woodland fringes of Lake Nakuru.*

Opposite: *a typical landscape in the alpine heath zone.*

The amount of rainfall varies considerably across the country: western Kenya receives from 1016 to 1270mm (40 to 50in) a year; the central highlands and Rift Valley, 762 to 1016mm (30 to 40in); while the northern and eastern areas are lucky if they receive 254mm (10in) a year.

Plant Life

The country's coastal strip, although only a few miles wide, has a rich and varied vegetation: mangroves grow in the tidal bays and creeks, and mangrove poles are an important export commodity. Along the coastline coconut palms, cashew-nut trees and sisal plantations dominate.

Remnants of the once-extensive coastal forest still remain (the **Arabuko-Sokoke** near Malindi has been proclaimed a forest reserve thus protecting this rapidly dwindling indigenous tract).

The coast's fertile land quickly gives way to dry woodland and then to arid bush country, which covers almost two-thirds of Kenya. Extensive montane forests remain in the central highlands, surrounded by rich agricultural land where wheat, maize, coffee and other crops are cultivated. Further west, in the highland bordering Lake Victoria, the major tea-growing area is centred on the town of Kericho. On Lake Victoria's shore to the north of Kisumu, **Kakamega Forest** is a remnant of the once-great rainforest that stretched from Africa's west coast to its east.

Of special interest within Kenya's diverse vegetation zones is the highest-occurring one on the country's mountain slopes – the alpine heath zone. Three distinctive vegetation belts ring Kenya's mountains: grassland, forest and finally the weird and wonderful alpine sector.

The forest zone follows the grasslands at around 2440m (800ft) and consists of bamboo and giant *Podocarpus* species (yellowwoods); this slowly gives way to leafy forests of twisted lianas and hagenia trees draped with orchids and Spanish moss, also known as 'old man's beard'. At the upper limit of this zone – around 3050m (10,000ft) – giant St John's wort (*Hypericum* sp.) with its bright yellow flowers begins to appear. Open areas of tussock grass featuring giant heaths (*Erica arborea*) also hung with strands of old man's beard now occur. Growing amidst the coarse grasses are everlasting flowers (*Helichrysum* sp.), turquoise delphiniums, and proteas – one of which produces a spiky yellow flower that resembles cat's claws, and is thus often referred to as 'lion claws'. Higher up are the fascinating giant lobelias and groundsels with, in the wetter areas, red-hot pokers and fiery gladioli.

At these high altitudes the climate is severe, with hot, summer conditions during the day and icy winter temperatures at night.

> **DISAPPEARING FOREST**
>
> Kenya is having a difficult time conserving her forests. Certain trees are required for the timber trade, but the forests are also under pressure from the human population, which is cutting down trees to make way for the planting of crops. Forests occurring within national parks are well protected. The unique Kakamega Forest is only partially protected; a small part is national park area, with the rest a reserve that is constantly under threat: a few years ago part of the forest was cleared for the growing of tea.

Kenya has 57 national parks,
reserves and marine reserves;
almost 10% of the country's
land area is devoted to
wildlife conservation. The
national parks are owned
and run by the government.
A portion of the revenue
earned is allocated to the
local people living in the area;
no human settlement is
allowed. Local county coun-
cils own the **national
reserves**; wildlife is protected and has precedence,
some human habitation is
permitted, and livestock may
share the area at times. As
for **game sanctuaries** and
conservation areas,
landowners can establish
such areas to protect a particular animal or certain plant
life. They are allowed to use
the rest of their land for
other purposes; a good
example of this is Lewa
Wildlife Conservancy.

Wild Kingdom

Kenya's wildlife heritage is for many people its prime
attraction. The best-known wildlife areas are **Amboseli
National Park**, which is dominated by the snow-covered
Mount Kilimanjaro, and the **Masai Mara National
Reserve**, famous for its abundance of game and its many
predators. Other impressive wildlife areas are the three
national reserves to the northeast, set in arid bush country along the banks of the area's only river, the Ewaso
Nyiro: they are **Samburu**, **Buffalo Springs** and **Shaba**.
These reserves are notable for the unusual species they
contain: the endangered Grevy's zebra, herds of beisa
oryx, the long-necked gerenuk and the very striking
reticulated giraffe.

To the south and east of the country lie **Tsavo East**
and **Tsavo West** national parks which are bisected by
the main Nairobi–Mombasa highway. Together, the
parks form one of the largest wildlife areas in the entire

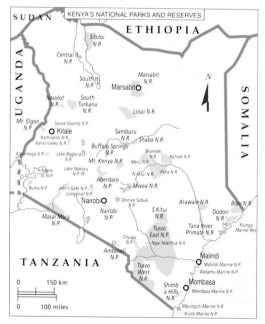

Opposite: *a lioness at rest
in the Masai Mara reserve,
part of the famed Serengeti
ecosystem. For three or four
months each year the
annual migration brings
more than two million
large herbivores onto the
Mara grasslands, and the
predators flourish.*

world – 20,812km² (8035 sq miles) – in contrast to the tiny **Saiwa Swamp National Park** which is only 2km² (half a square mile) in size, and is possibly the world's smallest national park. Another park deserving a mention is **Lake Nakuru**, famous for its spectacular flamingos: sometimes as many as 1.5 million make their home there.

Kenya's numerous and varied birdlife (1075 species) is attracting increasing numbers of ornithologists and bird-watchers, and is the fastest growing sector of the tourist industry. Sixty-six different birds of prey have been recorded (excluding owls); among these are 19 eagles, from the mighty martial to the tiny pygmy falcon. Eight species of vulture are found in Kenya, namely the palm nut, African white-backed, Rüppell's, hooded, Egyptian, lappet-faced and white-headed species, and finally, the rarest, the lammergeyer.

Conserving Kenya's Natural Heritage

Like every other African country, Kenya's wildlife areas, forests and special habitats are continuously being threatened, mostly by an expanding population's need for more land, by increasing urbanization and industrial

---

WHERE TO SPOT THE BIG FIVE

● Lion: a nocturnal hunter, but easiest cat to see in the Masai Mara during the day.
● Leopard: shy and nocturnal, it can however usually be seen in the Masai Mara, Samburu and Lake Nakuru reserves on early morning and late afternoon drives.
● Elephant: seen in most wildlife areas (except Nairobi and Saiwa Swamp parks); best place is Amboseli, around swamps at midday.
● Buffalo: most dangerous of Africa's animals, can best be seen in the Masai Mara and Aberdare national parks.
● Rhino: both black and white species, most confined to protected areas; see them in Nairobi, Nakuru and Aberdare parks; Solio Ranch and Lewa Conservancy.

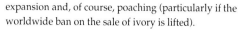

KENYA'S ORNITHOLOGICAL HERITAGE

Kenya has 1075 bird species. Only Zaïre in Africa – four times larger in area than Kenya – has more species. Kenya holds the record for the largest number of birds seen in a 24-hour period: 340, seen by Terry Stevenson, John Fanshaw and Andy Roberts (a team from the USA has recorded a higher total in South America, but a substantial amount of the birds were only heard and not seen). Kenya also holds the world record for the greatest number of birds seen in a 48-hour period: 496, seen by Don Turner, David Pearson and the world-famous wildlife film maker, Alan Root.

Below: *the colourful Hartlaub's turaco.*

expansion and, of course, poaching (particularly if the worldwide ban on the sale of ivory is lifted).

But there have been signs of hope. Since Dr Richard Leakey and the Kenya Wildlife Service took over the running of the national parks (Dr David Western replaced Dr Leakey in 1994, and Dr Leakey was reappointed as director in 1998), there has been a dramatic drop in poaching; rhino have not been poached for over two years. Entry fees for the national parks have been raised substantially and a proportion of this now goes directly to the people living adjacent to these wildlife reserves. The money is used to help the local people build health clinics, schools and improve the roads. There are plans to fence the parks (at the time of writing, work had started on the Aberdare National Park). This has proved to be very popular with the local people as the fencing stops the wildlife from raiding their *shambas* (small farms).

The East African Wildlife Society raises large sums of money to fund various wildlife research programmes. Also strongly active, and perhaps most important of all, the organization Wildlife Clubs of Kenya teaches the citizens of tomorrow the importance of conservation. Many national parks now have educational facilities, exhibits and interpretation centres. The Nairobi National Park has a very active education centre where groups of schoolchildren can experience wildlife conservation lectures and film shows.

Birding Hot Spots

Kakamega Forest: a visit to this forest is a must for every keen bird-watcher; many bird species not normally found elsewhere

in Kenya can be spotted here (blue-headed bee-eater, yellow-billed barbet, brown-eared woodpecker, dusky tit, Cameroon sombre greenbul and yellow-bellied wattle-eye).
Lake Baringo: over 400 species have been recorded here; not to be missed is an early morning walk with Lake Baringo Club's resident ornithologist

Above: *a bevy of vulturine guineafowl makes its way through the Samburu scrub north of Mount Kenya.*

and a boat trip along the lake shore (Verreaux's eagle, Goliath heron, Hemprich's and Jackson's hornbill).
Samburu-Buffalo Springs reserves: many species found only in the north and east of Kenya can be seen here (pygmy falcon, Somali bee-eater, buff-crested bustard, vulturine guineafowl, magpie starling and the localized Donaldson Smith's sparrow weaver).
Mount Kenya: Naro Moru River Lodge, at the base of Mount Kenya, is a bird-watcher's dream; it is not uncommon to see 10 different sunbird species on one visit to the area (the tacazze sunbird is the highlight). Other birds to be spotted include African black duck, emerald cuckoo, red-fronted parrot, giant kingfisher, Hartlaub's turaco, cinnamon-chested bee-eater, mountain wagtail and white-starred forest robin.
Mountain Lodge: in addition to the birds listed for the Naro Moru River Lodge, this night game-viewing spot on the slopes of Mount Kenya has Doherty's bush shrike, grey-headed Negro finch and Abyssinian crimsonwing.
Other places are **Lake Nakuru** for flamingos and shorebirds, **Lake Naivasha** for a variety of waterbirds and **Masai Mara** for vultures, eagles and other birds of prey; **Arabuko-Sokoke** conceals the world's rarest owl, the Sokoke scops owl.

Above: Maasai family members outside their home.

HISTORY IN BRIEF

As new evidence comes to light, the theory that East Africa – or Kenya, for that matter – is the cradle of mankind is gaining strength among scientists. Believed to be the first signs of ancient man in Kenya is the collection of stone tools found – and later some 400 hominid fossils – by anthropologist-palaeontologist Dr Richard Leakey at the desolate **Koobi Fora** excavation site on the eastern shores of Lake Turkana. One particular skull is dated 2.5 million years ago.

The first indigenous people to wander across Kenya in search of food were hunter-gatherers who were later forced out or assimilated by later arriving people. **Kikuyu** legend weaves stories around pygmies who, they recounted, lived in the forests to which the Kikuyu were slowly migrating. The **Ndorobo** people, a small tribe who still hunt with bows and arrows, and gather honey in traditional ways, are very likely descendants of these early people.

As a result of migrations from north Africa around 3500 years ago, the region was slowly being settled by people of three different origins, classified mainly by the language they spoke: the Cushitic, Nilotic and Bantu peoples. The Cushites were nomadic pastoralists moving down from Ethiopia, while the Nilotic tribe, also pastoralists, originated from the Nile valley (the Southern Nilotes settled in the Lake Turkana area and are the ancestors of the present Turkana and Maasai peoples). The Bantu people were iron-makers and agriculturalists (which they still are today), and they form the vast majority of present-day Kenyans. Unfortunately, little is known of these tribal movements as no written records appear to have been kept.

KENYA'S INDIGENOUS PEOPLES

• The **Bantu** tribe is made up of two groups: eastern and western. The eastern group is composed of the Kikuyu, Embu, Meru and Kamba, while the western comprises the Abaluyia and the Kisii.
• The **Nilotic** people are split into three groups: the highland group, which includes the Kipsigis, Nandi and Tugen; the plains group represented by the well-known Maasai and the Samburu; and the lake group, the Luo, who probably moved into present-day Kenya as recently as 400 years ago from the southern Sudan.
• The Somalis make up the majority of the **Cushitic** peoples.
• Other groups are the Galla and the Rendille.

The Birth of Swahili

The arrival of Islam on the coast around the 9th century through the interaction of passing traders left a rich cultural and architectural legacy. Between the 10th and 15th centuries, as a result of the large trade network that covered the Indian Ocean, a series of cities and towns was established along the East African coast, from Somalia in the north to Mozambique in the south. The history of this settlement by Arab and Persian peoples was recorded in Kiswahili (a name derived from the Arabic word *sahel*, for 'coast'). Eventually, the architects of these cities integrated with the coastal Africans creating an Arab-African culture that today is known as Swahili.

In 1498 Vasco da Gama, the Portuguese sailor-explorer, called at Mombasa to pick up a navigator who would guide him to India (his arrival was not welcomed by the Arabs and he was forced to sail on to Malindi). Da Gama's travels paved the way for other adventurers to explore the East African coast. Following on from this, the coastal peoples were increasingly subjected to

GALLA TRIBE

The Galla people originated from southern Ethiopia. Galla means 'wandering'; they are indeed highly mobile, constantly in search of water and grazing for their herds, which include camels. Their simple, dome-shaped huts are made from doum palm leaves, woven into mats, and laid onto pliable saplings, which are placed in a circle in the ground and tied together in the centre. They now live in the area around the Tana River in Eastern Kenya.

Below left: *Lamu's marketplace, next to the Old Fort.* **Below:** *one of Lamu's beautifully carved doors.*

THOMSON'S EXPEDITION

Joseph Thomson's Rift Valley explorations proved of some importance; it was he who named the Aberdares (after Lord Aberdare, president of the Royal Geographical Society), a mountain range rising above the Kinangop Plateau, which he climbed while at Lake Naivasha. Passing around the northern edge of the Aberdares and on to the Laikipia Plateau, he saw Mount Kenya, so confirming Krapf's discovery. He also came across a waterfall in this region, which was named Thomson's Falls after him (now renamed Nyahururu). Next, he walked to Lake Baringo, where he spent some time mapping the area. He then headed westwards, crossing the Kerio Valley, the Uasin Gishu Plateau and finally reaching Lake Victoria, where he made the decision to turn back.

pressure throughout the 16th and 17th centuries, not only from the Portuguese but also from the fierce Galla warriors, a migratory nomadic people originating from Ethiopia.

The Portuguese eventually captured Mombasa in 1505 and in 1593, they commenced building Fort Jesus; here they held sway until 1698 when the fort was captured by Sayyid Said, the Sultan of Oman and Zanzibar. During Portuguese rule there had been little contact with inland tribes because of hostility and fear, which was effective in keeping Kenya largely free of the slave trade that was well underway during that period.

First European Explorers

The first Europeans to explore Kenya were probably **F.L. Krapf** and **F. Rebmann**, two German missionaries working on behalf of the Church Missionary Society. In 1847 Rebmann explored inland as far as the Taita Hills. In the following year, on 11 May, Rebmann became the first European to record having seen the snow- and ice-covered Mount Kilimanjaro. In 1849 Krapf saw Kilimanjaro for the first time, and later, from a hill near Kitui, he sighted Mount Kenya. Then in 1882 a German doctor, **Gustav Fischer**, who was embarking on a scientific collecting expedition, entered Kenya along the Rift Valley from Tanzania and eventually walked as far north

Opposite: *a close wildlife encounter, with Mount Kilimanjaro providing a magnificent backdrop.*
Right: *flamingos congregate at Lake Bogoria in the Baringo district of the Rift Valley. Europeans first explored the area in the 1880s, when Joseph Thomson led a Royal Geographical Society expedition to Lake Victoria.*

as Naivasha. On his way back to the coast he passed through Hell's Gate, where his name is still remembered in the form of a column of rock called Fischer's Column.

The next explorer was **Joseph Thomson**, who led a Royal Geographic Society expedition in 1883. From the coast he walked through what is now Amboseli National Park and on to Ngong, near present-day Nairobi, which was then a stopping-off point on the edge of the Rift Valley for ivory caravans. From Ngong he descended into the Rift Valley, which he penetrated as far north as Lake Baringo. Here, he cut westwards to Lake Victoria, where he then decided to turn back. Thomson stopped off first to visit the now famous Elephant Caves on Mount Elgon, then made his way to Lakes Baringo, Nakuru and Naivasha, before finally returning to Mombasa.

The next European explorer to pass this way was **James Hannington** who had been appointed Bishop of Buganda (in present-day Uganda). Hannington discovered a lake that Joseph Thomson had missed, which was later named Lake Hannington (now known as Lake Bogoria) in his honour. Hannington was later murdered when he arrived at the Nile.

Count Samuel Teleki von Szek and his companion **Lieutenant Ludwig von Höhnel** were the next explorers to follow Thomson's route and in 1887 arrived at the foot of Mount Kenya, which Teleki tried unsuccessfully to climb. They then went on to Lake Baringo and continued northwards to discover a new lake, which they named Lake Rudolf, after the crown prince of Austria. The following year in 1889, **Frederick Jackson**, who later became Sir Frederick Jackson and the first governor of the Colony of Kenya, led an expedition sponsored by the Imperial British East Africa Company to explore the territories it had been granted.

Above: *one of the grand old steam work-horses on display in Nairobi's evocative Railway Museum.*

THE LUNATIC LINE

In order to build the Uganda Railway – dubbed the 'Lunatic Line' by poet Henry Labouchère – thousands of workers were brought over from India (mainly Punjabis who were of the Sikh religion) owing to the problems experienced with recruiting local tribespeople to do the heavy work. During construction, hundreds of these Indian workers died of disease, malaria being the main culprit, and at least 28 were killed by lion. Heavy rains washed away miles of embankment; excessive heat was a big problem in the Taru Desert area, while bitterly cold weather, ice and sleet had to be endured at the Mau summit.

Formation of the Imperial British East Africa Company

Meanwhile, during this time of exploration, the scramble for Africa had begun. In 1877 the Sultan of Zanzibar offered William MacKinnon (later 'Sir') of the British East Africa Association a concession to administer mainland East Africa as his vassal; the offer was not accepted. In 1885, at the Berlin Conference attended by 13 European nations and the USA, it was decided that the Sultan's rule did not extend beyond the 10-mile strip along the East African coast. The Sultan again offered the mainland to the British East Africa Association in 1887; this time it was accepted, with the power to exercise full judicial and political authority and to levy customs duties. The company was granted a Royal Charter in April 1888 and renamed the Imperial British East Africa Company.

In 1890 the Anglo-German Agreement was signed, giving interior Tanganyika to the Germans, and the whole of Uganda and interior Kenya to Britain. Uganda became a British protectorate in 1894; it was considered to have great potential, and more importantly, it would enable Britain to control the source of the River Nile. Uganda covered a much larger area at this time: its eastern areas included much of modern western Kenya, stretching as far east as Naivasha in the Rift Valley.

The Building of the Uganda Railway

Early in 1885 the British Parliament decided to build a railway 965km (600 miles) long from Mombasa to Kisumu (then part of Uganda). Also in the same year, Britain took over the administration of the Imperial British East Africa Company and the 16km (10 miles) coastal strip on behalf of the Sultan of Zanzibar. As a result, all the land from the coast to the Ugandan border

Left: *Kikuyu in ceremonial mode. Largest of Kenya's ethnic groups, the Kikuyu began farming in the fertile area south of Mount Kenya some 400 years ago, later coming into conflict with European settlers in quest of good land.*

became a protectorate known as the British East African Protectorate. The building of the Uganda Railway was a mammoth task, costing the British Government £5 million – a lot of money in those days. Work was started in 1895, the first rail laid in 1896, and it took four years to reach what's now Nairobi, finally reaching Kisumu in 1901.

The railway not only ensured better access to Uganda but also opened up Kenya to the early settlers. It was about this time that Lord Delamere settled in the Rift Valley on a 40,500ha (98,840 acres) ranch near Nakuru. Over the years, despite Delamere's decreasing wealth and after failures and setbacks, he proved that the Highlands were fertile and very suitable for settlement.

In 1902 the border between Uganda and Kenya was adjusted to its present position, leaving the Uganda railway firmly in Kenya. It was not until 1931 that the railway eventually reached Kampala, Uganda's capital.

Kenya became a protectorate in 1905, when its administration was transferred from the Foreign Office to the Colonial Office and then became the East African Protectorate.

After World War I there was a big influx of European settlers; unfortunately most knew little of farming; farms were either given away to lottery winners or sold at a nominal cost on long-term credit.

Rumblings of Discontent

In 1920, the status of Kenya was changed from a protectorate to a crown colony, except for the coastal strip which remained a protectorate under lease from the Sultan of Zanzibar. At this time the settler population was about 9000, and it appeared that Kenya was on its way to becoming a permanent 'white man's country'. But there were also signs of African disenchantment. In 1921, the Young Kikuyu Association was formed by Henry Thuku, a telephone operator at the treasury; in the following year, the association drew up a petition containing a number of grievances concerning land, and

JOMO KENYATTA

A Kikuyu, Jomo Kenyatta wasborn in 1882, north of Nairobi; educated at mission school, at 29 joined Nairobi Municipal Council as water-meter inspector; became involved in politics, changed name to Jomo Kenyatta, went into self-imposed exile in England in 1931; returned to Kenya in 1946, elected head of KAU a year later; arrested October 1952 by colonial government and incarcerated; while in jail, elected president of KANU; released Aug 1961, in Nov led delegation of KANU delegates to London to discuss Kenya's future; first general elections held May 1963; Kenyatta elected MP for Gahundu; Kenya granted internal self-government 1 Jun, Kenyatta first prime minister. Independence on 12 Dec 1964, Kenyatta became first president, succeeded by Daniel arap Moi in August 1978.

the carrying of a *kipande*, or registration card. The petition led to Harry Thuku's arrest. A crowd gathered outside the Central Police Station where he was being held, shots were fired and at least 23 Africans were killed or died later of their injuries. Thuku was later deported.

The settlers suffered a further setback when a British Government White Paper revived the old policy of 'Africa for the Africans'. Called the Devonshire White Paper, it stated: 'Kenya is an African territory … the interests of the African native must be paramount, and that if and when those interests and the interests of the immigrant races should conflict, then the former should prevail.' In the same year Mzee Jomo Kenyatta became a member of the committee of the East Africa Association (Mzee, a term given to Kenyatta by his people, is one of respect meaning 'father' or 'elder').

There was much discontent among the settler population, and there was even talk of rebellion, but as their numbers were never significant enough, the talk soon fizzled. In 1925, due to pressure, the name of the East Africa Association was changed to the Kikuyu Central Association; in 1928 Mzee Kenyatta became its secretary and started the Kikuyu newspaper *Mwigwithania* (the reconciler). The following year Kenyatta went to England to make personal representation to the British

Government about Kikuyu grievances and in 1930, before returning to Kenya, he published their injustices and demands in the British press. He returned to Britain in 1931 to continue his work, and Harry Thuku was released from detention. In 1932 tribal reserves were established, to be administered along tribal lines – Maasailand is an example. In the same year, Jomo Kenyatta returned to England to give evidence before the Carter Commission.

During 1940 the Kikuyu Central Association, the Ukamba Members Association and the Taita Hills

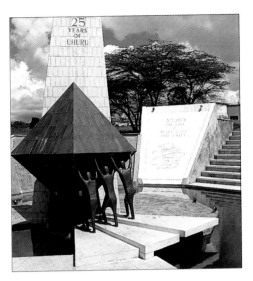

Opposite: *Jomo Kenyatta (left), father of modern Kenya, and Dr Jonas Savimbi of UNITA.*
Left: *the 24m (79ft) monument in the Uhuru Gardens, on the way to Nairobi National Park, where Kenya finally gained its freedom from colonial rule. Surrounding the monument are lush grounds laid out within a 'map' of the country.*

Association were banned and their leaders arrested. However in 1944, the first African, Mr Eliud Mathu, was nominated to the Legislative Council, replacing two Europeans overseeing African interests. Late in 1946 Kenyatta returned to Kenya and in the following year replaced James Gichuru as president of the Kenya Africa Union (KAU), previously known as the Kenya African Study Union.

Mau Mau Uprising

During 1948 the first stirrings of the Mau Mau freedom fight began, and in 1952 Jomo Kenyatta together with five of his comrades were arrested; on 20 October, a State of Emergency was declared.

Armies of freedom fighters made up mostly of Kikuyu moved into the forests of Mount Kenya and the Aberdares to wage guerrilla warfare on the European population. This rebellion lasted until 1957, but the emergency was not declared over until 1960. During this time, changes were taking place. In 1957 eight African members were elected to the Legislative Council, and in 1959 a turning point in African representation on the Council occurred when 25 African members were elected with 15 Asians, 5 Arabs and 46 Europeans. African membership continued to rise and non-African membership fell.

> **MAU MAU**
>
> The Kikuyu settled around Mt Kenya, the Aberdares and north of Nairobi. These areas also attracted European settlers. Trouble started with the slaughter of a European farmer's cattle in 1953, followed by the killing of a number of Kikuyus for their loyalty to the colonial government. The rebellion became known as Mau Mau; other tribes were also involved – mostly Luo and Maasai. The rebellion was only put down with the help of the British army in 1956.

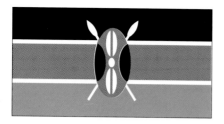

Above: *Kenya's national flag was formally raised for the first time, in Nairobi's Uhuru Gardens, on 12 December 1963.*

Freedom at Last

In March 1960 the Kenya African National Union (KANU) was formed and in May, while Mzee Jomo Kenyatta was still being held in prison, he was elected its president. This was followed by the formation of the Kenya African Democratic Union (KADU). The State of Emergency ended.

In February 1961 the general elections, in which Africans participated for the first time, resulted in a KANU victory with 67% of the vote against KADU's 16%. In August, Kenyatta was released from detention and in November led a delegation to England.

The year 1963 was the climax of the struggle for freedom. On 1 June, internal self-government (*Jamhuri*) was proclaimed with KANU forming the government and Jomo Kenyatta the first prime minister. During Kenyatta's inaugural speech, he gave Kenya the national motto *Harambee*, meaning 'let's all pull together'. In August Kenyatta addressed European settlers in Nakuru, convincing them to stay and contribute to an independent Kenya.

At midnight of 12 December, Kenya obtained its Independence: Uhuru, or freedom. In a colourful historic ceremony, attended by Prince Philip representing the Queen, the Union Jack was lowered for the last time and the black, red and green flag of Kenya raised.

A year later Kenya became a republic with Jomo Kenyatta as its first president. Kenyatta led the country along a moderate path, preached reconciliation with the European population and tolerence towards the Asian community, encouraging foreign investment and close links with the West.

On 22 August 1978, Mzee Kenyatta died at his Mombasa home. Nominated by KANU on 6 October 1978 as the sole candidate for president, then vice-president Daniel Toroitich arap Moi succeeded Jomo Kenyatta in an orderly fashion. President Moi's new national slogan is *Nyayo*, 'to follow in the footsteps'.

DANIEL ARAP MOI

Born in 1924 in Baringo district; was a school teacher before entering politics in 1955 when elected member of Legislative Council for Rift Valley; became Kenya's third vice-president in Jan 1967; after Kenyatta's death automatically elected new president; major achievements include introduction of free education and free milk for all primary school students, and doubling of number of primary schools; in 1981 elected chairman of the OAU (Organization of African Unity), a position held for an unprecedented two terms.

900-1499 Arab/Africa civilization flourishes on east coast.
1498 Vasco da Gama sails to Mombasa.
1593 Portuguese start building Fort Jesus at Mombasa.
1698 Army of Sultan of Oman and Zanzibar captures Fort Jesus from Portuguese.
1848–49 First European sightings of Mount Kilimanjaro and Mount Kenya.
1877 Sultan of Zanzibar offers British East Africa Association concession to administer mainland East Africa.
1883 Joseph Thomson's expedition up Rift Valley.
1888 Sir Frederick Jackson's exploration of Kenya.
1895-1901 Construction of Uganda Railway; reaches Lake Victoria at Port Florence (now Kisumu).
1902 Uganda-Kenya border readjusted to present position.

1908 Kenya becomes East African Protectorate.
1920 Kenya becomes a crown colony.
1929 Kenyatta visits England to air Kikuyu grievances.
1944 First African elected to Legislative Council.
1948 Mau Mau uprising.
1952 State of Emergency.
1959 25 Africans elected to Legislative Council.
1960 Political parties KANU and KADU formed.
1963 Internal self-government granted on 1 Jun, followed by full Independence on 12 Dec; Kenyatta first prime minister.
1964 Kenya a republic 12 Dec, Kenyatta first president.
1974 Swahili becomes official language of Parliament.
1976 Idi Amin, Uganda's president, claims large portions of Sudan and Kenya.
1977 Hunting banned.

1978 President Jomo Kenyatta dies; Daniel arap Moi sworn in as new president.
1979 President Moi decrees that all rhino in Kenya be protected.
1982 Attempted coup by Kenya Air Force.
1989 Dr Richard Leakey made director of Department of Wildlife; President Moi burns 12 tons of ivory in public ceremony in Nairobi National Park.
1991 Constitution amended, opening way for registration of opposition parties.
1992 First multiparty elections held in Dec.
1994 Dr Richard Leakey resigns as director of Kenya Wildlife Service. President Moi appoints Dr David Western as new director.
1998 Dr Richard Leakey re-appointed as director of Kenya Wildlife Service.

GOVERNMENT AND ECONOMY

Kenya is a republic within the Commonwealth with the president, as commander-in-chief of the Armed Forces, heading the National Assembly, which forms the Legislature. The president must be a member of the National Assembly and is normally elected through a general election process, which follows the dissolution of Parliament. The vice-president and the Cabinet are appointed by the president and must also be members of the Assembly. Elections for both the president and the National Assembly are held every five years.

Since 1969 Kenya has been a one-party state. In November 1991, however, Kenya reverted to a multiparty state. For administration purposes, Kenya is divided into eight provinces (of which Nairobi is one), each headed by a provincial commissioner. These eight provinces are divided into 41 districts, each administered by a district commissioner.

COMPOSITION OF NATIONAL ASSEMBLY

The National Assembly consists of a single chamber with 188 elected members, 12 nominated members, a speaker and an attorney general. The speaker is elected by the National Assembly; the attorney general is usually a civil servant appointed by the president. Candidates for a national election, unless nominated unopposed, are selected at a Party preliminary election. The government has 28 ministries, each headed by a minister and two assistant ministers, and administered by a permanent secretary.

Kenya's Wealth

Kenya is one of the most prosperous African nations, with a record of stability and sound government since Independence. Despite the fact that only 18% of the country's land is fertile and has cultivation potential, the economy is firmly based on agriculture which accounts for two-thirds of the country's exports. This is backed by tourism, manufacturing and commerce. Kenya is the third largest tea producer in the world, the largest producer of pyrethrum (a natural insecticide) and a major exporter of coffee, cut flowers and vegetables.

Tourism continues to be a major source of revenue and employment despite a levelling off in the number of visitors – mainly due to the recession in Europe and the United States, negative publicity in the overseas press, and rising travel costs. Most visitors are from Germany, followed by Britain, the USA and Switzerland. In 1991 earnings from tourism were US$1904 million from 804,600 visitors.

Kenya has a strong manufacturing sector, producing many consumer products that were once imported. A number of motor-vehicle assembly plants supply both a local and an export market. Last, but certainly not least, is the *Jua-kali* sector, the name given to the roadside businesses that are such a common feature these days in the towns and villages of Kenya. These businesses provide essential employment opportunities and produce cheap manufactured goods, mostly from scrap, roadside garage facilities and other items for the lower-income people. *Jua-kali* means 'hot sun', as the workers operate outside in the blazing heat.

Infrastructure

The port of Mombasa is the major gateway for East Africa, serving not only Kenya but also Uganda, Rwanda, Burundi, eastern Zaïre, southern Sudan, and also northern Tanzania. The port has 18 berths, two bulk oil jetties and a container terminal.

The Kenya Railways system provides 2085km (1295 miles) of railway line for both passenger and freight services. The passenger network runs from Nairobi to Mombasa, Nairobi to Kisumu, and Nairobi to Kampala in Uganda. Several branch lines are for freight only.

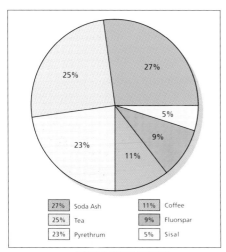

27%	Soda Ash	11%	Coffee
25%	Tea	9%	Fluorspar
23%	Pyrethrum	5%	Sisal

KENYA'S MAJOR EXPORTS

Kenya Airways, the national carrier, has a well-developed international and domestic network, and owns a modern fleet of aircraft (Airbus A300s and Boeing 737s). There are two international airports, Nairobi's **Jomo Kenyatta** and Mombasa's **Moi International**. In addition, there are over 150 local airports and airstrips, served by both Kenya Airways and a number of private-schedule and charter airlines. Among these airlines are Air Kenya, Africair, Safari Air and Prestige Air Services.

Of Kenya's 63,000km (39,148 miles) of roads, 13% are bitumen-surfaced. Over half of all freight traffic is transported by road, especially to Kenya's neighbouring countries. Public transport is mainly by country bus or by taxis known as matatus (*see* panel). Unfortunately, Kenya's accident rate is extremely high.

> ### MATATUS
>
> Matatus are privately owned taxis; originally small cars such as Peugeot 404s, they are now predominantly ex-tour-company minivans and larger trucks complete with a locally-made body. What they all have in common is that they're grossly overloaded (16 passengers in a 9-seat minivan) and are driven at breakneck speed. The origin of the meaning of the word 'Matatu' appears to be that it used to cost 30 cents (three 10-cent coins) to travel in Nairobi: *tatu* is the Swahili word for three .

Health Services
In 1991 (the most up-to-date figures available) Kenya had 277 hospitals, 357 health centres and 1712 dispensaries, as well as a number of mission hospitals and clinics in the country's more remote areas. There is, in Kenya, one doctor for every 6850 people, one dentist for every 38,600, and one nurse for every 900 people. Leading hospitals are the Nairobi Hospital, Aga Khan, Gertrude's Garden Children's Hospital, M.P. Shah and the Mater Misericordia.

Education
At Independence, Kenya had 5000 primary and 222 secondary schools, 8 technical institutes, 35 teachers' colleges and 1 technical college. By 1991, these figures had risen to 15,196 primary and 2647 secondary schools, 38 technical institutes, 22 teachers' training colleges and four universities.

Below: *Kenya's major centres are connected by regular and inexpensive buses known as matatus.*

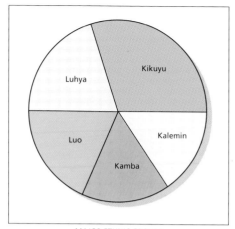

MAJOR ETHNIC GROUPS

THE PEOPLE

Man's earliest ancestors may well have originated as long as five million years ago in what is now northern Kenya. One wouldn't be far wrong in saying that the country's indigenous population represents more diversity than any other African country; approximately 30 languages are spoken in Kenya.

The most populous ethnic group is the Kikuyu, which numbered 3,202,800 at the last census; the smallest group is the el-Molo, living on the shores of Lake Turkana; they are probably less than 500 strong. Kenya's population has increased two and a half times since Independence and in 1993 was estimated to have reached at least 24.4 million.

Although the urban population continues to increase as people move to the cities and towns in search of jobs, better education opportunities and health facilities, at least 80% of Kenya's population lives in the rural areas. Life expectancy now stands at 60 years; more than half the population is below the age of 14, and this inevitably puts a heavy burden on education and health facilities.

Below: *sisal plantations in the Mogotio area. Other important national crops include tea, coffee, pineapples and pyrethrum.*

Culture

The majority of Kenyans are ambivalent toward their culture; they would prefer to have the world perceive them as a part of modern and progressive society than as stereotyped tribal warriors.

Religion

Along the country's coast and in its eastern provinces, most Kenyans are followers of Islam. **Islamic** sects make up 30% of Kenya's population, the remainder are **Christians** of various denominations. Almost every Christian sect is represented, as well as a number of **African Christian** groups which owe no allegiance to any of the world's Christian denominations. There has been an upsurge in these indigenous sects, and they are viewed with some suspicion by the government, who consider many of these sects to be radical.

COMMON SWAHILI WORDS	
English	**Swahili**
Hello	Jambo
How are you?	Habari?
I'm fine/good/well	Mzuri
Thank you	Asante
Please/excuse me	Tafadhali
Yes	Ndiyo
No	Hapana
Today	Leo
Tomorrow	Kesho
Hot	Moto
Cold	Baridi
Hotel	Hoteli
Room	Chumba
Bed	Kitanda
Shop	Duka

Most followers of Islam are of the Sunni branch, who have been able to attract reliable funding from Saudi Arabia for schools and hospitals. Among the Asian people, the most influential is the Ismaili community, followers of the Aga Khan. The Aga Khan has been liberal with funding in Kenya; as a result, many hospitals and schools are named after him. There is also a large following of **Hindus** of various sects.

Language

Kenya's official language is **English**, with **Swahili** the lingua franca readily understood by the majority of the people. In addition, all will speak their tribal mother tongue, such as Ki-Kikuyu and Ki-Maasai.

Left: *a Muslim fruit merchant displays his wares on a Mombasa sidewalk. All the major faiths are represented in Kenya: nearly 2000 religious organizations are registered within the country. Most of the people are Christians; Islam has the largest minority following.*

Kenya has a number of beautifully scenic golf courses at various altitudes, from sea level right up to the nine-hole Molo Hills Hotel golf course, at 2740m (8989ft). The newest is that at the Windsor Golf and Country Club; the oldest is the Royal Nairobi; its 'Royal' title was bestowed on the then Nairobi Golf Club in 1935 by King George V. The Muthaiga and Karen golf clubs each have championship courses. Kisumu Golf Club, on the shores of Lake Victoria, has a very interesting rule which could only apply in Africa: 'If the ball comes to rest in dangerous proximity to a hippopotamus or a crocodile, another ball may be dropped at a safe distance, but no nearer the hole, without penalty.'

Sport and Recreation

To many people around the world, the words 'sport' and 'Kenya' mean one thing: athletics. Kenya's world-class middle- and long-distance runners have long dominated the running tracks of the world. The legendary Kipchoge 'Kip' Keino and Naftali Temu were the first in a long line of Kenya's runners to make a name for themselves worldwide in important international events (including the Olympic Games). Kenya has also done particularly well at boxing on an international level. But for most Kenyans, football (soccer) is the number-one sport. Kenya's national soccer team, the **Harambee Stars**, has won the East and Central African Championships eight times since 1967, and in 1987 it was runner-up to Egypt in the fourth All Africa Games. Kenya's football clubs have upheld a very good record in international tournaments, winning nine East and Central African Club Championships since 1974. The most successful football clubs are Gor Mahia (who in 1987 won the Nelson Mandela Cup in the African Cup Winners), AFC Leopards and Kenya Breweries.

Other popular sports in Kenya are hockey, cricket, golf, tennis, rugby and squash. Both freshwater and deep-sea fishing, and polo attract the sports enthusiast and, of course, so does the world-famous Safari Rally held every Easter, when the world's leading rally drivers battle it out over 4500km (2795 miles) of rugged road and track.

Kenya offers an endless selection of sports opportunities for both the active player and the spectator. There are over 40 different sporting associations and management bodies in Kenya to look after a wide variety of activities and events.

Food

Most visitors to Kenya are surprised by the quality of food served at safari lodges and camps: in the mobile safari camps, cooks (*mpishis*) prepare it in old ammunition boxes covered in hot ashes. Breakfast and lunch are usually enjoyed in the shade of a tree, adding to the occasion. Breakfast consists of fresh paw-paw, pineapple, melon and delicious finger-sized bananas as well as fruit juices and porridge. English traditional bacon and eggs is also available. Often the cook is on hand to cook omelettes exactly to order. Lunch offers a selection of cold meats, fish and salads as well as a hot meal. Indian curry for Sunday lunch has become traditional. Saturday lunch often features African dishes such as *irio* (mashed peas, potatoes and maize), *nyama choma* (roast meat), *ugali* (stiff maize porridge), *sukuma wiki* (cooked spinach mixed with tomato and onion), *kuku* (chicken), *matoke* (steamed bananas) and *githeri* (mashed beans and maize). International cuisine is usually served at dinner.

Visitors staying at the coast will sample Kenya's wonderful seafood: oysters, lobsters, crab and a host of sea fish. Nairobi offers the visitor a bewildering choice of restaurants of different nationalities. True Swahili cuisine is best found at the coast.

DRINKS ARE SERVED

World renowned, Kenya's beers are Tusker, Whitecap, Pilsner, Tusker Premium and Tusker Export. The first three come in 500ml bottles, while Tusker Premium and Tusker Export are in 300ml bottles. Wine drinkers are well catered for as wines imported from all over the world are available. Kenya now has its own vineyards on the shores of Lake Naivasha, which are producing credible wines. After-dinner liqueurs – 'Kenya Gold', a coffee liqueur, and 'Ivory Cream', a coffee-cream liqueur – complete the mouthwatering delights on offer in Kenya.

2
Central Kenya

Kenya's central highlands are dominated by the imposing peaks of **Mount Kenya** and the fertile, forested slopes of the **Aberdare** mountain range. A region of high plateaus, rolling green foothills and moorlands, its most distinctive feature is a rich diversity of giant alpine flora in the mountainous upper reaches. Among the plant species are thickets of bamboo, gnarled hagenia trees, giant heather, tussock grass and groundsels (senecio), some of which grow to over 10m (33ft).

The **Aberdare National Park** itself lies mostly above 3048m (10,000ft); because the Aberdares form a barrier to the prevailing easterly winds, the rainfall on the upper slopes is as high as 2000mm (80in), making this a major water catchment area. The region's well-watered foothills support undulating plantations of coffee and tea. Two major rivers cross the area, the east-flowing Athi, and the Tana which is fed by streams running off the slopes of Mount Kenya and which supplies the country with its main source of hydroelectric power.

Nairobi, the United Nations regional headquarters, forms the area's hub and is important internationally as both a commercial and a communication centre. It offers visitors many worthwhile sights, and there is lots to do. Of the city's many mosques and temples, don't miss seeing the interesting – and photogenic – **Jamia Mosque**. And even though most tourists passing through the city are safari-goers, **Nairobi National Park** with its varied wildlife grazing against the backdrop of the city skyline should be included in one's intinerary.

CLIMATE

Although it is situated only 33km (21 miles) south of the equator, Nairobi lies at an altitude of 1675m (5496ft) and therefore enjoys a **pleasant year-round** climate with cool evenings and mornings, and an average daytime temperature of 24–29°C (75–85°F). From June to August it is often **cloudy, overcast** and **cool** but the other months, even in the rainy seasons, are usually **bright and sunny**.

Opposite: *Nairobi's attractive skyline.*

NAIROBI

Driving from the airport into Nairobi, one of the most prominent buildings on the skyline is the **Kenyatta Conference Centre** (its main hall can seat 4000 delegates); a public viewing platform on the 28th floor affords sweeping vistas across the city. The birth of Nairobi occurred less than 100 years ago, on 30 May 1899, when the chief engineer of Uganda Railway Construction, George Whitehouse, chose the spot for the railhead ('Mile 327') roughly halfway between Mombasa and Kampala, before tackling the difficult Rift Valley Escarpment. Prior to this, apart from the Maasai who watered their cattle in the river, the first European to live in the area was Sergeant Ellis of the Royal Engineers, who operated a telegraph office there. With the arrival of the railway, Nairobi quickly grew and by 1907 had become the capital of British East Africa.

Nairobi is now the largest city in east and central Africa, with a population of over two million. Often referred to as the 'city in the sun' or 'city of flowers,' the mostly broad streets and open areas, dominated by modern high-rise buildings, are lined with bougainvillea, jacaranda and hibiscus. The quiet suburbs of **Muthaiga**, **Limuru**, **Karen** and **Langata** have large homes set in beautiful spacious gardens, all of which contrast with the shanty towns which exist in and alongside the city.

National Museum ***

The National Museum is a must for every visitor to Nairobi. Originally known as the Coryndon Museum after Sir Robert Coryndon who was the main benefactor in its early days, it is perhaps best known for its connection with Dr Louis Leakey, the famous palaeontologist. The museum is well laid out, with cultural and historic sections, and good displays on birds, insects, reptiles, fish and mammals. The work of Joy Adamson is well represented with exhibits of her tribal portraits, and her Kenya flower and plant watercolours.

In the grounds of the museum is a **snake park** and an **aquarium**, both very popular with visitors. Some of the snakes are in open pits, while others are behind glass.

The National Museum is open daily from 09:30 to 18:00; from Monday to Friday there are voluntary guides who speak a number of languages to help visitors find their way around.

Above: *the Delamere Terrace of the Norfolk Hotel in Nairobi.*

Railway Museum **
The museum is close to Uhuru Highway, but is best approached from the railway station. Among the old locomotives on display outside the museum buildings is the carriage Charles Ryall was dragged out of by a maneating lion in Tsavo National Park. Ryall, a young police superintendent who volunteered to shoot the lions taking their toll of railway workers, fell asleep and became a victim himself. The museum houses a very interesting collection of memorabilia tracing the railway's history, including wonderful old photographs.

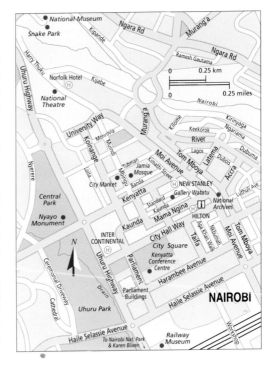

Nairobi National Park •••

Kenya's first national park at the time and only 8km (5 miles) from the city centre, Nairobi National Park was opened in 1946. This unique area, entirely within the city limits, is only 120km² (44 sq miles) and is home to an amazing variety of wildlife: 80 mammal and over 500 bird species have been recorded.

Fenced on three sides, the fourth boundary is formed by the Athi River, affording access to migrating game. Unfortunately Kitengela, once a traditional Maasai grazing area across the river, is slowly being settled which will hinder any future migration.

Most of the park is made up of open plains and scattered acacia bush, with a handful of man-made dams holding permanent water and intersected by a number of small seasonal rivers; in the west, an extensive area of highland forest contains olive and Cape chestnut trees.

Nairobi National Park is perhaps the best place to see the endangered black rhino, which occurs in good numbers (approximately 40 individuals) and is quite tame. It is also a good place to see and photograph Africa's largest antelope, the eland, which unusually is not at all shy or skittish here. Masai giraffe, buffalo, warthog and

---

NAIROBI ARBORETUM FOREST RESERVE

The arboretum is located in the heart of Nairobi near State House, and covers an area of 32ha (79 acres). There are almost 300 species of tree, both indigenous and exotic; all are labelled. The birdlife is good, featuring many highland forest species. A troop of Syke's monkeys also live in the area. Recently the 'Friends of Nairobi Arboretum' was formed, its aim to restore the reserve to its original state; this welcome rehabilitation is presently in progress. The arboretum also has a picnic area and a number of trails (visitors are advised to go in a group). Entrance is free of charge.

Below: *the Nairobi National Park.*

both Thomson's and Grant's gazelle are all common. Predators are well represented: lion and cheetah are quite a common sight, leopard are occasionally spotted in the highland forest. Strangely, hyena are seldom encountered, but it is not unusual to spot silver-backed jackal. During the dry season, there is a large influx of game – mainly wildebeest, kongoni (Coke's hartebeest) and zebra – from the Athi-Kapiti Plains.

Nairobi Animal Orphanage •

Located just inside the national park's main entrance gate, the orphanage was founded in 1963 to look after, and later return to the wilderness, sick and abandoned wild animals. Although this is still the main aim of the orphanage, a number of the animals are now permanent residents – among these a pair of tigers – so in many ways it is really very much a zoo. Any abandoned young elephants and rhinos are cared for nearby by author and conservationist Daphne Sheldrick. Her experiences while rearing a variety of African wildlife, particularly elephants, are told in her books *The Tsavo Story* and *An Elephant Called Eleanor*. Visitors wishing to view any animals in residence should call Daphne at tel: (02) 891996 for an appointment. Nearby is the **Wildlife Education Centre** which shows wildlife films to children on weekend afternoons and holidays.

> **CAPE CHESTNUT**
>
> The Cape chestnut (*Calodendrum capense*) is one of the most beautiful flowering trees in the highlands of Kenya. It grows up to 20m (66ft) high and during the summer when it flowers, the forests are filled with beautiful rosy-pink blossoms. The trees are particularly common along the Rift Valley Escarpment near Nairobi.

Above: *residents of Nairobi National Park graze within a stone's throw of the city. Tallest of the buildings is the Kenyatta Conference Centre, whose 28th floor has an observation platform.*

Giraffe Manor ★★

Giraffe Manor, 18km (11 miles) from Nairobi, along the route to the Blixen Museum, was the home of Jock and Betty Leslie Melville, who in 1976 turned their home into the **Langata Nature Education Centre** and founded the African Fund for Endangered Wildlife (AFEW). The purpose of the centre was to help preserve the Rothschild's giraffe which was threatened at the time, and also to educate young Kenyans about conservation. Originally two Rothschild's giraffe – Daisy and Marlon – were transported to the centre from western Kenya, where the human population was spreading increasingly into their territory. A circular wooden building housing a small lecture theatre has been constructed, around which is a raised platform from where visitors can feed and observe the giraffe; this has proved very popular with children. One can stay overnight at Giraffe Manor.

Worth visiting nearby is **Utamaduni**, a large house which contains a number of rooms selling various Kenyan crafts. It also has a very good coffee shop.

Set in peaceful scenic grounds is **Ostrich Park**, an arts and crafts village near Utamaduni. Ostriches reared here are a big attraction, as are the wood carvers, and carpet and basket weavers, all of whom can be watched at work.

Karen Blixen Museum ★★

This museum, once the home of Baroness Karen von Blixen, is located in the Nairobi suburb of Karen, which was named after her. Also famous as Isak Dinesen, the author of *Letters From Africa, Shadows on the Grass* and *Out of Africa* (this was turned into a major motion picture starring Meryl Streep), Karen Blixen lived here from 1914 to 1931. The house has been beautifully restored to its

---

Above: *the one-time home of Karen Blixen has been carefully restored and now serves as a museum.*
Opposite: *walking through emerald tea plantations in Kenya's high, rolling Limuru uplands.*

former state. Most of the furnishings are original but a few items, including the cuckoo clock and the bookcase (belonging to Dennis Finch Hatton) are replicas, made specially for the film *Out of Africa*. The house, open daily, is set in a large, colourful garden which was part of the old coffee farm. The view behind the homestead is dominated by the Ngong Hills, loved so much by Karen; the name 'Ngong' is a mispronunciation of the Maasai name for the hills, 'Enkongu e Mpakasi', meaning 'source of the Embakasi River'. Nearby is a small restaurant called the Karen Blixen Coffee Garden, once part of the coffee estate and home to the estate manager. It still retains its atmosphere from the past and the food is excellent. There is also a small gift shop.

Limuru Uplands

Limuru, 30km (18 miles) north of Nairobi, is at a bracing altitude of 2225m (7300ft) and set among rolling green hills covered with tea and coffee plantations. Tea, the main crop in the area, was first planted near here in 1903;

in 1910 a Mr Mitchell was responsible for the planting of the first commercial tea estate. Picking takes place most mornings, and only the new, young, tender shoots are plucked, giving the bushes their characteristic flat-topped shape. One can visit a tea estate by prior arrangement; Mr Mitchell's daughter organizes tours and lunches at her **Kiambethu Tea Estate**.

Limuru town is the home of Bata Shoe Company, which produces nine million pairs of shoes a year.

Thika

Forty-five kilometres (28 miles) north of Nairobi is the town of **Thika**, made famous by author Elspeth Huxley's *Flame Trees of*

BOMAS OF KENYA

The Bomas is a cultural centre set in 33ha (82 acres) of ground near Langata, 10km (6 miles) from Nairobi. The centre is dominated by a large circular building which can hold 3500 people; here visitors can watch a display of dance and song by professional dancers representing various Kenyan ethnic groups. Outside is a display of various different tribal homes illustrating different construction methods. In the main building, a restaurant serves ethnic foods. The Bomas are open daily, performances take place every afternoon.

COLOBUS MONKEY

These magnificent black-and-white monkeys are common in both the Aberdare and Mount Kenya national parks. They can usually be observed in the forest, leaping spectacularly – arms and legs outstretched – from tree to tree in search of food. Colobus monkeys differ from others in that they have no thumb; they feed almost exclusively on tender young leaves, spending the rest of the day grooming each other or resting. Young monkeys are born completely white, remaining that way for about a month, after which they slowly turn black and white. The colobus is a protected species.

Thika. The Blue Posts Inn, featured in the book, is still in operation and is worth a visit. In the hotel grounds are the **Chania Falls** which were used as the location for a Tarzan movie some years ago. Nowadays Thika is best known for its Del Monte pineapple plantations, the largest in the world (Kenya is the world's third largest pineapple producer). The town also has a vehicle assembly plant handling British Land-Rovers among others.

Twenty kilometres (12 miles) away on the Thika to Garissa road are the popular **Fourteen Falls**. Although they are not high (only 27m; 89ft), they can be quite spectacular, especially after the rains. Surrounded by dense tropical vegetation, the falls are a popular picnic spot at weekends.

Ol Doinyo Sabuk National Park ·

Near to the Fourteen Falls is the entrance to Ol Doinyo Sabuk National Park, itself a large forest-covered hill

2146m (7040ft) high. Ol Doinyo Sabuk, meaning 'sleeping buffalo' in Maasai, has only one track suitable for motor vehicles, winding its way to the summit through dense highland forest. The view on a clear day is wonderful – Mount Kenya and Nairobi can both be clearly seen. About halfway along this rough track is a panoramic bluff which offers wonderful views over the countryside. Here are three marble plaques, set on slabs of rock; they are the graves of Sir William Northrup Macmillan, his wife and their servant Louise Decker. Sir William, a wealthy American who loved the spot, was one of the early settlers in the area and owned the nearby 8049ha (19,890 acres) Juja Ranch. Although the park has a good population of game including buffalo, bushbuck, leopard

Left: *the renowned Treetops Lodge in the Aberdare park.*
Opposite: *the lovely Chania Falls at Thika, about which author Elspeth Huxley wrote so movingly. The area is notable for its vast pineapple plantations.*

and colobus monkeys, it is often very difficult to spot them because of the thick forest. There are many interesting birds, among them Hartlaub's turaco, white-starred forest robin and Narina trogon. It is advisable not to leave your vehicle unattended or to visit the area alone.

ABERDARE NATIONAL PARK

The Aberdare National Park, 100km (62 miles) north of Nairobi, covers an area of 767km² (296 sq miles). Now officially called **Nyandarua** (a Kikuyu name meaning 'a drying hide'), the Aberdares were given their original name by the explorer Thomson, who first saw the mountains in 1884 and named them after Lord Aberdare, then president of the Royal Geographical Society.

The park consists of the Aberdare mountain range running north to south, and a thickly forested salient which extends down the eastern slopes. On the eastern and western sides, montane forest slowly gives way to bamboo and hagenia at the higher levels. In the north is **Ol Doinyo Satima**, the highest peak at 3995m (13,100ft), and in the south the **Kinangop**. Between the two is an undulating moorland at an altitude of 3000m (9840ft), with scattered rocky outcrops, forest patches, highland bogs and streams. The moorland is covered in tussock grass, with areas of giant heaths, groundsels (senecios) and forest patches of rosewood, St John's wort and bamboo. A number of ice-cold streams cross the moorland,

---

BEAUTIFUL WATERFALLS

● Of the waterfalls in Aberdare National Park, the most accessible and widely photographed are the Chania Falls – sometimes known as Queen's Cave Waterfall after a visit by Queen Elizabeth II, who had lunch in a wooden pavilion overlooking the cascade.
● The Gura Falls, Kenya's highest at 457m (1500ft), are the most spectacular but unfortunately it is only possible to stand at the top of them, so their true magnitude cannot be seen.
● The Karura Falls, situated opposite the Gura, drop down to merge at the confluence of the two rivers a little further on.

Lord Baden-Powell, founder of the Boy Scouts movement, first visited Kenya in 1935. While staying in the small town of Nyeri, he is quoted as saying, 'The nearer to Nyeri, the nearer to bliss.' In 1938 he retired, returning to Nyeri to live in a cottage named Paxtu, specially built for him in the Outspan Hotel grounds. He and his wife, Lady Olave, lived here until his death on 8 January 1941. They are both buried facing Mount Kenya, in the nearby churchyard of St Peter's Church. Inscribed on Lord Baden-Powell's tombstone is a circle and dot, the Boy Scout symbol for 'gone home'. With permission from the Outspan Hotel one can visit Paxtu, which remains much as it was in the Baden-Powells' time.

eventually cascading down the slopes in a series of waterfalls. These streams hold both brown and rainbow trout, and there are two fishing camps on the moorland to cater for keen anglers.

The heavy rainfall in this catchment area makes the tracks very difficult to navigate and four-wheel-drive vehicles are essential. Animal life is prolific, but the thick forest habitat impedes game-viewing. Elephant, rhino, buffalo, giant forest hog, bushbuck and both colobus and Syke's monkeys are all common. Predators are well represented, among them lion, leopard, hyena and serval (many of them melanistic). Birdlife too is abundant and varied: cinnamon-chested bee-eaters nest in holes alongside the park's tracks, the crowned eagle – Africa's most powerful – is common in the forest where it preys on suni (a tiny antelope, smaller than a dik-dik), while mountain buzzards circle over the moorlands and Jackson's francolins, only found in Kenya, forage for food in the coarse tussock grass.

The most convenient way to visit and experience the Aberdares is to spend a night at **The Ark** or **Treetops**, night game-viewing lodges located in the Salient (*see* p. 41). The whole of this wonderful area is surrounded by small African farms (*shambas*) and large coffee estates. Because of the conflict between wildlife and farmer, the whole of the national park is in the process of being surrounded by an electric fence, powered by water-driven generators.

The enormous cost of this project is mostly being supported by local donations; an organization called Rhino Ark arranges fund-raising events such as motosport and golf.

MOUNT KENYA NATIONAL PARK

Mount Kenya, at 5199m (17,058ft) the country's highest mountain, has its higher slopes permanently covered in snow and ice, even though it sits astride the equator. The national park comprises the mountain above the 3200m (10,500ft) contour plus two salients astride the Naro Moru and Sirimon routes. Called 'Kirinyaga' by the Kikuyu to whom it is sacred, the first European to climb Mount Kenya was Sir Halford Mackinder, in 1899. An old extinct volcano, it is made up of three peaks: **Batian** (the highest), **Nelion** and **Lenana**. Of these peaks, the original hard centre core is all that remains; the bulk of the volcano has been eroded away with time.

Although conceived as a recreation area, the park has a good and varied population of wildlife, and is of geological and botanical interest. Elephant, buffalo and rhino are frequently seen as one slowly climbs upwards, and even when one is in the alpine zone just below the main peaks, there is wildlife in the form of giant rock hyraxes, begging for food if given the chance! Birdlife too is varied. Walking through the forests you are sure to see a flash of vivid red as a Hartlaub's turaco flies ahead; you will no doubt hear the high-pitched squawks of flocks of red-headed parrots, and be startled by the raucous call and rushing sound of a silvery-cheeked hornbill's wings. The forest-covered mountain slopes below the park's boundary, containing many large

CLIMBING MOUNT KENYA

Mount Kenya is becoming increasingly popular with mountaineers from all over the world (Reinhold Messner, the first man to climb Mount Everest without oxygen, did much of his high-altitude and ice training on Mount Kenya). The main central peaks, Batian and Nelion, require ropes and ice axes, and a certain degree of proficiency; Lenana is suitable for climbers with little experience. The four main routes to the peaks are: Naro Moru, the Sirimon and Timau tracks on the mountain's western slopes, and the Chogoria route on the eastern slopes. One can take a circular route or use a different track on the return leg (only for the experienced climber). Vegetation varies from dense forest and bamboo jungle to gnarled hagenia trees draped with 'old man's beard'. Contact the Naro Moru River Lodge for details.

Above left: *Mount Kenya, viewed from the Aberdare National Park.*
Opposite: *the spectacular flowers of the* **Erythrina** abyssinica *which appear in the dry season.*

Podocarpus and lichen-covered olive trees, merge, as the altitude increases, into a zone of bamboo, some as high as 15m (49ft). This in turn blends into vegetation comprising mostly giant heath that often grows to tree size at this altitude. The area then becomes moorland covered in spiky tussock grass with giant lobelia and groundsels, some of which grow to a height of 4.5m (15ft). Growing among the tussock grass are patches of everlasting flowers, gladioli, delphiniums and red-hot pokers.

To the west of Mount Kenya is the **Laikipia Plateau**, mostly dry country of rolling plains dotted with acacia trees. This is cattle-ranching territory with a number of large ranch properties still inhabited by a variety of wildlife. In 1991 the 165km^2 (64 sq miles) **Laikipia National Reserve** was set up in the area. Several of the cattle ranches such as Colcheccio, Solio (which has been very successful in breeding both black and white rhino), El Karama and Segera are now open to visitors and provide a different type of safari that offers horse riding, walking and fishing.

Night Game-viewing Lodges

Kenya has three night game-viewing lodges where powerful spotlights are directed onto a nearby waterhole and salt lick. Two of these tree hotels, **Treetops** and **The Ark**, are situated in the salient of the Aberdare National Park, while the third, **Mountain Lodge**, is on the slopes of Mount Kenya. Visitors to Treetops are first taken to Outspan Hotel in Nyeri for lunch; afterwards, guests are entertained by Kikuyu drummers in traditional dress. Visitors to The Ark lunch at the Aberdares Country Club.

MT KENYA SAFARI LODGES

Around the base of the mountain are a number of hotels and lodges:
- The plush Mount Kenya Safari Club, for guests who demand the utmost in comfort and luxury
- Mountain Lodge, a night game-viewing lodge similar to The Ark and Treetops
- The Naro Moru River Lodge, simple but beautifully situated, specializes in assisting mountaineers to climb the mountain safely; good for bird-watching
- The KenTrout Grill and Cottages for a delicious trout meal or for an overnight stay in rustic but comfortable surroundings; excellent value.

Top: *the Mount Kenya Safari Club.*
Opposite: *The Ark, a lodge that has a viewing walkway among the tree tops.*

At both venues, guests are transported to their respective night-viewing lodges. Mountain Lodge is similar, but differs in that you drive directly to the lodge where all meals will be are taken, giving you more time to enjoy the highland forest scene; it is also not such a rush to leave in the morning.

Because The Ark is deep inside the salient, the drive there often reveals colobus and Syke's monkeys, buffalo and elephant. On arrival, tea and cakes are served and often there is already game at the waterhole. Each lodge has a photographic bunker and/or open verandah where visitors can watch and photograph the wildlife. Flash photography is not allowed.

The Ark has a walkway among the tree tops, good for bird-watchers. A bird-feeding table attracts large numbers of birds, while underneath, waiting for scraps, is usually a black-tipped mongoose and occasionally a pair of suni. As the daylight fades, powerful spotlights are switched on. Dinner is served at eight, but guests keep their binoculars at hand as an interesting animal might appear at any time. It is important to be as quiet as possible. One need not worry about missing anything when retiring to bed, as a bell in each room will ring the minute an interesting animal is sighted. A warm fire burns all night (the lodges are at a height of around 2133m (6998ft) so nights can be very chilly); tea and coffee is also served the night through. Early the next morning, guests are transported back to the Outspan or Aberdares Country Club, where they meet up again with their safari guide and vehicle.

SAFARIS WITH A DIFFERENCE

Camel safaris run by a number of Laikipia-based companies, usually five or six nights; escorted by an armed safari guide, one either rides or walks alongside the camel, camping out each evening.
Horseback safaris for competent riders; one rides for five or six hours a day, camping each night. Safaris cannot enter national parks, but do ride through areas rich in wildlife; normally a visit to a national park in a four-wheel-drive is arranged.
Walking safaris from one to ten days; one walks in the cool hours of morning; in the afternoon a game drive is undertaken in a four-wheel-drive. Recently launched is an exciting walk along the edge of the spectacular Rift Valley north of Maralal.

Central Kenya at a Glance

BEST TIMES TO VISIT

From **December to mid-March** days are hot, sunny and dry, and nights are usually cool. Also nicest time to climb Mount Kenya, as peaks are normally cloud free. The main rainy season occurs mid-March to May, with a shorter period of rain in November.

GETTING THERE

Main Nairobi–Nakuru and Nairobi–Nanyuki **roads** are **tarred** and generally good. Other roads poor except some major toll roads through Nairobi and Mombasa. For security, try not to travel after dark.

GETTING AROUND

There are three types of **taxi** in Nairobi: the best but most expensive is a Mercedes from Kenatco Taxis; next, the black London-type cab; finally, taxis with a thick yellow line along the side (old but cheap). Kenatco Taxis charge a set price per km, tel: (02) 225123, 221561 or 338611, or at Jomo Kenyatta International Airport, tel: 822356. It is customary to bargain with the others, but be sure to agree on the price before getting in.

To get to the national parks, join an **organized tour**. It is possible, though, to **hire a car** in Nairobi and visit the parks on your own (major car-hire firms are represented). Try Avis, tel: (02) 336703/4, airport tel: 822186, fax: 339111; or Hertz UTC, tel: (02) 333233, airport tel: 822339.

WHERE TO EAT

If one joins a safari to the national parks and reserves, all meals are catered for by the lodges at which guests are staying. Visitors staying in self-help *bandas* can usually buy a midday meal at a safari lodge.

Nairobi
Alan Bobbe's Bistro, Koinange St: the best of French cuisine, tel: (02) 226027/4945 or 336952.
Foresta Magnetica, Corner House, Kimathi and Mama Ngina sts: Italian cooking, tel: (02) 728009 or 223662.
Tamarind Restaurant, Harambee Ave: renowned for its seafood, tel: (02) 338959 or 217990.
Minar Restaurant, Banda St: Indian fare, tel: (02) 229999.
Trattoria Restaurant, Wabera St: Italian cuisine, tel: (02) 340855, 223662/3.
La Galleria, Casino, Museum Hill: Italian food, tel: (02) 742600 or 744477.
Safeer, Pan Africa Hotel: spicy Indian, tel: (02) 336803.
Carnivore, Langata Rd: famous for its game dishes, tel: (02) 501775 or 501779.

Hotel Restaurants
Ibis Grill and **The Lord Delamere**, Norfolk Hotel: nouvelle cuisine at former, international menu at latter, tel: (02) 335422.
Mandhari, and **Cafe Maghreb,** both located in the Nairobi Serena Hotel: international cuisine, high standard, tel: (02) 710511.

The Tate Room, New Stanley Hotel: offers fine cuisine, tel: (02) 333248.
Le Bougainville, Safari Park Hotel: international menu, tel: (02) 802493; Korean, Japanese, French and African cuisine also served.
Windsor Room, Windsor Golf and Country Club: French-influenced menu, tel: (02) 802300.

WHERE TO STAY

Nairobi
Norfolk Hotel, Harry Thuku Rd: the rich and famous have stayed here; Nairobi's meeting place, tel: (02) 250900, fax: 216796.
Nairobi Serena Hotel, Central Park, Kenyatta Ave: set in beautiful gardens, its restaurants recommended, tel: (02) 725111, fax: 725184.
Safari Park Hotel, Thika Rd: large and lavish, set in 64 acres of land, tel: (02) 802493/7, fax: 802477.
Nairobi Safari Club, University Way: distinctive high-rise fountain in foyer, tel: (02) 330621, fax: 331201.
Windsor Golf and Country Club, Garden Estate: elegant, looks onto beautiful golf course, tel: (02) 802300, fax: 802322.
New Stanley Hotel, Kimathi St: a meeting place for travellers in Nairobi, tel: (02) 333233, fax: 217294.
Nairobi Hilton, Mama Ngina St: tall, circular, tower-like hotel with rooftop pool, tel: (02) 334000, fax: 339463.

Central Kenya at a Glance

Giraffe Manor, Mukoma Road, Nairobi: tel: (02) 891078, 890948.

Limuru Uplands
Kentmere Club, near Tigoni: country inn atmosphere, set in lovely gardens, tel: (0154) 42101.

Aberdares
Aberdare Country Club, Nyeri: elegant country home set in landscaped gardens, book through Lonrho Hotels.
Outspan Hotel, Nyeri: the site of Baden-Powell's home, it is still used as a suite for guests, book through Block Hotels.

Mount Kenya
Mount Kenya Safari Club, nine-hole golf course; bird observation towers, pools, book through Lonrho Hotels.
Sweetwaters Tented Camp, on Ol Pejeta Ranch: solitude in luxury thatched tents set in rhino sanctuary, book through Lonrho Hotels.
Naro Moru River Lodge, Naro Moru: set in Mt Kenya foothills, book through Alliance Hotels.
Ken Trout Grill & Cottages: guest houses on peaceful farm, call telephone operator (900) and ask for Timau 14, or tel: (02) 228391.

RANCHES
Loisaba Wilderness: c/o Mellifera Bookings, PO Box 24397, Nairobi; tel: (02) 574689/567251, fax: 564945.

Sangare Ranch: book through Savannah Camps & Lodges.
Patrick's Camp – Solio: book through Bush Homes.
Ol Ari Nyiro Ranch: contact the Gallman Memorial Foundation, PO Box 45593, Nairobi; fax: (02) 521220.
El Karama Ranch: self-catering *bandas*, book through Let's Go Travel.

NIGHT GAME-VIEWING LODGES
Aberdares
The Ark: tree hotel built in form of Noah's Ark, book through Lonrho Hotels.
Treetops: wooden hotel on stilts, visited by Queen Elizabeth and Prince Philip, book through Block Hotels.

Mount Kenya
Mountain Lodge: on stilts in rainforest; book through Serena Central Reservations.

TOURS AND EXCURSIONS

Camel safaris: Camel Trek Ltd, tel: (02) 891079, fax: 891716; Desert Rose Camels Ltd, tel: (02) 884259/882124, fax: 212160; Just The Ticket, tel: (02) 74155/6/7, fax: 740087.

Horseback safaris: Safaris Unlimited (Africa) Ltd, tel: (02)

891168/890435, fax: 891113; Offbeat Safaris Ltd, book through Bush Homes of East Africa Ltd.
Walking safaris: Kentreck Safaris Ltd, book through Let's Go Travel, tel: (02) 340331, fax: 336890; Alliance Hotels central booking office, tel: (02) 332825, fax: 219212; or contact Kobo Safaris in Nairobi, tel: (02) 568438 or 562108, fax: 560496.

USEFUL ADDRESSES

Savannah Camps & Lodges, PO Box 48019, Nairobi; tel: (02) 229009, fax: 330698.
Alliance Hotels, PO Box 49839, Nairobi; tel: (02) 337501, fax: 219212.
Block Hotels Ltd, PO Box 47557, tel: (02) 335867, fax: 340541.
Bush Homes of East Africa Ltd, PO Box 56923, Nairobi; tel: (02) 571647 or 571661, fax: 571665.
Lonrho Hotels Ltd, PO Box 58581, Nairobi; tel: (02) 216940, fax: 216796/6896.
Let's Go Travel, PO Box 60342, Nairobi; tel: (02) 340331, fax: 336890.
Serena Central Reservations, PO Box 48690, Nairobi; tel: (02) 711077, fax: 718103.

NAIROBI	J	F	M	A	M	J	J	A	S	O	N	D
AVERAGE TEMP. °F	68	68	70	70	66	64	63	63	68	66	66	66
AVERAGE TEMP. °C	20	20	21	21	19	18	17	17	20	19	19	19
Hours of Sun Daily	9	9	8	6	5	5	4	4	6	7	6	8
RAINFALL ins	2	1	3	6	5	1	0	1	1	2	5	3
RAINFALL mm	50	37	85	154	125	30	14	19	20	49	132	77
Days of Rainfall	16	8	3	12	15	15	8	10	4	12	9	8

3
Western Kenya

Although this is the country's most highly populated region – and also the most productive with its vast rolling tea plantations and large wheat and maize-growing areas – Western Kenya is the least visited.

Only fairly recently has **Lake Victoria**, source of the Nile and the world's second largest freshwater lake, started arousing interest among visitors, because of the establishment of a number of exclusive new lodges there. Kenya's border with Uganda cuts through the lake's northeastern edge, and continues northwards to slice through the centre of **Mount Elgon**'s volcanic crater.

In contrast to the flatlands surrounding Lake Victoria's shores are the richly fertile slopes of the **Mau Escarpment** rising to the east, mantled with emerald tea plantations; rainfall on the Mau massif is abundant and regular. Sited in these highlands, the town of **Kericho** forms Kenya's tea capital.

The region's dense population is attributed to the Gusii people living in the highlands around **Kisii** (they are believed to support one of the highest birth rates in the world); the Luo, accomplished fishermen living around Lake Victoria's shores; and the Luhya of **Kakamega**, where the only remaining tropical rainforest in East Africa is to be seen.

Western Kenya's most famous area is, of course, the **Masai Mara National Reserve**, with its rolling grassland plains, acacia woodlands and scrub thickets which harbour a marvellously abundant variety of wildlife; and the open plains make game-viewing a pleasure.

CLIMATE

The main **rainfall season** in the Lake Victoria basin is from **March** to **June**, and from **September** to **November**, but it can rain there almost any month. Strangely, in the tea-growing highland areas around Kericho, most rain falls between April and September. In the Narok district and the Masai Mara, the heaviest rain falls between November and May.

Opposite: *game-viewing by balloon in the splendid Masai Mara National Reserve.*

DON'T MISS

*** A safari to the Masai
Mara National Reserve
*** A hot-air balloon trip
over the Mara plains
*** A day's fishing trip to
Lake Victoria
** A visit to a Masai
manyatta.

MASAI MARA NATIONAL RESERVE

Kenya's premier wildlife area, the famous Masai Mara National Reserve, is a six-hour drive west of Nairobi. Lying at an altitude of 1650m (5414ft), it covers an area of 1510km^2 (580 sq miles) and forms the northern extension of the Serengeti National Park in Tanzania. The Mara, as it is generally known, is a Maasai word meaning 'spotted' or 'dappled'; it is a mosaic of rolling grassland dominated by red oat grass, small bush-covered hills, and along the Mara River and its tributaries flowing towards Lake Victoria, riverine bush and forest.

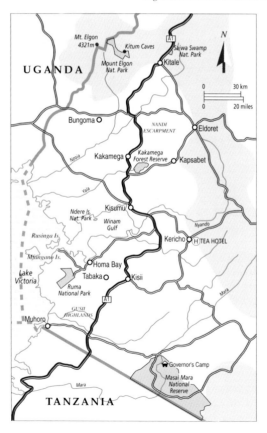

The reserve is well known for its black-maned lion, as well as its abundant resident wildlife, and is one of the few places where it's possible to see the 'big five' during a morning's game drive. However, it is perhaps more famous for its annual wildebeest migration – possibly Africa's greatest wildlife spectacle. The wildebeest population is now thought to number 1.4 million; accompanying them into the Mara may be as many as 550,000 gazelle, 200,000 zebra and 64,000 impala. Added to this are rhino, elephant, buffalo, warthog, giraffe, topi, kongoni (Coke's hartebeest), eland, leopard, cheetah, hyena and jackal – 95 species of mammal in all. Many of the cheetah are so tame they seek shelter from the hot sun under

UGANDA
Mount Elgon
Nat. Park

Lake
Victoria
•Kisumu
Homa Bay
•Kericho
Ruma
National Park
•Kisii

TANZANIA
Masai Mara
National Reserve

Left: *tame cheetah in the Masai Mara. The park, perhaps the country's finest wildlife area and haven for the 'big five', is especially noted for its black-maned lion as well as its great wildebeest migrations.*

one's vehicle and several even climb onto the roof to get a better view of any prospective prey. For the bird enthusiast, almost 500 species have been recorded: among these are 16 species of eagle plus many hawks and falcons, six species of vulture, eight of stork, four of bustard (including the kori bustard, the world's heaviest flying bird), and nine species of sunbird. With this combination of wildlife and wonderful scenery, all under a great African sky, it is easy to see why the Masai Mara has become so popular among visitors.

It's possible to visit Lake Victoria while staying at the Masai Mara Reserve. At dawn, a light aircraft takes tourists to spend a morning fishing or sightseeing on the lake, usually returning after lunch.

Balloon Safaris ★★★

A popular event and an experience of a lifetime for visitors to the Masai Mara (and to the Taita Hills Lodge in southern Kenya) is a balloon flight. Participants gather at dawn at the launch site where they can watch the giant balloons being slowly inflated by motor-driven fans. The burners are then lit and, with a roar, the balloons quickly take shape. It is time to climb into the basket; the pilot instructs everyone on ballooning rules, and the burners are put on full power. Slowly, almost imperceptibly, the balloon leaves the ground and you are looking at the rising sun and the African bush below. The pilot soon

> **UP, UP AND AWAY**
>
> The world's first scheduled passenger service by balloon was launched in 1976 from Keekorok Lodge by Alan Root, the famous wildlife film maker, and the late balloon pilot, Dudley Chignal. Now, at least six lodges offer hot-air balloon flights, most of which are followed by a glorious champagne breakfast, making Kenya the only country in the world to offer such a high number of passenger balloon flights. It is now also possible to spot wildlife from the air by microlight aircraft.

CEREMONIAL RITES

No Maasai ceremony takes place without a bull, an ox or a cow, as the animal's blood plays an important role: while the animal's head is tightly held, the jugular vein is cut using the tip of an arrow or by shooting the arrow directly into the vein (the arrow has a leather thong wrapped around it just behind its tip to prevent it penetrating too far). Once the blood has been collected in a gourd, the vein is simply pinched and plugged with a wad of dung and mud. The blood is usually mixed with milk, but is also drunk untainted by warriors, by women who have just given birth, or by a person who has undergone circumcision rites.

CIRCUMCISION AND MARRIAGE RITES

Maasai girls are circumcised at puberty. Although a ceremony is held, it is limited to family as girls are not separated into age groups; circumcision takes place in the mother's house. Like the boys, the Maasai girls dress in black robes smeared with oil, and around their heads they wear a band which has long links of metal beads hanging from it to cover the eyes. After circumcision the girls are allowed to marry, but because men may only enter into marriage once they become elders, the girls' husbands are normally much older than they are.

points out animals and birds which mostly ignore the balloon unless it passes immediately over them. On a recent flight from Governors Camp in the Masai Mara reserve, a rare Pel's fishing owl was spotted on a nest which also contained a large young owl; this is the first breeding record in Kenya of the bird.

After about an hour, the balloon lands in an open area; the retrieving party arrives and before long a low dining table is set up and a full breakfast cooked over the balloon burners. While the food is being prepared, the pilot opens a bottle of champagne, and with everyone's glass full, a toast to the successful flight is proposed. Eating a cordon bleu breakfast surrounded by Africa cannot be beaten. After breakfast, guests are taken on a game drive while travelling back to their lodges.

The Maasai People

The Maasai are pastoralists, herding cattle, sheep and goats; they also keep donkeys as beasts of burden. The majority of the Maasai still remain firmly attached to their traditional life. After children, the most important aspect of their lives is cattle, which they believe were given to them by their god *Enkai*; a Maasai of modest wealth will own at least 50. (He will, however, only be considered wealthy if he also has children.) The beasts are rarely slaughtered for meat (special ceremonial occasions aside); instead they provide the Maasai people with all their needs: milk and blood for nourishment, hides for bedding and for making sandals, and as payment in the case of a dowry or fine.

The Maasai live in an *enk'ang*, or kraal – often wrongly called a *manyatta*, which is a collection of huts housing Maasai warriors. Low, igloo-shaped huts are constructed by the women out of thin branches and grass, which they cover with a mixture of cow dung and mud. The *enk'ang* is surrounded by a strong thorn-bush fence, and each evening cattle, sheep and goats belonging to all the families are herded into this enclosure until morning. The huts are usually divided into two or three alcoves: one is used as a sleeping area for very young calves, lambs and kids; the others form the Maasai sleeping areas and a cooking area.

Above: *Maasai woman.*
Opposite: *migratory wilde-beest in the Masai Mara.*

A cultural feature of Maasai life is the male's passage through four traditional phases, each one marked by an important ceremony. The first one, called the *alamal lengipaata*, is performed just before circumcision. Because the circumcision ceremony only takes place every 12 to 15 years, the age of the boys taking part in the rites varies considerably. At this time, the group picks one of its members as a leader, who then retains the title throughout the lives of that particular group. The first phase is followed by *emorata*, or circumcision, initiating the boys into warriorhood. During the ceremony, the boys may show no sign of pain; to do so would be a disgrace. After a period of healing, they become warriors and are known as *morans*. They then become junior elders through the ceremony of *eunoto*, after which they may marry. Finally, with the *olngesherr* ceremony, they become senior elders whose duties are to preside over Maasai affairs. Traditionally the Maasai have no chiefs or headmen; all decisions are made by the senior elders.

> ### PASSAGE TO MANHOOD
>
> Once male circumcision has taken place, a period of healing follows during which the boys daub their faces white and wear black robes. They use a small bow to shoot birds, which are fashioned into a special headdress – one way in which to prove their manhood and skills. A headdress can have as many as 50 birds. These circumcised young men travel all over Maasailand, and at the end of this period, the warriors grow their hair long, cover their bodies with ochre and dress in their finery.

LAKE VICTORIA

Visitors to the Masai Mara would hardly believe that only a few hours' drive away lies Lake Victoria, and the most populated area of Kenya. The major town in the area is **Kisumu**, Kenya's third largest. Like Nairobi, it owes its existence to the Uganda Railway which reached there in 1901; at the time the town was called Port Florence, after the wife of the chief railway engineer.

Kisumu sits on the shores of the **Winam Gulf**, a part of Lake Victoria. The lake covers an area of 68,000km² (26,255 sq miles) and is on average only 78m (255ft) deep. Living around its shores are the Luo people, who are both cultivators and expert fishermen (they some-times refer to themselves as *Jonam*, the 'lake people'). They have adopted and still use today the boat style that originated from the traditional lateen-sailed dhows used by Arab slave-traders during the early part of this century.

During the day, the Luo fish for Nile perch (*mbuta*) and tilapia. The former was introduced into the lake from Lake Albert in Uganda some years ago and unfor-tunately has caused a drop in the population of many of

HOMA BAY

The town of Homa Bay is 150km (93 miles) from Kisumu; from here one can hire a boat to visit Mfangano, Rusinga and Takawiri islands. This is also a base from which to visit Ruma National Park, a half-hour away. Originally known as Lambwe Valley, the park was established as a reserve primarily to protect roan antelope (a few do occur in the Masai Mara). The reserve lies in a long, narrow, tsetse-fly-infested valley; its wildlife species include oribi (another uncommon ante-lope in Kenya), Rothschild's giraffe, Jackson's hartebeest, topi, buffalo and zebra. It also has an interesting variety of birds.

the lake's smaller indigenous species; some have disappeared completely. Although the perch is a much larger fish and provides a lot of meat, tilapia is much preferred for its taste. At night fishermen throw out nets for a small sardine-like fish known as *omena*. They paddle out onto the lake and place floats holding bright kerosene lights on the water. The light attracts the fish, which are then caught using nets; these *omena* are spread out on the ground during the day to dry in the sun. The sight of the rainbow-coloured nets heaped along the shore and thousands of fish and African kites wheeling above is a feature of all the Luo lakeside villages.

Until recently very few tourists visited Lake Victoria, but with the opening of three small tourist lodges, the lake is slowly being rediscovered. Most tourists tend to be fishermen who fly to the lake from the Masai Mara for a pleasant day's angling.

The most beautiful of the lodges, **Mfangano Island Camp**, which comprises six cool, thatched-roof cottages styled after local Luo houses, is situated in a shady spot on Mfangano; there are others on Rusinga and Takawiri.

In the north of the Winam Gulf, about 30km (19 miles) across the water from Kisumu, is the tiny **Ndere Island National Park**, a rarely visited spot. It was gazetted a national park to protect its natural vegetation and bird-life; besides its hippo and crocodile population, it also harbours a small herd of impala.

SOAPSTONE CAPITAL

Inland from Homa Bay, situated in the Gusii highlands, is the town of Kisii, best known for its soapstone. The highlands' Gusii people are considered to be among the most artistic of Kenya's ethnic groups, and have produced some skilled soapstone sculptors. They also have one of the highest population densities in Kenya (and, supposedly, one of the highest birth rates in the world). The soapstone quarries, which supply much of the world with their rose-tinted product, lie a few miles south of Kisii, near Tabaka village.

Opposite and left: *fishing canoes near Dunga, a Luo village at Lake Victoria, the country's most densely populated region. Giant Nile perch have depleted the lake's smaller and tastier species, but the catches are still excellent and the fishing industry thrives.*

Kericho, Tea Centre

High in the western highlands, 98km (61 miles) from Kisii, is the town of Kericho, centre of Kenya's tea industry. Tea was first grown near here from Ceylonese and Indian plants in the 1920s; Kenya is now the world's third largest tea producer. The best place to see the plantations and watch the leaves being picked is from Kericho's renowned **Tea Hotel**, perched in the centre of the estate and surrounded by manicured lawns. Behind this elegant complex, originally built by Brooke Bond, visitors can walk amid the shoulder-high tea bushes and photograph the pickers with their wicker baskets.

In another highland area 73km (45 miles) north of Kisumu is the town of **Kakamega**, centre of the Luhya people. Kakamega's past claim to fame is the gold rush it experienced in the 1930s, which unfortunately didn't last very long. Gold is still found here, but only in small amounts. Nowadays Kakamega is known for its nearby forest which is unique in Kenya. Relict of a tropical rainforest that once extended from West to East Africa, it is home to trees, plants, animals and birds found nowhere else in Kenya. Forty-five square kilometres (17 sq miles) of the forest have been declared a national reserve.

Above: *the view across the tea plantations around Kericho. In addition to the estates there are many smallholdings, established as part of a unique farming scheme launched in 1963. Kenya is the world's third largest producer of tea.*
Opposite: *inside one of Mount Elgon's tube caves; the droppings are those of elephants, who visit the caverns in quest of mineral salts.*

MOUNT ELGON

Driving north from Kakamega, the immense bulk of
Mount Elgon, its base over 80km (50 miles) across, soon
dominates the skyline. It is Kenya's second highest
mountain; the tallest peak, at 4321m (14,177ft), is actually
in Uganda (Kenya's border bisects Elgon), the second
highest in Kenya at 4310m (14,140ft) high. Part of the
mountain, which is actually an extinct caldera, is a
national park – one of the most scenic and unspoilt in the
country. Elgon's lower slopes are forest-covered, containing some of Kenya's finest *Podocarpus* sp. trees, which
slowly give way to beautiful afro-alpine moorland with
giant heaths and groundsel. The crater floor, at an altitude of 3500m (11,480ft) comprises a luxuriant groundsel
forest and has a number of hot springs which form the
source of the Suam River.

One of Elgon's special features is that hiking and trout
fishing are permitted in the national park. Mount Elgon
also has a number of lava tube caves, some several hundred feet deep. Three are accessible, these being Kitum,
Chepnyali and Mackingeny. Although the latter cave is
the most spectacular, Kitum is the best known as it
formed the subject of a wildlife film. Because mountain
vegetation lacks minerals which are essential to the

AFRO-ALPINE VEGETATION

The height of the alpine
heath zone differs from mountain to mountain depending
on rainfall and the direction
of prevailing winds. Fascinating are the belts of giant
heaths hung with strands of
old man's beard; giant lobelias, some 3m (10ft) high,
give way to giant groundsels
which can grow to 9m (30ft).
These high-altitude plants are
specially adapted to withstand frost at night; the senecios, for example, close up
tightly, only opening when
the warm sun strikes them.

health of all wildlife,
local elephants have for
hundreds of years vis-
ited Mount Elgon's caves,
particularly Kitum, to
gouge into them – some-
times for quite long
distances – in their con-
stant search for essential
mineral salts.

Other mammals also
requiring these minerals,
such as buffalo, bush-
buck and duiker, have
followed the elephants'
path into the caves.

SAIWA SWAMP NATIONAL PARK

Due east of Mount Elgon and 26km (16 miles) northeast of Kitale is Saiwa Swamp National Park, Africa's smallest national park (being only 2km², or half a mile in size).

Saiwa was made a national park to protect a population of rare sitatunga antelope. It consists of a narrow swampy valley filled with rushes and sedges, bordered by a narrow band of riverine forest – an ideal habitat for the sitatunga which has evolved specially adapted hoofs to live in this environment. A nice feature of this park is that there are no roads, so visitors do all their viewing of animals and birds on foot.

Several observation towers have been built along the edge of the swamp to enable visitors to view the wonderful sitatunga, and other animals such as the De Brazza, Syke's and colobus monkeys, olive baboon, bushbuck, reedbuck, suni and otters.

Just north of Saiwa, the village of **Kapenguria** is renowned for the publicity it received in 1953 when Jomo Kenyatta was tried and convicted for his alleged role as head of the Mau-Mau movement.

Below: *a male sitatunga makes its way through the Saiwa Swamp.*

Western Kenya at a Glance

To visit Masai Mara, almost any time is good, though heavy rains from end March to May, and again in November to early December, can make travel difficult. **July to September** normally coincides with the wildebeest migration. Rain can occur in any month at Lake Victoria, usually late afternoon.

Air Kenya operates daily scheduled flights to **Masai Mara** from Wilson Airport, tel: (02) 501601/2/3/4; or call Africair, tel: (02) 501210, 501219/26, fax: 609619. To get to **Lake Victoria**, Kenya Airways has daily **flights** to Kisumu, tel: (02) 823456.

There is a good (but busy) **road** from Nairobi to Kisumu. In **Masai Mara** all luxury tented camps and lodges have **four-wheel-drive** vehicles. To visit **Mfangano** and **Rusinga islands**, most visitors fly in from Masai Mara. You can also drive to Rusinga Island across a causeway from Mbita Point. Passenger boats run to Mfangano from Kisumu, via Homa Bay; cars can be parked at the district officer's office.

Masai Mara Reserve
Governors Camp: luxury tents on banks of Mara River, book through Musiara Ltd.

Little Governors Camp: small camp, beautiful setting, book through Musiara Ltd.
Kichwa Tembo Camp: built on edge of small riverine forest patch with sweeping views, book through Conservation Corporation Africa.
Siana Springs, outside reserve: luxury double tents, book through Conservation Corporation Africa.
Mara Serena Lodge, near Mara River: based on traditional Maasai architecture, book through Serena Hotels.
Mara Safari Club: tented lodge on banks of Mara River, book through Lonrho Hotels.
Mara Intrepids in reserve: double tents on Talek River bank, book through Prestige Hotels Ltd., tel: (02) 716628, fax: 716457.
Mara River Camp outside reserve: permanent tented camp (16 double tents) in beautiful spot on Mara River, book through Savannah Camps & Lodges.

ISLAND CAMPS
Mfangano Island Camp: beautiful, exclusively small lodge under giant figs in secluded bay, book through Musiara Ltd.

Rusinga Island Camp: three rondavels, book through Mellifera, PO Box 24397, Nairobi, tel: (02) 567251, fax: 577851.

Lake Victoria
Homa Bay Hotel, Lake Victoria: modern, tel: (0385) 22070 or 22132.
Sunset Hotel, Lake Victoria: overlooks lake, book direct, tel: (035) 41100/1/2/3.
Kericho Tea Hotel: historic colonial edifice, book direct, tel: (0361) 30004.
Mount Elgon Lodge: book through Msafiri Inns.

Conservation Corporation Africa, PO Box 74957, Nairobi; tel: (02) 441001-5, fax: 746826/740676.
Lonrho Hotels, PO Box 58581, Nairobi, tel: (02) 216940, fax: 216796.
Msafiri Inns, PO Box 42013, Nairobi; tel: (02) 223488.
Musiara Ltd, PO Box 48217, Nairobi; tel: (02) 331871/2, 331041, fax: 726427.
Prestige Hotels, tel: (02) 338084, fax: 217278.
Serena Hotels, tel: (02) 711077, fax: 718103.
Savannah Camps & Lodges, PO Box 48019, Nairobi; tel: (02) 229009, fax: 330698.

KISUMU	J	F	M	A	M	J	J	A	S	O	N	D
AVERAGE TEMP. °F	73	75	75	73	70	68	68	70	70	72	73	72
AVERAGE TEMP. °C	23	24	24	23	21	20	20	31	31	22	23	23
Hours of Sun Daily	9	9	8	8	8	8	7	7	7	8	8	9
RAINFALL ins	3	4	5	7	7	6	4	3	3	4	5	4
RAINFALL mm	86	94	128	172	183	142	94	87	82	96	126	104
Days of Rainfall	7	10	11	17	13	8	7	8	8	10	13	9

4
Great Rift Valley

The **Great Rift Valley**, part of an immense fracture in the earth's crust running 6440km (4000 miles) from Jordan to Mozambique, slices through Kenya from north to south. One of the most impressive features on earth, its stretch through Kenya encompasses the most dramatic, spectacular and varied scenery, unsurpassed anywhere in Africa.

Several volcanoes, now mostly dormant, occur in the valley, although just over the border in Tanzania, one volcano, Lengai, is still very active. Kenya is successfully harnessing the potential of volcanic activity in a number of ways: steam jets issuing from the lower slopes of **Mount Longonot** in **Hell's Gate National Park** power turbines which now produce approximately one-fifth of Kenya's power requirements. To the east of Longonot, at the top of the escarpment, carbon dioxide gas seeping to the earth's surface is further evidence of volcanic activity; the gas is collected, compressed into a liquid state and bottled. It is also made into dry ice for refrigeration.

The Great Rift Valley can be both inhospitable, with its gruelling lava terrain, searing temperatures and seething hot springs; and life-nurturing, with its rich, arable farmlands yielding coffee, fruit and other edible products.

Another distinctive feature is its large number of alkaline lakes, all very different and some, such as **Nakuru** and **Bogoria**, famous for the breathtaking sight of their pink flamingos; world-famous American ornithologist, Roger Tory Peterson, described Nakuru as 'the world's most fabulous bird spectacle'.

CLIMATE

The Rift Valley can be visited year-round, bearing in mind the **rainy season** (March to May), followed by rain again in November. Around Lakes Nakuru, Elmenteita and Naivasha, the weather often turns **cloudy** in the afternoon, followed by a rain shower. Temperatures vary considerably, mostly depending on altitude. At the higher altitudes, nighttime temperatures can drop below 10°C (50°F).

Opposite: *lesser flamingos feeding at Lake Bogoria.*

DON'T MISS

*** Flamingos at Lake
Nakuru or Lake Bogoria
*** A visit to Lake Naivasha,
most beautiful of the lakes
*** A stay at Lake Baringo's
Island Camp
** A climb up Mt Longonot,
Kenya's youngest volcano
** Night game-viewing at
Delamere camp.

GREAT RIFT VALLEY

Although still not fully understood, the Rift Valley was initially formed 20 million years ago when continental drift was taking place. Violent subterranean forces prised the earth's crust apart, causing the collapse of the land between parallel fault-lines. A Scottish geologist, John Walter Gregory, was the first to recognize the Rift Valley; he came across it in 1893, at a spot near **Lake Naivasha**, but because of trouble with the Maasai, Gregory moved on northwards to **Lake Baringo**. Here he took samples of rock from the valley floor and from the top of the surrounding escarpments, and found them to be similar. It

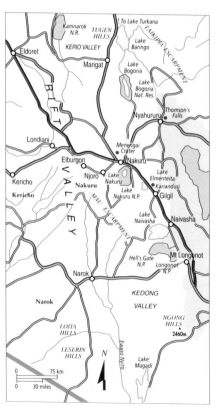

was he who named his discovery the Rift; although there are other similar rifts in the world, Gregory believed this to be the greatest, and it became known as the 'Great Rift Valley.'

Where the Rift Valley enters Kenya, the floor lies at an altitude of 198m (650ft), with little sign of steep escarpments, but at Lake Baringo to the south, the valley rises to 914m (3000ft) and is just over 16km (10 miles) wide; to either side, spectacular escarpments rise several thousand kilometres. The valley floor continues to rise until it reaches just over 1829m (6000ft) in the central highlands, before dropping down again to **Lake Magadi**, on the border with Tanzania.

Lake Turkana

Of the Rift Valley's lakes, Lake Turkana (formerly Lake Rudolf) in the extreme north is the most dramatic. With a length of 318km (198 miles) and a width of around 56km (35 miles), it's one of the largest alkaline lakes in the world.

Count Samuel Teleki von Szek, a Hungarian sportsman, geographer and wildlife enthusiast, and his companion Lieutenant Ludwig von Höhnel, first discovered Lake Turkana in 1887, naming it Lake Rudolf in honour of Crown Prince Rudolf, heir to the Austro-Hungarian empire, a man who had taken great interest in their expedition. At the time the lake was known to the local people as *Basso Narok* (black lake).

Turkana, often referred to as the 'jade sea' because of the blue-green, jade-like colour of its water, is surrounded by harsh, rugged, dry desert country with spectacular scenery that's almost constantly whipped by strong winds. The lake's waters are only slightly alkaline (the water is drinkable), and as a result support some aquatic vegetation and a large population of fish and birds, as well as crocodiles which prey on them. Huge Nile perch – some as large as 90kg (200lb) – occur in the waters, proving that at one time the lake was connected to the Nile system. Tigerfish and tilapia species are also present in the lake.

Unfortunately the lake's level has dropped quite dramatically. The reason is that the two major rivers flowing into the lake, the Omo (running into the lake's northern end from Ethiopia) and the Turkwel (entering the lake on the western shore) have both been dammed for irrigation and hydroelectric schemes. Added to this is the fact that for a number of years now, rainfall in the northeast has been very poor and irregular. Ferguson's Gulf, a shallow bay of water which was thought to be an important breeding area for fish, has for some years been totally dry, leaving the **Lake Turkana Fishing Lodge** stranded and the nearby fish-processing plant, built by the Norwegians, redundant.

Sibiloi National Park **

Covering an area of 1570km² (600 sq miles) the Sibiloi National Park has a surprising number and variety of wildlife, despite its being

---

EL-MOLO TRIBE

The el-Molo, Cushitic people living along the southeastern corner of Lake Turkana's shore and once believed to be a dying race, now exceed 500 in number as a result of intermarriage with the Turkana and Samburu peoples, and access to medical help from a nearby mission station. Through this intermarriage, however, their tribal language is disappearing.

Below: *an elaborately beaded Turkana girl.*

SIGNS OF PREHISTORIC MAN

Around Lake Turkana's shores is abundant evidence of prehistoric animals and ancient man: a part of the eastern shore has revealed traces of man and his predecessors going back 3 million years, and is referred to as the 'cradle of mankind'. The area, known as **Koobi Fora**, is now protected and forms part of **Sibiloi National Park**. The park's headquarters here house a museum where some of the fossils are displayed. It's possible to visit the nearby sites if you gain permission from the National Museum in Nairobi.

Below: *Lake Turkana and its volcanic South Island.*

extremely arid and windblown. It includes lion, Grevy's zebra, beisa oryx, gerenuk, Grant's gazelle and a unique family member of the topi, called tiang.

Birdlife, too, is varied and at times plentiful, especially during the European winter months, when the lake shore is home to large numbers of wading birds, among them black-tailed godwits and redshanks. For the really keen bird-watcher, the birds found in the arid bush are perhaps the most interesting: swallow-tailed kites, Heuglin's and kori bustards, Lichtenstein's sandgrouse, Somali and carmine bee-eaters and both crested and short-crested larks are just a few of the wonderful birds found in this area.

Turkana's Volcanic Islands

Lake Turkana has three islands, all of them volcanic. **North Island**, small and rocky, is inhabited only by snakes. Midway down the lake is **Central Island** – a national park – formed from three still-active volcanoes which occasionally belch out steam and smoke. Each of the volcanoes is flooded; the result, three interesting

lakes which serve as breeding grounds for possibly the world's largest crocodile population. The lakes are named after their most prominent features: Crocodile, Flamingo and Tilapia. The third island, appropriately named **South Island**, is the largest; it is also a national park. Volcanic ash covers most of it, making it most desolate except for a few feral goats. At night its volcanic vents often glow, and have inspired the el-Molo people to relate stories of evil spirits.

Few people visit Turkana's southern shore, an area of scorched, black lava and one of the most inhospitable places on earth. The shoreline is dominated by **Teleki's Volcano** and **Nabuyatom Cone**, which form part of 'The Barrier' separating Turkana from the Suguta Valley, one of the world's hottest locations: midday temperatures average between 72–77°C (130–140°F). The terrain is so difficult that there is virtually no access between the east and west shores. The least known of the Rift Valley lakes, **Lake Logipe**, lies in the Suguta Valley; it can, at times, rival famous Lake Nakuru with spectacular numbers of flamingos.

Mention must be made of **Mount Kulal**, which has been designated an International Biosphere Reserve – one of three such reserves in Kenya. Mount Kulal's cool, forested slopes, rising to 2416m (7927ft) just a few short miles from Turkana's sunbaked southeastern shore, are an incredible contrast. A fascinating mountain with two peaks separated by a deep gorge and a knife-edge ridge, Kulal is the main cause of the very strong winds that are such a feature in this area. The winds usually start to blow during the late morning, slowly becoming stronger until by nightfall they are almost gale force; they suddenly cease before dawn.

Above: *a 'rock desert' of lava near Lake Turkana.*

A MODERN MYSTERY

Lake Turkana's el-Molo people are known to weave their stories of intrigue around the hiss of the island volcanoes, but a real mystery did occur on South Island in 1934. At that time, Vivien Fuchs (later 'Sir') of Antarctic fame led an expedition to the island, returning to the mainland after three days, from where he sent another member to join the colleague he'd left behind. However, neither man nor trace was ever seen again, and their disappearance has yet to be satisfactorily explained.

MOLO RIVER SAFARI

As a guest at **Lake Baringo's Island Camp**, the highlight of your visit will be an early morning boat safari up the Molo River; you encounter birds, crocodiles, wild Africa: an experience of a lifetime. If, during your visit, the Molo River isn't flowing, a walk along the dry riverbed with an Njemps guide from the camp is another wonderful excursion. At the end of your stay, an overriding memory of Island Camp will be the sun rising over the Rift Valley escarpment at dawn, with perhaps a lone Njemps fisherman slowly paddling his way across the lake.

Below: *bougainvillea festoons the grounds of the Lake Baringo clubhouse.*

Lake Baringo ★★★

Continuing southwards along the Rift Valley is Lake Baringo, a freshwater lake and now a major tourist resort lying deep in the valley.

Although surrounded by semidesert, the scenery is rugged and majestic. To the east of the lake rise the dramatic Tugen Hills, birthplace of President Moi, and to the west is the Laikipia Escarpment. Unfortunately the lake's waters are stained brown: considerable overgrazing by goats has stripped the soil of its groundcover, and during heavy rains, the fine volcanic silts are washed into the lake. They are so fine that much of the silt never settles, resulting in murky water. Even so, the lake holds a good fish population – mainly tilapia and barbel – plus herds of hippo and many crocodile.

Lake Baringo's water is fresh, in spite of there being no obvious outlet. When Gregory explored the lake in 1893, he concluded that Baringo was at one time connected to Lake Turkana, but that volcanic activity had lifted the northern end of the lake, cutting off its outlet. It is believed today that the outlet lies submerged; 50km (31 miles) north of Baringo, at Kapedo in the middle of

Lake Baringo
Eldoret

Lake Bogoria Nat. Res.

Nakuru
Kericho   Aberdare
                                     National
Lake   Park
Naivasha   Naivasha

Hell's Gate   Mt. Longonot
Limuru   N.P.

Lake Magadi

---

hot, dry, barren country, is an oasis of doum palms with
hot springs and a 9m (30ft) waterfall: this is believed
to be Lake Baringo's outlet.

Nowadays, Baringo is regarded as the bird-watching
centre of Kenya, with over 450 species recorded. Not
only is there a proliferation of waterbirds, but there is
also a wonderful variety of birds in the acacia bush bordering the lake, many of them difficult to see elsewhere.
Whether you are a bird-watcher or not, an early morning
walk here should really not be missed.

Other activities at Lake Baringo are fishing (tilapia,
barbel, catfish), water-skiing and wind-surfing; facilities
and hiring equipment are available at Island Camp.

Njemps People

The Njemps, numbering less than 9000, are related to
both the Maasai and the Samburu, but have become
sedentary rather than nomadic. Although the Njemps
own cattle and goats, because of the harsh climate they
rely heavily on fishing, mostly from small canoes, for
their livelihood. These canoes are sometimes used to
carry sheep and goats over considerable distances to
other islands, where they can forage for food; the image
of a solitary Njemps fisherman slowly paddling his craft
across the water is a distinctive and lasting one.

FISHING FOR A LIVING

The unique canoes used by
the Njemps tribe are made
from ambach, a lightweight
wood which grows around
the lake shore. Lengths are
bound together – traditionally with wild sisal but increasingly with nylon cords –
into a peaked bow and open
stern. A separate deck of
ambach is then constructed
to fit into the bottom of the
canoe, where the fisherman
sits. This flimsy but buoyant
vessel is propelled by small
hand paddles which look
inefficient but appear to
work well for the fishermen.
They also fish standing in the
water, often with crocodile
nearby; but it's an almost
unheard of occurrence that a
person has been attacked by
one, presumably because the
predators are so well fed!

Top left: *a young Njemps
boy paddles his lightweight
canoe over the placid
waters of Lake Baringo.
His people are related to
the Masai.*

ALKALINE LAKES

Almost all of the Rift Valley lakes are soda or alkaline as they have no outlet. Their composition of trona, or sodium carbonate, rather than sodium chloride (common salt) is as a result of rivers, streams and springs having flowed into them for thousands of years through mineral-rich volcanic rocks and soils. However, Lakes Baringo and Naivasha are surprisingly fresh although they have no obvious outlets. Lake Turkana, too, is only slightly alkaline. Some of the alkaline lakes do contain common salt, which is produced in commercial quantities.

Below: *a jetting geyser shrouds Bogoria's lake shore in steam.*

Even though the Njemps cultivate, eat fish and have abandoned the *manyatta* tradition (young warriors living in separate groups), Maasai cultural traits remain dominant. They dress and decorate themselves in the Maasai fashion, their songs and dances are similar, and they practise circumcision and retain the warrior system.

Lake Bogoria ∗∗∗

Just south of Baringo is Lake Bogoria (formerly known as Lake Hannington); the lake and surrounding area is a national reserve. Lying close to the base of the Ngendalel Escarpment, which rises 610m (2000ft) above the lake, Bogoria is scenically the most spectacular and dramatic of all the Rift Valley lakes. Long, narrow, and deep, it is strongly alkaline and surrounded by dense, impenetrable thorn bush. Around the lake shore are a number of geysers and hot springs, which at dawn can sometimes form a thick mist. When one stands near one of the geysers and peers across the lake through the clouds of hot swirling steam to the towering wall of the escarpment, it is easy to imagine how the earth split apart to form the dramatic, chiselled sweep of the Rift Valley.

There are times when Lake Bogoria is home to thousands of flamingos; to watch skeins of them flying along the lake towards the geysers and hot springs where they drink and bathe is a wondrous sight not easy to forget. John Walter Gregory, when he visited the lake during his explorations, called it 'the most beautiful sight in Africa.'

Above: *a jackal and a young waterbuck on the shore of Lake Nakuru.*

During some years, lesser flamingos build their cone-shaped mud nests at Bogoria, and though they occasionally lay eggs, they strangely have never been known to breed there. Bogoria is also home to a variety of mammals: common zebra, Grant's gazelle, impala, klipspringer, dik-dik and the magnificent greater kudu, which is both prolific and tame.

Lake Nakuru ***

Across the equator, southwards of Bogoria, lies the Rift Valley's most famous lake, Nakuru. Known all over the world for its flamingos, it is also alkaline and is recognized as being one of the natural wonders of the world.

In 1961, the southern two-thirds of the lake was established as a sanctuary to protect the flamingos, and in 1967 Nakuru was declared a national park, the first one in Africa to be set aside for the preservation of birdlife. The park's area was extended in 1969 to encompass the whole lake, and since then has been extended once more; it now covers an area of 188km² (73 sq miles).

Lake Nakuru is now also a rhino sanctuary, harbouring a population of 44 black and 28 white rhino; but the flamingos, of course, have always been the main attraction. At times there may be almost two million

---

RIFT VALLEY VOLCANOES

The length of the Rift Valley is studded with dormant volcanoes varying in age, size and shape. Some of them have the classical cone shape (Mt Longonot is a good example), while other much older ones can sometimes be difficult to identify as volcanoes, because the original crater has been eroded away with time and only the hard central plug remains. Examples of these, starting in the north of the country, are: North, Central and South islands in Lake Turkana, Teleki's Volcano, Kakorinyo, Silali, Londiani, Menengai, Eburru, Longonot, Suswa, Olorgesailie, and Shomboli on the Tanzanian border.

flamingos in residence, forming a stunningly beautiful deep-pink band around the edges of the lake shore.

During 1960 a small fish which is tolerant to alkaline water, *Tilapia grahami*, was introduced into the lake to control mosquito larvae. These tilapia have since multiplied both in number and in size, attracting lots of fish-eating birds such as pelicans, cormorants and herons. Although over 400 species of bird have been recorded at Nakuru, they are not the only attraction the lake has to offer; over 50 species of mammal have been recorded and it is perhaps the best place in Kenya to see leopard.

Some years ago a number of endangered Rothschild's giraffe was translocated here; they have multiplied and are now a common sight.

Troops of black-and-white colobus monkeys can be seen in the yellow-barked acacias (*Acacia xanthophloea*) in the southern part of the sanctuary. This is also a good area to see the magnificent crowned eagle, Africa's most powerful. Along the eastern shore of the lake stretches a magnificent forest of tree euphorbias (*Euphorbia candelabrum*), unique in Kenya. It is, in fact, the largest single euphorbia forest in Africa.

FLAMINGOS

Two flamingo species occur on most of the Rift Valley lakes: the greater and the lesser flamingo, the latter outnumbering the former by 200 to one. Although they frequent the lakes that are alkaline, they use any fresh-water source flowing into the lake, and hot springs that are not strongly alkaline, for bathing and drinking. What makes these birds so attractive is the deep coral hue of their legs and beaks, and their salmon-pink plumage. During courtship displays, flamingos spread their wings to reveal the vibrant colour underneath.

Lake Elmenteita ⋆⋆

Smallest of all of the Rift Valley's lakes is Lake Elmenteita; shallow and alkaline, it has two small seasonal rivers flowing into it. The lake is surrounded by an almost lunar-like landscape of extinct volcanoes and lava flows; it is also very attractive, its water often edged with pink flamingos.

Elmenteita lies on Soysambu Estate, owned by Lord Delamere whose father was one of the early settlers in Kenya. The estate, which still harbours good numbers as well as a variety of game, is now the **Soysambu Wildlife Sanctuary**, complete with a luxury permanent tented camp. Only visitors staying at the camp, however, are permitted to visit the sanctuary.

On the western side of the lake is a number of secluded bays with small lava islands, which were, for several years, used by greater flamingos as a nesting site. Although flamingos usually make their nests out of mud, at Lake Elmenteita they would lay their eggs on the lava, only adding a few pieces of grass. However, for

Opposite: *African spoonbills crowd the shoreline of Naivasha, the purest of the Rift Valley's lakes. The waters are home to more than 400 bird species.*
Below: *the black-and-white colobus, a prominent resident of the forests.*

a number of years now these islands have been taken over by white pelicans, Kenya's only breeding colony. Because Elmenteita has no fish, the pelicans have to commute to nearby Lakes Nakuru and Naivasha to obtain their food.

To the south of the lake is **Eburru**, an old volcano which has at least 200 steam jets around its base. These jets are an important source of fresh water in the area, obtained by condensing the steam.

Nearby is **Kariandusi**, a prehistoric site first worked on by Dr Louis Leakey in 1928. There is also a mine here, where diatomite (deposits of ancient microscopic aquatic organisms) is extracted. Diatomite is used for water filters in industry.

Above: *part of the grace-fully embowered grounds of the Lake Naivasha Country Club, to the west of the once notorious aristocratic playground of 'Happy Valley'.*
Opposite: *The waters of Lake Naivasha are too chilly for crocodiles, but hippos seem to find them congenial enough.*

The 'Happy Valley' Set

The infamous 'Happy Valley' is an area between the western slopes of the Aberdares and the town of **Gilgil**, but the real centre used to be along the **Wanjohi River**. It is a beautiful, wide, grassy valley set at the foot of the Aberdares and looking out over the Rift Valley.

Soon after World War I a number of titled and aristocratic Euorpeans settled here. The first of these was Josslyn Hay (later Lord Erroll) who eloped to Kenya from England with Lady Idina Gordon; the scandal of their affair forced them to leave England in April 1924. Idina was eight years older than Hay and twice married.

Thus was Kenya's reputation launched as a place beyond society's official censure. There were soon stories of wild champagne and wife-swapping parties, endless orgies and drug abuse (cocaine and morphine).

These early settlers built themselves wonderful homes and were soon receiving European visitors with a taste for gambling and promiscuity. It was around this time that the area became known as 'Happy Valley', a term probably given to it by the London gossip columns; and it was here that the saying, 'Are you married, or do you live in Kenya?' originated.

Lake Naivasha ★★★

Lake Naivasha is the highest and the most beautiful of the Rift Valley lakes. At 1910m (6200ft), the water is fresh and the lake is fringed with dense clumps of papyrus (ancient Egyptians once used this to make paper). Kingfishers use the papyrus as a perch, and herons hide in it while searching for food.

Dominating Naivasha (known by the Maasai as *En-aiposha* – 'heaving' or 'to and fro' – a reference to how turbulent Naivasha can get in the afternoon) is **Mount Longonot**, a dormant volcano, while **Crescent Island**, at the lake's southern end, is part of the rim of an ancient submerged volcano. The island is a private game sanctuary open to visitors, who may walk among the game (there are no predators or dangerous animals).

Naivasha is yet another area popular for bird-watching (over 400 species have been recorded). It is also a favourite weekend retreat for Nairobi residents, who come here to sail, water-ski and fish. There are no crocodile in the lake as the water is too cold for them due to altitude, but there is a number of hippo. Early settlers introduced tilapia and later, black bass to control its increasing numbers. Both of these fish are preyed upon by one of the largest concentrations of fish eagle in Africa. Other not-so-popular introductions into the lake are Louisiana crayfish, which are thought to damage the fish, and the coypu, a South American rodent, which has eaten the beautiful water lilies; now floating weeds cover much of the surface. The lake's fresh water (it is assumed that Naivasha, like Baringo, has an underground outlet) is used extensively to irrigate

MOUNT LONGONOT

At 2776m (9108ft) Mount Longonot is the highest of the Rift Valley volcanoes. Visitors wishing to climb its crater should leave their car at the Longonot police station, although this means a walk of almost 7km (4 miles) to the start of the climb. The walk up to the crater's rim takes about four hours, and although very narrow, it is possible to walk around the entire rim. There is a track down to the crater floor, but beware of buffalo hiding in the thick scrub!

the richly fertile volcanic soils that exist in the surrounding areas. A variety of vegetables, fruit and flowers is grown, mostly for export, earning important foreign exchange.

Along the lake shore, vineyards produce grapes for the country's fledgling wine industry.

Lake Magadi ⋆⋆

The most southerly lake in Kenya's Rift Valley is Lake Magadi, a Maasai word meaning 'soda lake'. At an altitude of 579m (1900ft), Magadi is one of the world's most inhospitable lakes, a shimmering pink-coloured hellscape of overpowering heat and smell, with temperatures well over 38°C (100°F).

The lake is the second largest source of trona (sodium carbonate) in the world (the Salton Sea in the United States is the largest). Magadi differs from the other Rift Valley alkaline lakes in that its deposits well up from below the earth's surface. These deposits have been mined for the last 80 years by the Magadi Soda Company; production is now 220,000 tonnes annually, and the lake is still maintaining its enormous soda output. The trona is processed at Magadi into soda ash and sodium chloride (common salt); the soda ash is exported mainly to the Far East and Southeast Asia.

Although the vegetation around the lake is dry desert scrub, receiving only 380mm (15in) of rain in a good year, there is a surprising amount of wildlife. Giraffe, gerenuk, Grant's gazelle and wildebeest are all found here. Birdlife too can be spectacular, particularly near any of the hot springs: flamingo (thousands of lesser flamingos bred at the lake in 1962), pelican, stilt, avocet and the localized Magadi plover (chestnut-banded sand plover) are just a few of the many birds recorded in the area.

The Rift Valley's Flamingos

There is nothing more synonymous with the Rift Valley than its flamingos. These magnificent birds occur on all the valley lakes; although their favourite haunts are those that are strongly alkaline, they do occasionally occur in small numbers on the freshwater lakes. Both the lesser and the greater species are found in East Africa, the greater flamingo being a larger bird, the lesser occurring in larger numbers (it is believed there may be as many as four million lesser flamingo and somewhere between forty to fifty thousand of the greater species living on the lakes). It is not unusual to find 1.5 million resident at Lake Nakuru.

The two species do not compete with one another: greater flamingo feed mostly on aquatic invertebrates and crustacea in the mud on the lake bottom, while lesser flamingo feed almost exclusively on a blue-green alga called spirulina which hangs suspended in the top millimetre or so of the water. Flamingos' bills are adapted for this very specialized diet. The lesser flamingo's lower mandible, which lies uppermost when the head is bent over while feeding, is lightweight and acts as a float, keeping the bill at the optimum depth. Both mandibles are lined with fine bristly lamellae which act as filters, and the tongue is round, acting as a pump. Water is drawn into the bill through the action of the tongue, causing the laminae to lie flat. The water is not swallowed (the alkalinity makes it poisonous) but is pumped out again, at which the laminae stand erect, retaining the spirulina. The greater flamingo's bill is very similar but differs in that the laminae are fewer and much coarser.

It is estimated that each lesser flamingo eats 184g (6.5oz) of spirulina a day; this means that a million birds at Lake Nakuru consume around 184 tonnes in a single day – about 66,300 tonnes a year! Add to this figure an estimated 2550 tonnes of fish consumed by white pelicans – and it illustrates just how productive an alkaline lake such as Lake Nakuru can be.

Opposite: *the lone Masai is crossing the soda settling ponds of the Magadi Soda Company. Despite the heat and harsh surrounds, the area sustains a surprising wealth of wildlife.*

Below: *flamingos in their thousands flock to the Rift Valley's lakes.*

Great Rift Valley at a Glance

BEST TIMES TO VISIT

Almost **any time of year** is suitable, but during rainy season, state of roads can make driving difficult, particularly in national parks and reserves.

GETTING THERE

Practically all Rift Valley areas south of Lake Baringo easily accessible by ordinary **saloon car**. Visitors to Lake Turkana and northern areas can make use of **Turkana Bus**, run by Safari Camp Services; converted four-wheel-drive Bedford trucks depart every week from Nairobi (this economically priced safari one of best ways to visit Turkana), contact Safari Camp Services, PO Box 44801, Nairobi; tel: (02) 228936 or 330130.

WHERE TO EAT

Visitors to the Rift Valley are fully catered for at the lodges in which they are staying.

WHERE TO STAY

Lake Turkana

Oasis Lodge at Loiyengalani on lake's eastern shore: most comfortable lodge in the area, two pools fed by fresh water from a spring, book through Bunsen Travel, PO Box 45456, Nairobi; tel: (02) 221992/3/4, 333771/2/3, fax: 214120.

Lake Baringo

Island Camp, on Olkokwe Island in centre of lake: luxury permanent tented camp under shady acacias, wonderful views across lake and escarpment; occasional evening barbecues around pool very popular; book through Let's Go Travel.
Lake Baringo Club, on lake shore near Kampi ya Samaki: rooms overlook lake across lawns where hippos graze at night; small but attractively sited pool; book through Block Hotels.

Lake Bogoria

Lake Bogoria Hotel near reserve's northern entrance gate at Loboi: first class, book direct, tel: (02) 249055.

Lake Nakuru

Lion Hill Lodge, on eastern shore: well-appointed rooms on steep hillside all have views over lake; sauna and pool; book through Sarova Hotels.
Lake Nakuru Lodge near southeastern corner of lake: good lake views; book through Let's Go Travel.

BUDGET ACCOMMODATION

Lake Turkana

Safari Camp Services, Loiyengalani: accommodation available at their base; also two campsites; write to PO Box 44801, Nairobi.

Lake Bogoria

Fig Tree Camp Site in reserve: most popular of a number of shaded campsites, enquire at reserve gate.

Lake Nakuru

Two public plus three private sites (need to be booked in advance by professional safari companies).

Lake Naivasha

Fisherman's Camp on lake shore: primarily campsite, but also number of self-catering bandas available, plus others on hillside overlooking lake; book through Let's Go Travel.
Burche's Camp & Marina on lake shore: self-catering accommodation, 4-bed cottages plus rondavels and bandas; book direct, PO Box 40, Naivasha, tel: (0311) 21010.

Lake Elmenteita

Delamere Camp on lake's northeast shore: small, exclusive permanent tented camp in Soysambu Wildlife Sanctuary (sanctuary open to Delamere Camp guests only); write to PO Box 48019, Nairobi, tel: (02) 335935 or 831684, fax: 216528.

Lake Naivasha

Lake Naivasha Country Club (formerly The Lake Hotel) on lake shore opposite Crescent Island: set among yellow-barked acacias, green lawns and beautiful gardens, book through Block Hotels.
Loldia House, on Naivasha's north shore: old settler's house, part of group who own Govenors Camp, welcoming atmosphere, cuisine excellent; book through Musiara Ltd.
Longonot Ranch House on Kedong Ranch, between Hell's Gate and Longonot national parks: colonial-style house overlooking Lake Naivasha; working cattle ranch with

Great Rift Valley at a Glance

abundant plains game; book through Safaris Unlimited (Africa) Ltd.

Mundui, home of Lord and Lady Cole: accommodation in large cottage near main house; set in private game reserve containing plains game and large variety of birds; book through Bush Homes of East Africa.

Elsamere, former home of Joy Adamson: small museum and research centre, accepts guests if rooms available and if they're members of conservation organization; write to PO Box 1497, Naivasha; tel: (0311) 30079.

Crater Lake Tented Camp on shore of Lake Songasoi (within ancient volcanic crater near Lake Naivasha): luxury double tents; walks and ox-wagon safaris; book through Southern Cross Safaris, tel: (02) 225255/336570.

TOURS AND EXCURSIONS

Bird-watching: resident naturalist at Lake Baringo Club organizes walks mornings and afternoons (morning walk along base of nearby cliffs highly recommended to bird-watchers and keen walkers); Baringo also runs bird-watching boat trips, although awnings restrict upward viewing; Delamere Camp has bird hides on the lake shore; escorted walks by Naivasha Country Club; vultures nest on cliffs of Hell's Gate gorge in Hell's Gate National Park, nearby Naivasha.

Boat trips: run by Island Camp (the Njemps act as excellent and knowledgeable guides); Lake Naivasha Country Club (includes visits to Crescent Island); Loldia House; and Safariland.

Game-viewing: Delamere Camp has a small tree house where guests can stay overnight to watch leopard attracted by bait; also on offer is a sundowner excursion to a cliff above the lake, and night game drives using powerful spotlights to view nocturnal animals, some rarely seen by visitors; Longonot Ranch House offers night game drives; plains game can be viewed in Hell's Gate National Park; Fischer's Column has a colony of hyrax, visitors permitted to walk around.

Horse riding: Loldia House and Longonot Ranch House have facilities for horse-riding enthusiasts.

Lake Excursions: Island Camp takes visitors to an Njemps village, where they can photograph the people; visits to other parts of Baringo, and nearby Lake Bogoria also available; Loldia House organizes visits to Hell's Gate and Nakuru national parks.

Photographic talks: Lake Baringo Club holds a pre-dinner slideshow and commentary on Lake Baringo's birds every evening, and shows a wildlife video after dinner.

Walking: guided walks arranged by Island Camp (using Njemps guides), Delamere Camp, Loldia House, and Longonot Ranch House.

Watersports: Island Camp has water-skiing and windsurfing facilities; Loldia House offers fishing.

USEFUL ADDRESSES

Safaris Unlimited (Africa) Ltd, PO Box 24181, Nairobi, tel: (02) 891168/890435, fax: 891113.

Block Hotels, PO Box 47557, Nairobi, tel: (02) 335807.

Bush Homes of East Africa Ltd, PO Box 56923, Nairobi; tel: (02) 571647/571661; fax: 571665.

Let's Go Travel, PO Box 60342, Nairobi; tel: (02) 340331, fax: 336890.

Musiara Ltd, PO Box 48217, Nairobi; tel: (02) 331871/331041.

Sarova Hotels, PO Box 30680, Nairobi; tel: (02) 333233.

NAKURU	J	F	M	A	M	J	J	A	S	O	N	D
AVERAGE TEMP. °F	64	66	65	63	63	62	62	62	61	61	61	62
AVERAGE TEMP. °C	18	19	18	17	17	16	16	16	16	16	16	17
Hours of Sun Daily	9	8	7	6	7	8	7	7	7	6	6	8
RAINFALL ins	1	2	4	6	4	3	4	4	4	3	3	1
RAINFALL mm	34	38	90	160	110	67	95	88	110	59	63	30
Days of Rainfall	5	7	9	16	15	11	12	15	12	12	13	6

5
Northern and Eastern Kenya

This area, once known as Kenya's Northern Frontier District (NFD), is a vast expanse of hot semidesert terrain. It is a country of sand rivers whose courses are marked by clumps of doum palms, of rocky hills and isolated mountains which rise sheer out of the hot, dry plains. Two rivers flow through the area: the **Tana**, Kenya's longest river, which eventually flows into the Indian Ocean, and the **Ewaso Nyiro** which slowly disappears into the Lorian Swamp.

Northern and eastern Kenya are rich in mammal and bird species not found elsewhere, and fortunately there are a number of national parks and reserves to protect them. A group of nomadic tribes also lives in this difficult region – the Somali, Gabra and Samburu – herding camels, sheep and goats.

Most visitors to this part of Kenya are drawn by the **Samburu** and **Buffalo Springs** reserves. A special feature, too, is the practice by lodges within the reserves to attract leopard at night by placing bait in a tree across from the lodge. Powerful spotlights directed at the bait allow guests to watch this nocturnal animal at work.

The **Samburu** and **Samburu Serena** lodges also feed crocodiles, while guests look on. Staff at Buffalo Springs Lodge succeed in drawing the rarely seen African civet, and the occasional striped hyena, by putting out food at night close to the lounge.

It is better to visit these remote parts of Kenya with a reputable safari operator, who will always ensure that places considered unsafe will be completely avoided.

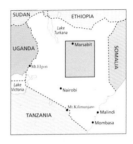

Opposite: *the reticulated giraffe, resident of the northern region.*

DON'T MISS

*** Samburu and Buffalo
Springs reserves
*** Shaba National Reserve
*** Lewa Wildlife
Conservancy
** Meru National Park
** Marsabit National Park.

Opposite, left: *the gerenuk
feeds at a higher level
which is out of reach of
other browsing animals.*
Opposite, right: *accommodation on stilts at the
Samburu Intrepids Camp.*

Samburu and Buffalo Springs National Reserves •••

These two small scenic reserves range in altitude from
800 to 1230m (2625 to 4036ft). They sit astride the Ewaso
Nyiro River (a Samburu name meaning 'river of brown
water') and are dominated by the sheer-walled **Ol
Lolokwe** and the rocky hills of Koitogor and Lolkoitoi.
The river, bordered by a green ribbon of riverine forest
made up mostly of tamarind trees, doum palms, Tana
River poplars, and the *Acacia elatior*, is the lifeblood of
this dry, arid region.

In the **Samburu National Reserve** north of the river, a
narrow plain quickly gives way to rocky hillsides which
are home to many leopard, while **Buffalo Springs
National Reserve** is mainly a rolling plain of volcanic
soils with dry riverbeds lined with doum palms.

The latter reserve has two small but important rivers
flowing through it: the Isiolo River which never dries up
(the Ewaso Nyiro occasionally does) and the Ngare
Mara. There are also the crystal clear
springs which give the reserve its
name. Unfortunately, their beauty has
been spoilt; one of the springs has had
an unsightly wall built around it and its
water piped to the nearby small town
of Archer's Post, while another has a
smaller wall around it and is used as a
swimming pool by campers. Fortunately, one small spring has been left
in its natural state and its waters flow
into the nearby Ewaso Nyiro River,
providing a magnet for wildlife.

Near Buffalo Springs is a wonderful
area called Champagne Ridge, covered
with flat-topped umbrella thorn trees
(*Acacia tortilis*) which are characteristic
of the area. On either side of the river
are extensive areas of salt bush (*Salsola
dendroides*), which few animals eat
because its leaves taste salty, but it does
provide cover for lion and cheetah.

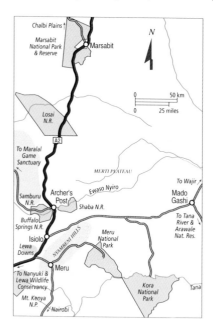

It is the unique wildlife that attracts the many tourists to this wonderful area and, although there are no large spectacular herds, there is a wide variety. Four special mammals – gerenuk, Grevy's zebra, beisa oryx and reticulated giraffe – are all quite common and although there is some seasonal movement out of the reserves, you can usually count on seeing them. Other mammals include Burchell's zebra, buffalo, impala, common waterbuck, dik-dik (both Kirk's and Guenther's), Grant's gazelle, klipspringer, both greater and lesser kudu and warthog.

The highlight of any visit to Samburu and Buffalo Springs is to watch the large numbers of elephant – who are unperturbed by safari-goers – drinking and bathing in the shallow waters of the Ewaso Nyiro River. Crocodiles – some of them very large – and the occasional hippo are present in the river, although it is not an ideal environment for hippos as the dry bush to either side of the river provides them with very little food.

To the north of Samburu National Reserve is a forested range of mountains, **The Matthews**. A variety of game, including elephant, occurs in these mountain forests. The highest point, **Matthews Peak**, at 2375m (790ft) was named by Count Samuel Teleki in appreciation of help received on his expedition from Sir Lloyd Matthews, who was at the time commander-in-chief of the Sultan of Zanzibar's army.

THE GERENUK

This shy, graceful gazelle gets its name from the Somali language and means 'giraffe-necked', while its Swahili name *swara twiga* translates as gazelle-giraffe. Its outstanding characteristic features are long legs and a long, slender neck. The gerenuk's head is small for the animal's size; in front of the eyes are two preorbital glands which emit a tar-like substance that's deposited on twigs and bushes to mark the gazelle's territory. It feeds by standing erect on its hind legs, long neck stretched upwards, sometimes using its front leg to pull the vegetation down to an attainable level. Nibbling at such heights, it avoids competing with other gazelles and most antelopes. Gerenuks rarely drink water, obtaining all their moisture requirements from the food they eat.

Above: visitors on a horse-back safari in Lewa Wildlife Conservancy, south of Samburu National Reserve. The conservancy has had much success in protecting both black and white rhino.

A FLOWERING DESERT

In the thorn scrub and on many of the rocky outcrops grows the desert rose (*Adenium obesum*), whose colourful pink flowers are a beautiful contrast in this arid environment. Other common but interesting plants are the *Callalluma speciosa*, a succulent that produces balls of black flowers which give off a smell of rotten meat, thus attracting pollinating flies; the *Calotropis procera*, a tall plant with cabbage-like fleshy leaves that doesn't appear to be eaten by any mammal; and the red-flowering Erythrina trees, loved by sunbirds.

Camel Safaris in Samburu **

Camel safaris are a fairly recent innovation in Kenya and take place in Samburu country north of Nairobi. They are really walking safaris, where camels are used to carry all the equipment and food and, of course, an occasional tired walker. Guests are transported from Nairobi to a pick-up point deep in Samburu territory, where they meet their guide and the camels with their handlers, Samburu warriors wearing their traditional colourful clothes, which all adds to the mood of the occasion.

Walking is at a leisurely pace and the guide and Samburu warriors soon point out wildlife, including colourful birds, insects, flowers and interesting plants that most safari-goers miss. Although a variety of game is usually seen on this type of safari, one does not get as close to the game as on a conventional vehicle safari to a national park or reserve. Even so, the walk in the African bush with only the sounds of nature or the soft singing of your Samburu guides is something special. Each evening, camp is set up near a river or waterhole and guests have the choice of sleeping with only a mosquito net between them and the stars, or sleeping in a tent. Take the first option! You will never experience anything like it in your life! Food is prepared in the camp and tastes all the better when eaten outside under a big African night sky. These special safaris usually last from five to six days. For details of camel safaris, *see* p. 47.

Shaba National Reserve ***

Although Shaba, lying to the east of the Samburu and Buffalo Springs reserves, is only separated from them by a major highway, it is a very different habitat. With an area of 280km² (108 sq miles), it is scenically dramatic; here the Ewaso Nyiro, instead of coursing through a plain, runs through deep gorges and waterfalls. **Mount Bodech** and **Shaba Hill** dominate the landscape, and the plains are dotted with springs, small swamps and rocky hills. The wildlife is similar to the other reserves, but generally not as plentiful.

Shaba is perhaps best known as the onetime home of author Joy Adamson who rehabilitated a leopard called Penny here. The story is told in Joy's book *Penny, Queen of Shaba*. It was at Shaba that Joy was murdered.

Lewa Wildlife Conservancy ✱✱✱
South of Samburu is Lewa Downs, now called Lewa Wildlife Conservancy, owned by the Craig family. Originally a cattle ranch where wildlife was encouraged, it now carries an abundant and amazing variety, ranging from elephant and rhino to leopard and tiny dik-dik.

It is at Lewa that Anna Mertz, with the help of the Craigs, has established the **Ngare Sergoi Rhino Sanctuary**. Protecting both the black and white species, it is surrounded by an expensive solar-powered electric fence and is patrolled by armed game rangers – over 50 in all – equipped with radios. Recently the fence was extended to encircle the entire ranch area, a total distance of 35km (22 miles), and Lewa Downs was renamed.

LET LEWA BE YOUR HOST

Lewa Wildlife Conservancy offers accommodation in the form of three stone-built cottages next to the main ranch house. Each cottage has two rooms and a verandah with wonderful views over the surrounding countryside; another home is also available to guests. Meals are eaten with the Craig family, consisting mostly of fresh, home-grown ingredients. Also at Lewa is the new Lerai Luxury Tented Camp, which has 12 tents. Of interest on the ranch is a prehistoric site that has many Acheulian hand-axes strewn all around.

Left: *two elegantly beaded Samburu girls. The Samburu, a nomadic cattle-owning people, traditionally inhabit the northern region between Lake Turkana and the Ewaso Nyiro River.*

DOUM PALM

The doum palm, which can grow to 15m (49ft), is the only member of the palm family to have a divided trunk. The trees are riparian, occurring along the coast and in the arid areas of northern and eastern Kenya along seasonal river courses. Their fruit is much prized by animals, particularly baboon and elephant; humans occasionally eat it too. Elephants swallow the seeds whole, thus distributing them over large areas. Local people carve the seeds into buttons and other decorative items, which can look remarkably like ivory. The palm's sap is used to make a coarse alcoholic drink, the leaves for covering traditional huts, and for weaving baskets and mats.

There is now a total of 26 black and 27 white rhino in the conservancy, with the figure slowly rising as the population increases naturally. Cattle and sheep are still raised on the ranch, their numbers varying depending on the seasons. Wildlife includes greater kudu, reticulated giraffe, eland, hartebeest (a Mount Kenya subspecies), both Grevy's and common zebra, gerenuk, impala, Grant's gazelle, bushbuck and buffalo.

One of the main attractions of a stay at Lewa is being able to walk or ride on horseback among the wildlife. It is also one of the few places in Kenya which runs night game drives using powerful spotlights.

Meru National Park ★★★

To the east of Samburu, Buffalo Springs and Shaba lie the Nyambeni Hills, and beyond them is Meru National Park. The approach to Meru by road is quite dramatic; the road winds its way through the hills, a very densely populated area, and through coffee and tea plantations, and groves of miraa trees (*Catha edulis*). The leaves of this tree are chewed as a mild stimulant, which is exported to Somalia where it is known as *khat*.

The scenery changes dramatically as the road descends in altitude and suddenly one is in wild, remote country. Meru National Park was first gazetted in 1966 by the local council – the first African council to do so. The park covers an area of 870km² (335 sq miles); rainfall varies greatly, most falling in the western area and slowly decreasing eastwards.

Meru was made famous by the book and film *Born Free*, a story about the lives of Joy and George Adamson and Elsa, the lioness. Joy also reared a cheetah called Pippa here, which became the subject of another book titled *The Spotted Sphinx*.

Meru National Park is still an area of unspoilt wilderness, and despite its good network of well-maintained roads, it instils the feeling of real Africa. The park's attraction lies in the diversity of its scenery, and its wide variety of habitats ranging from forest, dry bush and grasslands to swamps and numerous rivers which are lined with doum palms, tamarind trees and various acacias. The Rojewero River, roughly bisecting the park, is the most beautiful. Along its banks, bird-watchers should look out for the rarely seen Peter's finfoot, the unusual palm-nut vulture, and Pel's fishing owl.

Meru's wildlife, although not as approachable as in the more visited parks, is varied and often numerous. Lion, leopard and cheetah may be sighted, as well as elephant and buffalo; hippo and crocodile are plentiful

GREVY'S ZEBRA

A distinctive animal with fine stripes and large ears, the Grevy's zebra is a threatened species found only in northern Kenya, Ethiopia and Somalia (its status in the last two countries is unclear). Its numbers have been severely reduced by poachers, and it is now being threatened by domestic livestock competing for food and water. Thought to be more closely related to the horse than to other zebra species, Grevy's zebra were apparently trained to pull carts during Roman times. They are protected in a number of Kenya's national parks and reserves, but at certain times of the year, the females and their young migrate out of the protected areas, unfortunately coming into conflict with nomadic herders.

Opposite: *a group of Grevy's zebra in the Samburu National Reserve.* **Above:** *the Meru's attractive Adamson's Falls.*

THE SINGING WELLS

Near Marsabit are the famous Singing Wells, dug by the Boran people who herd camels, cattle, sheep and goats. The men descend into the wells – many as deep as 15m (50ft) – and form a human chain to pass water in buckets, made out of giraffe skin, to one another. The water is poured into troughs where the livestock are waiting to drink. The name originates from the singing of the men as they pass the buckets along, helping them keep up a steady rhythm.

in the river. Burchell's and Grevy's zebra occur, as do reticulated giraffe, gerenuk and a number of antelope.

The Tana River forms Meru's southern boundary and it is here that the Adamson's Falls are located; they are named after George Adamson, whose final home was across the river in the **Kora National Reserve**.

Kora National Reserve

Kora National Reserve consists of inhospitable, dry acacia thorn bush, interspersed with granite kopjes. Between 1983 and 1984 a joint expedition of the National Museums of Kenya and The Royal Geographical Society studied this little known area, which proved to be a remarkable ecosystem virtually untouched by man. The book *Islands in the Bush* written by the expedition's leader, Malcolm Coe, records their findings.

It was in the Kora reserve that George Adamson, from 1970 onwards, made his final home. Still rehabilitating lions to the wild up to the time of his death, he was gunned down and murdered on 20 August 1989 by poachers.

Unfortunately there are virtually no roads or tracks in the reserve but the Kenya Wildlife Service has plans to build a bridge across the Tana from Meru National Park, and then open up Kora National Reserve to visitors.

Tana River National Reserve

The **Tana River** and **Arawale** national reserves are two little known and seldom visited wildlife areas on the river Tana, both more accessible from Malindi on Kenya's north coast (they lie 160km, or 99 miles, and 130km, or 80 miles, respectively north of Malindi). The Tana River National Reserve was established principally to protect two endemic primates, the red colobus and the crested mangabey. These monkeys occur nowhere else in East Africa and are threatened mostly by a decrease in habitat caused by man. Besides the seven different primates in the reserve, other mammals to be seen are elephant, lion, giraffe, common waterbuck, lesser kudu, hippo and crocodile.

Kenya's only herd of rare Hunter's hartebeest occurs in the dry thorn bush of the Arawale National Reserve. No visitor facilities exist – not even a gate!

Marsabit National Park and Reserve **

Also a little visited refuge, this reserve covers a total area of 1555km² (600 sq miles). Marsabit Mountain (meaning 'place of cold') is a cool, forested oasis rising out of the hot, dry **Chalbi Desert** plains. The thickly wooded slopes contrast sharply with the desert landscape, and the difference in temperatures causes thick mists to form each evening, which do not clear until early afternoon. These mists provide Marsabit's forests with moisture.

The park is studded with volcanic craters, the largest being **Got Bongoti**, and many are filled with fresh water. The best known, **Lake Paradise**, was home to Osa and Martin Johnson for four years where, in the 1920s, they made some of the world's first wildlife films.

Although difficult to see, wildlife is plentiful in the mountain forest: this includes a number of magnificent greater kudu, elephant, buffalo, reticulated giraffe and lion. The birdlife is good and it is probable that the rare lammergeyer, or bearded vulture, nests here.

Above: *the endearing and widely distributed little vervet monkey.*

Opposite: *Lake Paradise, one of a number of water-filled volcanic craters in the Marsabit park.*

AHMED, THE ELEPHANT

Marsabit National Park is perhaps best known as the home of Ahmed, a male elephant who was the proud owner of an enormous pair of tusks which touched the ground; President Jomo Kenyatta declared him a national monument, granting the impressive beast presidential protection until his death as a result of old age in 1974. Ahmed's body has been preserved and is on display in the Nairobi National Museum.

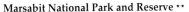

Maralal Game Sanctuary

On the northern edge of the Laikipia Plateau is the small town of Maralal, administrative centre of the Samburu District. A frontier town, it sits on the edge of a range of hills at an altitude of 1495m (4900ft) surrounded by beautiful cedar forests.

It was in Maralal that Jomo Kenyatta, Kenya's first president, was detained for a while by the colonial authorities. The house in which he was detained has been declared a national monument and is open to visitors. Two and a half kilometres (1.5 miles) out of town is the **Maralal Safari Lodge**, situated within the **Maralal Game Sanctuary**.

Below: *the view across the Laikipia plateau. Below the escarpment is Lake Bogoria, a limpid, ice-blue sheet of water whose eastern shore is flanked by the 610m-high (2000ft) Siracho Cliffs. The lake, described by one early traveller as 'the most beautiful in Africa', is perhaps the one least known to tourists.*

The lodge is mainly frequented by travellers on their way to or from Lake Turkana. It is set in the midst of a large forest glade near a waterhole which attracts large numbers of game such as the common zebra, eland, impala, buffalo and warthog. A short walk from the lodge is a hide where it's possible to see leopard, which are attracted to bait.

On the road to Turkana, 20km (12 miles) north of Maralal, is the **Lerogi Plateau viewpoint** with breathtaking vistas to the Rift Valley far below. The best time to experience this view is in the early morning.

Northern and Eastern Kenya at a Glance

Any time of the year; rain falls in March and in November, but during normal years is not heavy enough to make travel difficult or unpleasant.

As Samburu and Buffalo Springs reserves are remote and isolated, and in many places roads have been reduced to dirt tracks, visitors usually rely on **tours** organized by reputable safari companies.

Samburu National Reserve
Larsen's Tented Camp, on banks of Ewaso Nyiro River: tents raised on stilts, with good views over river; book through Block Hotels.
Samburu Intrepids Camp, upstream: similar to Larsen's, book through Prestige Hotels.
Samburu Lodge, Ewaso Nyiro River: modern lodge; leopard and crocodile attracted to bait; book through Block Hotels.

Buffalo Springs National Reserve
Buffalo Springs Lodge, only one in reserve: near small permanent waterhole, striped hyena attracted to bait; book through Moto Tours.
Samburu Serena Lodge, on banks of Ewaso Nyiro: leopard and crocodile; book through Serena Hotels.

Shaba National Reserve
Shaba Sarova Lodge on banks of Ewaso Nyiro: amid

oasis of sparkling springs, book through Sarova Hotels.
Kitich Camp in the Matthews mountains: permanent tents on banks of Ngeng River, book through Mellifera Ltd.

Lewa Wildlife Conservancy
Borana Lodge: six luxury thatched stone cottages, book through Tandala Ltd.
Lewa House: farmhouse, six thatched-roof cottages; book through Bush Homes.
Lerai Tented Camp: luxury permanent tented camp, 12 tents; book through Savannah Camps and Lodges.

Meru National Park
Leopard Rock Safari Lodge: PO Box 45456, Nairobi; tel: (02) 745926 for information.
Elsa's Kopje: eight thatched stone cottages near Mugwongo Hill; book through Cheli & Peacock.

Tana River National Reserve
Research Camp: limited tent accommodation; contact National Museums of Kenya.

Marsabit National Park and Reserve
Marsabit Lodge in park: overlooks waterhole; book through Msafiri Inns.

Maralal Game Sanctuary
Maralal Safari Lodge, situated at the northern edge of Laikipia Plateau: write to PO Box 70, Maralal; tel: (0368) 2060.

Block Hotels, PO Box 47557, Nairobi; tel: (02) 335807, fax: 340541.
Bush Homes of East Africa, PO Box 56923, Nairobi; tel: (02) 571647/49/61, fax: 571665.
Cheli & Peacock, PO Box 39806, Nairobi; tel: (02) 748307/327/633, 750721/1073, fax: 750225/740721.
Msafiri Inns, PO Box 42013, Nairobi; tel: (02) 229751/3488, fax: 227815.
Prestige Hotels, PO Box 74888, Nairobi; tel: (02) 338084, fax: 217278.
Sarova Hotels Ltd, PO Box 30680, Nairobi; tel: (02) 333248, fax: 211472.
Savannah Camps & Lodges, PO Box 48019, Nairobi; tel: (02) 331191, fax: 330698.
Serena Hotels, PO Box 48690, Nairobi; tel: (02) 711077, fax: 718103.
Tandala Ltd, PO Box 24397, Nairobi; tel: (02) 574689/567251/568804, fax: 564945.

MERU	J	F	M	A	M	J	J	A	S	O	N	D
AVERAGE TEMP. °F	73	75	77	75	71	71	70	71	75	77	71	71
AVERAGE TEMP. °C	23	24	25	24	22	22	21	22	24	25	22	22
Hours of Sun Daily	8	8	8	7	8	7	6	6	7	8	6	7
RAINFALL ins	3	1	5	11	3	0	0.5	0	0.5	5	13	5
RAINFALL mm	80	39	126	282	86	5	10	8	16	140	328	139
Days of Rainfall	7	6	8	17	10	3	3	3	4	9	17	12

6
Southern Kenya

Kenya's southern areas are the most popular. Most recognized, and made famous by the Hollywood movie moguls, the glistening snow-capped **Mount Kilimanjaro** dominates **Amboseli National Park**. At 5895m (19,341ft) it is Africa's highest mountain, and the first breathtaking view of its magnificent peak is one that stays with you forever. **Tsavo**, Kenya's largest national park cut through by the Nairobi–Mombasa highway, is famous for its magnificent wildlife and its quality lodges. Then there are the **Chyulu Hills** composed of gravelly lava soil, but with the onset of the rains a superficial cloak of green appears to transform the slopes into fragile but beautiful undulating grasslands.

Over the years, Amboseli has undergone a startling change in appearance: the swamps have increased dramatically in size and much of the beautiful acacia woodland has been destroyed. Theories abound as to the swamps' sudden expansion – underground movement, global warming and so on – but there is no doubt that Kilimanjaro's ice cap is receding. A contributing factor is the considerable clearing of forests on Kilimanjaro's slopes; water now runs off the mountain during heavy rains instead of the majority of it being absorbed. The destruction of the acacia woodlands has been blamed on the increase in the park's elephant population. Although this cannot be denied, the rising water table has brought mineral salts to the surface which are not tolerated by the trees, thus aiding their destruction. The parks do, however, have much to offer in terms of their wildlife.

CLIMATE

In southern Kenya it is generally **hot**, except for July and August which tend to be overcast. The more reliable **rains** fall during **November** (which is often cloudy) and December, but the main **rainy season** is actually from **March** to **May**.

Opposite: *elephants take to the road in the Amboseli National Park. Mount Kilimanjaro rises magnificently in the background.*

DON'T MISS

*** Visit Amboseli for its
elephants and unforgettable
views of Kilimanjaro
*** Join a safari to Tsavo
West (most scenic of the
two); famous for its red
elephants
*** Walk along the crest of
the volcanic Chyulu Hills for
spellbinding views
** Walk to Observation
Point in Amboseli for panor-
amic vistas
** Descend into the under-
water viewing tank at Mzima
Springs to watch the hippos
** Stay at Hilton-run Taita
Hills Game Sanctuary.

Amboseli National Park ***

Amboseli, situated due south of Nairobi, is Kenya's most visited wildlife area. Originally designated a reserve in 1948 and having an area of 3260km² (1259 sq miles), it was handed over to the Maasai in 1961, but because of conflict between the Maasai herds and the wildlife, the reserve was gazetted a national park in 1974 (at a frac-tion of its original size). Now 392km² (151 sq miles), the park centres on **Ol Tukai** (Maasai for the locally com-mon phoenix palm), an area containing several swamps which are a magnet for wildlife.

To compensate the local Maasai who traditionally watered their livestock in this area, a number of wells were sunk in a spot outside the national park with funds donated by the New York Zoological Society.

Most of the park consists of a dry, ancient lake bed and fragile grasslands with patches of acacia woodland, while in the southern area there is a number of small, rocky, volcanic hills. Around the swamps – Ol Okenya, Ol Tukai and Enkongo Narok – the vegetation is lush with yellow-barked acacias and phoenix palms.

Despite its changing habitat, Amboseli National Park is possibly the best wildlife area in the whole of Africa to experience ele-phants at close range. Left unharassed by poachers, elephants feeding and bathing in the swamps must form the highlight of any safari.

Cynthia Moss and Joyce Pool, with their many assistants, have undertaken extensive

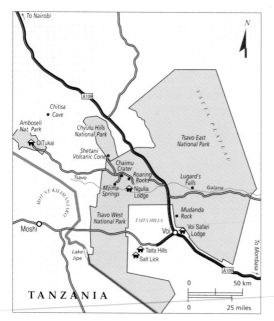

studies on these elephants; Cynthia herself has followed their movements for over 20 years, the most extended study of any one species by the same person in Africa.

Apart from elephant, the variety of game includes most species, from rhino, Masai giraffe, Grant's and Thomson's gazelle through lion, cheetah and leopard. In the drier areas of the park, away from the swamps, one can see fringe-eared oryx, gerenuk and eland. Birdlife is prolific too, especially in and around the many swampy areas. Both white and pink-backed pelicans, among many other waterbirds, share the open water areas with the beautiful pygmy goose which is quite uncommon in Kenya. Kingfishers and bee-eaters use the reeds along the swamps to look out for their quarry, and birds of prey are well represented, with the African fish eagle, martial eagle, pale chanting goshawk and the tiny pygmy falcon all occurring.

No visit to Amboseli is complete without a visit to Observation Hill, south of the airstrip. Walk to the top for a sweeping view over the whole of Amboseli spread out below. You will see the dust trails of animals walking across the expanses of dry plain to the water, and towards the south, an almost endless tract covered with acacias slowly merging into the base of Kilimanjaro.

Above: *the stone and cedarwood Amboseli Lodge, one of four lodges within the Amboseli park. The area is famed for its elephants.*

ACCOMMODATION IN AMBOSELI

The national park has good lodges, as well as other forms of accommodation:

- **Amboseli Serena**, in the form of a Maasai *manyatta*
- **Amboseli Lodge**, fashioned from stone and cedar wood
- **Ol Tukai Lodge**, a luxury 80-room lodge.

Outside the park:
- **Tortilis Camp**, luxury tented camp
- **Kimana** and **Kilimanjaro Buffalo** lodges; the latter, although some distance from the park boundary, has the best views of Mt Kilimanjaro.

Above: *Iltalal camp in the Chyulu Hills.*
Opposite: *a Grant's gazelle grazes in Meru National Park.*

Chyulu Hills National Park ★★★

The Chyulu Hills, lying to the east of Amboseli and running parallel with the main Nairobi to Mombasa road for 80km (50 miles), became a national park in 1983. The park comprises several hundred small, grass-covered volcanic hills that are only 400 to 500 years old, and a number of beautiful forested valleys. It is possible to walk along the crest of these hills, the highest of which is 4430m (14,535ft), from where the views of Kilimanjaro and the surrounding countryside are phenomenal. There is also a track through the hills, negotiable with a four-wheel-drive vehicle.

It is thought that rainfall percolating through the Chyulus, and so forming an underground river, feeds the famous Mzima Springs in nearby Tsavo National Park. A variety of wildlife, including the fringe-eared oryx, lives in this lovely area. Visitors wanting accommodation can choose between **Ol Donyo Wuas**, a small exclusive lodge, and **Iltalal Camp**, a permanent tented camp near the hills.

Immediately to the south of the Chyulus is a volcano named **Shetani** (the devil) whose black lava flows are only 200 years old, and the mighty Tsavo National Park.

TSAVO NATIONAL PARK

This very large national park immediately to the south of the Chyulu Hills is larger than Wales (and approximately the same size as the states of New Hampshire and Vermont combined). It has an area of 20,810km² (8035 sq miles) and varies in altitude from 230 to 2000m (755 to 6562ft). The main Nairobi to Mombasa road splits the park into two halves, **Tsavo East** and **Tsavo West**.

Although it was split mainly for administration purposes, the two areas differ remarkably. Tsavo East consists of miles of flat, dry thorn bush interspersed with magnificent baobab trees and dominated by the **Yatta Plateau**, the world's longest lava flow. In contrast, Tsavo West is much more scenic. Although it is also dry thornbush country interspersed with the occasional giant baobab, the vista is of volcanic mountains and hills, and outcrops with magnificent views. Along the **Tsavo River** the lush vegetation comprises doum palms, and tamarind and acacia trees.

For much of the year Tsavo burns dry and dusty; the red Tsavo dust blankets everything – including the elephants, which are known here for their red colour. Once numbering tens of thousands, the drought and serious poaching of the late 70s and early 80s have severely reduced the elephant population (now around 5000). However, their destructive effect on the environment (*see* panel on p. 97) has been lessened as a result, and the vegetation is recovering, in many places thicker than before. After the rain, Tsavo transforms almost overnight; the grass pushes up fresh shoots and many wildflowers, such as the pink-and-white *Convolvulus*, quickly appear.

Both of the parks have an excellent network of well signposted tracks, which are generally well maintained.

Tsavo West National Park ★★★
Tsavo West is the most visited section in Tsavo National Park, offering many attractions apart from its wildlife. The foremost is the famous **Mzima Springs** where up to 227.3 million litres (50 million gallons) of cool crystal-clear water flow out of the ground through porous volcanic rocks. This water is believed to originate from the Chyulu Hills via an underground river. Water from

SOME HORN FACTS

- The horns of all male antelopes (and many females) grow to various shapes, but never branch out to form antlers.
- Antelope horns are permanent, unlike a deer's antlers which are shed annually.
- Rothschild's giraffe males sometimes develop five horns (these are extra knobs that develop on the skull).
- Rhino horn is actually an outgrowth of the hide, composed of thickly compacted hair rather than bone.

Above: *lava flow in the Tsavo area.*
Opposite: *rock strata in the Tsavo East park.*

the springs is piped all the way to the town of Mombasa on the east coast. At Mzima there is a car park and visitors are permitted to walk to the springs' source and along a pathway which follows the newly formed river. The walk is a wonderful experience; if you are quiet you may be rewarded with the sight of animals coming down to the water's edge to drink, and you are sure to see hippo clearly as they lie in the cool water.

One can also watch for them through the windows of an observation tank sunk into the river, which allows the visitor to enter a cool, new, underwater world. Close to the tank's windows are likely to be a number of fish, mostly barbel species. Troops of black-faced vervet monkeys and many interesting birds inhabit the trees around Mzima. This is one of the few places where darters can be seen in Kenya.

Other interesting places to visit are the '**Roaring Rocks**', which get their name from the wind that hurtles through them. From here there are wonderful views over Tsavo from the top of a 98m (300ft) rock face; similar views can be experienced from the poachers' lookout. The volcanic **Chaimu Crater**, less than 200 years old and composed of black coke, is worth visiting and can be climbed if you are interested. This area is a good place to look out for klipspringer, a small antelope that's as agile as its Swahili name *mbuzi mawe* implies; that is, 'mountain goat'.

Besides the small but graceful lesser kudu, Tsavo's wildlife includes lion, leopard, cheetah, Masai giraffe, eland, fringe-eared oryx, buffalo, Burchell's zebra, yellow baboon, Coke's hartebeest and Grant's gazelle. Below **Ngulia Mountain** there is now a well-guarded rhino sanctuary containing a number of black rhino.

In the southwest corner of Tsavo West is **Lake Jipe**, 10km long and 3km wide (6 miles by 1.9 miles), which has the Kenya-Tanzania border running through it. Above the lake, the Tanzanian Pare Mountains form a dramatic backdrop, especially at sunset, and on clear days, Mount Kilimanjaro can be seen towards the northwest. Although there is a variety of game in the area, the birds attract most visitors. The lake shore is the best place in Kenya to see purple gallinules, black herons, pygmy geese, and occasionally lesser jacanas.

Tsavo East National Park **

Most of Tsavo East north of the Galana River is closed to the public; only a few professional safari companies are allowed to enter. The park has a good network of well-signposted tracks, and because the terrain is mostly dry, flat thorn scrub (the mountains and hills of Tsavo West are missing) and

RED ELEPHANTS OF TSAVO

Tsavo's red elephants, at one time numbering around 50,000, have dramatically changed the vegetation in the area. During a very severe drought in the late 60s and early 70s, the elephants ate virtually all the vegetation and badly damaged many of the baobabs. Together with the black rhino, they died of starvation in large numbers and were the subject of much debate on the issue of culling, both in Kenya and the rest of Africa. This controversial subject is still under earnest discussion.

BAOBAB TREE

The baobab (*Adansonia digitata*) is very common in both the Tsavo and Meru national parks, along the Kenyan coast, and inland east of the Rift Valley in areas as high as 1250m (4100ft). For up to nine months of the year the trees, some of which may be 3000 years old, are leafless. Called *mbuyu* by the Swahili, the baobab features in the mythology of many African tribes who believe that God threw the tree out of his garden where it landed upside down, explaining its present-day 'uprooted' appearance.

Below: *view of the 300km (186 miles) Yatta Plateau – one of the world's longest lava flows – from Tsavo East's Voi Safari Lodge.*

there are fewer visitors, it has the aura of untamed Africa. The monotonous scrub is occasionally broken by green vegetation along one or other of the rivers that cross the area.

The most interesting section to visit is that around **Voi**, the park's headquarters. Dominated by the beautifully designed **Voi Safari Lodge** set high on a bluff, the Kandara swamp and Voi River lie to the east. The vegetation is rich along the river and it is here that most of the wildlife occurs. To the north of the lodge is **Mudanda Rock**, a miniature of Australia's Ayres Rock. Two kilometres (1.2 miles) long, it stands out prominently from the surrounding plains. Below the rock a natural waterhole attracts a great deal of wildlife at times. There is a parking area to the western side of the rock, and a footpath leads to a spot where one can climb up onto it. From here the views over the plains are wonderful, and occasionally one can see animals drinking.

Approximately 60km (37 miles) north of Voi are **Lugard's Falls** on the Galana River. Actually a series of rapids, the falls are most dramatic and impressive after rain, when the river's flow is constricted in the narrow, rocky gorge. Below the falls, very large crocodiles are usually to be seen at **Crocodile Point**.

Left: *an ancient baobab –
the 'upside-down tree' of
African lore – rises above a
sisal plantation near the
town of Voi.*

Approximately 40km (25 miles) west of Voi is the
11,000ha (27,181 acres) **Taita Hills Game Sanctuary**, pri-
vately owned and run by the Hilton Hotel chain. This
area was once an abandoned sisal plantation but has
now been transformed into an exciting reserve containing a large variety of wildlife.

Nearby, the imposing craggy pinnacles of Taita's
granite hills are impressive.

Lodge Luxury in Taita Hills

Taita Hills: Built to resemble a German fort, the small
house is now a lodge, and is covered with a tangled mass
of bougainvillea. `James Stewart's house', a small wood-
en structure built for the film *A Tale of Africa*, stands
nearby and is open for tourists.

Salt Lick: Among the best in Kenya, this complex is
architecturally based on the traditional Taita home – elephants browse unperturbed beneath the clusters of rondavels that are perched on stilts and linked by raised
walkways. The lodge's waterhole attracts a wide variety
of wildlife.

Both lodges must count among the world's most distinctive conference centres, set as they are in the midst of
an array of African wildlife.

MAN-EATERS OF TSAVO

This is the title of a true
account, written by Colonel
J.H. Patterson, who was in
charge of building a bridge
over the Tsavo River for the
Uganda Railway in 1898. For
some time, workers were
continually being dragged off
into the night by two large
male lions; the workers
believed it was the Devil in
the shape of a lion, as the
mammals were quite fearless.
Eventually, in December
1898, after the mounting toll
included 28 Indian labourers
and a large number of
Africans, work on the bridge
was brought to a halt until
the lions were shot, the deed
having been carried out by
Colonel Patterson himself.

Southern Kenya at a Glance

This region experiences a warm climate **all year round**. The main rainy season normally occurs from the end of March to early May, and then again in November when it is often cloudy during the day.

Amboseli National Park

The **roads** into and out of Amboseli are generally very **bad**, but at the time of writing the Emali to Kimana road was being rebuilt; this road gives access to the Lemeiboti gate on the northeast boundary of the park. Most of the **park's roads** are in fairly **good condition**, but a strong vehicle is still recommended. During heavy rain some areas of Amboseli are flooded.

Chyulu Hills

To enjoy the Chyulus, a **four-wheel-drive** vehicle is required. **Cars** can be **hired** in Nairobi and Mombasa; try The Car Hire Company in Nairobi, tel: (02) 225255, fax: 216553; or contact Galu Safaris in Mombasa, tel: (011) 229524 or 209057, fax: 314226. The international airports and main hotels in Nairobi and Mombasa have Hertz representatives.

Tsavo National Park

Park **roads** are usually **excellent** – they are the best-maintained roads in any of Kenya's wildlife areas. A strong saloon car is suitable in normal conditions, but beware heavy rains, especially on tracks alongside the rivers.

Taita Hills Game Sanctuary

Roads in the sanctuary generally **good**; an ordinary saloon car is suitable.

Amboseli National Park

Amboseli Serena Lodge: built to represent Maasai dwelling, very pleasant and cool; has wonderful dining room and bar area; guest rooms a little small; unfortunately lodge does not face Kilimanjaro; book through Serena Hotels.

Amboseli Tortilis Camp: permanent tented camp; although outside park, very close to Kitirua gate; contact Cheli and Peacock, tel: (0154) 22551/2, fax: 22553.

Amboseli Lodge: large, noisy and busy, but faces Kilimanjaro; book through Kilimanjaro Safari Club.

Kilimanjaro Safari Lodge: also large, near Amboseli Lodge; rooms very close to each other, but afford wonderful views of Kilimanjaro; book through Kilimanjaro Safari Club, tel: (0302) 22004.

Kilimanjaro Buffalo Lodge: outside national park (20–30 minute drive on dusty, often rough, road); has stunning views of Kilimanjaro; book through Kilimanjaro Safari Club.

Ol Tukai Lodge: Amboseli's newest lodge, 80 large rooms, two of which are designed to accommodate disabled people; book through Let's Go Travel.

There are two camps and a lodge outside the park:
Kimana Lodge: book through tel: (02) 338888 or 227136, fax: 219982.

Kimana Leopard Camp and **Cottar's Kilimanjaro Camp**: book through Let's Go Travel.

Chyulu Hills

Ol Donyo Wuas: exclusive and small (eight guests), at foot of Chyulu Hills with wonderful views over surrounding countryside and on to Kilimanjaro; book through Richard Bonham Safaris.

Tsavo West National Park

Finch Hatton's Safari Camp: luxury permanent tented camp on banks of three spring-fed pools which feature hippo; 35 luxury tents raised on platforms facing pools; special views of Kilimanjaro from main building; old-fashioned, very high-class camp; book through tel: (0302) 22473.

Kilaguni Lodge: Kenya's first safari lodge (opened 1962); perfectly situated overlooking waterhole with magnificent views of Chyulu Hills and Kilimanjaro; during dinner the rarely seen striped hyena pays a visit; book through Express Travel Group.

Southern Kenya at a Glance

Ngulia Lodge: spectacularly situated on top of a rocky outcrop; the waterhole in front of the lodge is floodlit at night and each evening bait is put out close to the open-sided dining room for leopard and ratel (and the animals usually oblige); book through Kenya Safari Lodges and Hotels.

Lake Jipe Safari Lodge: built just a short distance from the lake, the lodge has wonderful views of Kilimanjaro and North Pare mountains; book direct, tel: (0147) 30219.

Tsavo East National Park

Tsavo Safari Camp on the banks of Athi River: this permanent tented camp can only be reached by rubber dinghy; it is a lovely relaxing spot with even a couple of tame fringe-eared oryx; book through Kilimanjaro Safari Club.

Voi Safari Lodge: set high on a rocky bluff overlooking a waterhole and the huge expanse of Tsavo; book through Kenya Safari Lodges and Hotels.

Tiva River Camp on the Tiva River: new permanent tented camp, offers walking safaris; book through Reachout Safaris.

Budget Accommodation

Ngulia and **Kitani** in Tsavo West offer two self-catering lodges; book through Let's Go Travel.

Aruba Lodge in Tsavo East offers self-catering facilities; contact Let's Go Travel.

Near the parks

Tsavo Inn on main Nairobi to Mombasa road, at Mtito Andei: 30-room inn; book through Kilimanjaro Safari Club.

Crocodile Camp just outside national park near Sala gate on banks of Galana River: crocodiles attracted to bait at night; book through Repotel.

Taita Hills Wildlife Sanctuary

To reserve accommodation at any of the following complexes, book through Hilton International, tel: (02) 332564.

Taita Hills Lodge: impressive-looking, made out of sand-bags and built to resemble fortress; covered in climbing plants; also offers guided walks and balloon flights.

Salt Lick Safari Lodge: excellent night game-viewing lodge; rondavel-shaped rooms built on stilts overlooking series of waterholes.

The Tents: small permanent tented camp in riverine forest along Bura River, 12 tents; in centre of camp is James Stewart House, a wooden structure built over river.

Useful Addresses

Express Travel Group, PO Box 40433, Nairobi; tel: (02) 225151/335850/339420, fax: 334825.

Future Hotels, PO Box 24423, Nairobi; tel: (02) 604321/2, fax: 604323.

Hilton International, PO Box 30621, Nairobi; tel: (02) 332564, fax: 339462.

Kenya Safari Lodges and Hotels, Nairobi; tel: (02) 340894/330820/229751, fax: 227815.

Kilimanjaro Safari Club, PO Box 30138, Nairobi; tel: (02) 227136 or 338888/89/90 or 337510, fax: 219982.

Let's Go Travel, PO Box 60342, Nairobi; tel: (02) 340331 or 213033, fax: 336890.

Reachout Safaris: PO Box 48019, Nairobi; tel: (02) 891457, fax: 216528.

Repotel, PO Box 46527, Nairobi; tel: (02) 227828.

Richard Bonham Safaris Ltd, PO Box 24133, Nairobi; tel: (02) 882521 or 884475, fax: 882728.

Serena Hotels, PO Box 48690, Nairobi; tel: (02) 711077, fax: 718103.

VOI	J	F	M	A	M	J	J	A	S	O	N	D
AVERAGE TEMP. °F	79	79	81	79	77	73	72	72	73	77	77	77
AVERAGE TEMP. °C	26	26	27	26	25	23	22	22	23	25	25	25
Hours of Sun Daily	8	7	7	7	7	7	6	5	6	8	7	7
RAINFALL ins	1	1	3	4	1	0	0	0	1	1	4	5
RAINFALL mm	36	32	76	94	34	8	6	10	18	30	102	130
Days of Rainfall	5	3	8	7	5	2	1	2	3	4	10	8

7
The Coral Coast

Mombasa is Kenya's second largest city and gateway to East Africa. Over hundreds of years, Mombasa's harbour has seen a passing parade of fascinating creeds and cultures: Chinese junks, Arabian dhows, Portuguese galleons, merchant ships, passenger ships and cruise liners from all over the world.

Mombasa Town, an island that is now connected to the mainland by a causeway, was at war for centuries as the various conquerors in possession of the island throughout the years held authority over the coast and control of the hinterland. Fort Jesus, guarding the entrance to the Old Harbour, is a constant reminder of those fearful days. Mombasa's history goes back at least twelve centuries, at which time it was the residence of the people of Zeng, an African kingdom; it later became an Arab settlement. Both in 1505 and 1528, Mombasa was attacked by Portuguese galleons and sacked; in 1593 the Portuguese began to settle and started building Fort Jesus, where they remained until 1631 when they lost Mombasa in an Arab revolt. They briefly reclaimed the fort from 1632 to 1696, when the Arabs again took control. But for a brief occupation in 1728, the Portuguese finally left, leaving the Arabs in control until 1895, when the coastal strip became a protectorate of Britain.

Besides its historical heritage, Mombasa has miles and miles of white beaches to the north and south, holding a multitude of attractions: magical coral reefs sheltering beautiful tropical fish, an abundance of game fish for deep-sea anglers, and the chance to sail aboard a dhow.

CLIMATE

Temperatures generally are **moderated by sea breezes**, ranging from an average low of 24°C (75°F) in July to an average high of 28°C (82°F) in March. The heaviest rain usually falls in May, with rain again at the end of October and early November. The sea temperature is always warm and varies between 27–30°C (80–86°F) depending on the season. Humidity varies from 74% in February to 84% in May.

Opposite: *palm-graced Tiwi Beach on Kenya's south coast.*

DON'T MISS

*** Snorkelling off the Lamu Archipelago
*** A ramble through Old Mombasa town
*** Dining on the famous Tamarind Dhow
*** *Son et lumière* show at Fort Jesus
*** A trip to explore the Gedi ruins
** A visit to Malindi resort.

OLD MOMBASA TOWN

The old town, hot and steamy, remains very much the same today as it was in the 19th century. Its narrow streets are lined with old Arab houses, many with traditional carved doors studded with brass, there are spice shops, coffee vendors and mosques, and dhows lying at anchor in the Old Harbour; although greatly reduced in numbers, they still ply their trade with various ports in Arabia as they have been doing for at least two thousand years. The dhows arrive, usually in early December on the northeast monsoon, with their traditional cargos of dates, dried kingfish and a few carpets and traditional chests. They leave eventually in the middle of May, at the latest, on the southeast monsoon with a cargo of *boriti* poles (mangrove), ghee and limes. Traditionally their main cargo would have been made up of slaves and ivory.

A Walk Through the Old Town •••

A good place to start is at **Fort Jesus**, which everyone should make an effort to visit. From the fort entrance, walk across the road, keeping **Mombasa Club** on your right, and on into Mbarak Hinaway Road. The shops along its length are now mainly filled with curios, but look out for shops selling spices and scents. You will pass **Mandhry Mosque**, Mombasa's oldest, built in 1570 (at one time there were almost 50 mosques in the Old Town

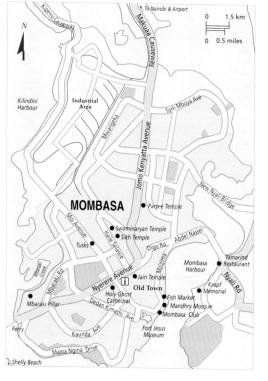

MOMBASA

To Nairobi & Airport
0   1.5 km
0   0.5 miles

N

Kipevu Causeway
Makupa Causeway

Kilindini Harbour

Industrial Area

Tom Mboya Ave.

Mikanjuni

Jomo Kenyatta Avenue

New Nyali Bridge

Parsee Temple

Moi Avenue

Swaminaryan Temple
Sikh Temple

Haile Selassie

Tusks

Digo Rd.
Abdel Nasser

Mizizima

Mombasa Harbour

Tamarind Restaurant

Nyerere Avenue

Jain Temple

Mbaraki Rd.

Mbaraki Coast

Mbaraki Pillar

Holy Ghost Cathedral
Dedan Kimathi Ave.

Old Town

Fish Market

Krapf Memorial

Nyali Rd.

Mandhry Mosque
Mombasa Mosque

Mombasa Club

Ferry

Kaunda Ave.

Fort Jesus Museum

Mama Ngina Drive

Shelly Beach

but today a little over 20 are still in use). You then reach **Government Square** and the **Old Harbour**, which have not changed much over the years. Here it is still possible to watch the loading of cargo onto the old trading dhows. After exploring Government Square and its interesting shops, turn into Thika Street and then left into Ndia Kuu which takes you back to the fort.

Fort Jesus ⁑

This 16th-century stronghold was built by the Portuguese to protect their trade routes to India. The architect was Italian, so the structure has all the features representative of an Italian fortress of the time. The fort, whose walls are 15m (50ft) high and 2.4m (8ft) thick, stands on an old coral ridge commanding the entrance to the Old Harbour.

At the end of the 17th century the Sultan of Oman sent an army to seize the fort; the siege lasted almost three years before finally falling into their hands. In 1728 the fort was recovered by the Portuguese without a struggle, but relinquished again later to remain under Arab rule until 1895 when Mombasa became a British protectorate. The fort was bombarded by the British Navy in 1878 and 1895; it later became a prison (1895) under British protection. On 15 August 1960, Fort Jesus was declared a national monument.

Above left: *Mombasa's Old Town, a place of mosques, spices and scents.* **Above:** *one of the cannons of Fort Jesus.*

PEOPLE OF THE COAST

Through the ages, tribes from across Africa have migrated to Kenya, whose east coastline in turn survived turbulent conquests from Arab, Persian and Portuguese quarters. As a result, the tribes around Mombasa are many and various. Mombasa's people are Swahili – a mixture of Arab, Persian and Bantu influences – and the majority are strongly Islamic. From Mombasa northwards to the Sabaki River is the Giriama tribe. Inland from Mombasa are the Duruma, and south are the Digo. North of the Sabaki River, along the banks of the Tana River, live the Pokomo, while further north are the Bajun and Somali peoples.

SHOPPING IN MOMBASA

The Floating Market: during an interesting cruise around Mombasa Island in the dhow *Husna*, local people in traditional dugout canoes approach with spices, crafts, kikois, and so on for sale.
Biashara Street for fabrics, kangas and kikois.
Mbarak Hinaway Road in Mombasa Old Town for spices and crafts, perfumes, carpets, and curios of all description.

Today, outside the fort's main entrance are two large guns from a more modern time, World War I. They are relics of a battle between two ships, the British *HMS Pegasus* which was sunk by a German cruiser, the *Konigsberg*, in Dar es Salaam Harbour in 1914. The German ship was eventually sunk by the British Navy.

Fort Jesus is popular among tourists and is open to the public daily.

Dhow Trips •••

An exciting excursion while staying in Mombasa is to take one of the many dhow trips on offer, particularly those operated by Jahazi Marine Ltd and Tamarind Dhow Safaris (the Tamarind Restaurant, located in both Nairobi and Mombasa, is the best-known seafood eating spot in Kenya). The **Tamarind Dhow** sails twice a day at 12:30 and 18:30, during which one of its legendary seafood meals is served on the open deck; a live band plays for the cruise guests.

Jahazi Marine also operates midday and evening trips. At midday, the dhow sails past Mombasa Old Town and the Old Dhow Harbour where, depending on the time of year, dhows from places as far away as India and the Arabian Gulf may be seen at anchor. Once past the Old Town, the dhow ties up to allow passengers to disembark for an exotic lunch at the gourmet **Harlequin Restaurant**. After lunch, a traditional African herbalist teaches the passengers about African herbs, which can be purchased from him after his talk. Everyone boards the sailing ship once more to head for Tudor Creek and meet the **floating market**; Africans in traditional dugout canoes approach the dhow to sell carvings, kikois, kangas, baskets and spices. After a lively bartering session, the

Right: *delicious lunchtime seafood fare aboard the Tamarind Dhow out of Mombasa. There is also an evening excursion; a live band entertains passengers.* **Opposite:** *exploring Watamu's coral gardens.*

dhow returns to Harlequin Restaurant, from where passengers are transported back to their hotels. On the evening cruise, guests enjoy snacks and drinks to the music of a live band. After just over an hour's cruise, the dhow ties up at the Old Dhow Harbour, where passengers disembark to take a short walk through the Old Town to Fort Jesus. Here they are met by an impressive tableau of men in old costumes holding aloft flaming torches; after a guided tour of the fort, guests enjoy an atmospheric *son et lumière* (sound and light) presentation of Mombasa's history. Finally, a wonderful Portuguese meal is served under the stars in the fort's courtyard.

Both the Tamarind Dhow and Jahazi Marine collect and return all guests to their hotels.

The Coral Reefs •••

The endless stretches of beaches to the north and south of Mombasa, lapped by the warm, blue Indian Ocean, ensure this city's continued popularity. From just north of Malindi down to Shimoni in the extreme south, the coast is fringed by a coral reef broken only occasionally in areas occurring opposite a river or creek where fresh water has hindered and killed the growth of the coral. The reef is generally only 640m (700yd) offshore and at low tide it is usually possible to walk across to it.

Snorkelling and scuba diving are popular pursuits along the reef and a number of marine national parks and reserves has been established to protect the underwater life and the wonderful coral. Apart from creating smooth, calm water along the beaches, the reef also keeps out any sharks that could be a menace to bathers. The only hazards that may be encountered are stonefish whose dorsal spines can cause a nasty sting, and sea

MBARAKI PILLAR

As you head straight towards the Likoni ferry, by turning right, you will arrive at the **Mbaraki Pillar**, a phallic-like tomb structure built of coral-rag some time before 1728. It is thought to be the burial place of the Sheik of Changamwe who, it is believed, was the head of one of the original 12 families living in Mombasa at that time.

urchins whose long-needled spines can be very painful if stepped upon. The beautiful pebbleless beaches are white and sandy; seaweed can be washed up on the sand after storms, otherwise they are remarkably clean.

The coastal climate is governed by two monsoons: the northeast called the **Kaskazi** blows from December to March and the southeast, called the **Kusi**, blows from April to November.

SOUTH COAST

The only way to leave Mombasa Island for the south coast is via the **Likoni motorized ferry**. Unfortunately, it is always very busy and delays of at least one hour can be expected during rush periods. Having been ferried

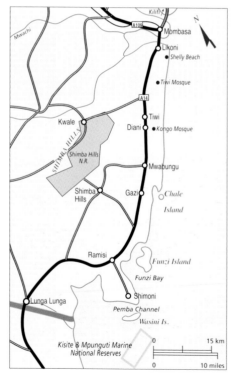

across, the first in a series of pristine beaches is **Shelly Beach** followed by **Tiwi**, then **Diani**, 35km (22 miles) south of Mombasa; Diani is the most popular of all the beaches. Here, at the Tiwi River mouth and standing in a grove of baobab trees is the 18th-century **Kongo Mosque**. It is still mostly intact and is used by the local people as a place of prayer.

Most of the holiday resort hotels are along Diani Beach, which is a real tropical paradise of coconut palms, white sandy beaches and an opal-blue sea. Many of the hotels are surrounded by huge baobabs like those at the new **Indian Ocean Beach Club**; one large specimen in the area, its girth measuring 22m (72ft), is protected by presidential decree. Also at Diani is the remnant of a once-large coastal wooded tract, **Jadini Forest**, which is inhabited by colobus monkeys and other wildlife.

A few miles inland from Diani Beach are the green rolling **Shimba Hills** which rise steeply from the coastal plain up to a height of 457m (1500ft); they are covered mainly with grassland and patches of forest, and offer wonderful views over the surrounding countryside.

The **Shimba Hills National Reserve**, 192km² (74 sq miles), was established in 1968 to protect one of the last breeding herds of sable antelope in Kenya, which were being threatened by the fast-expanding human population. Roan antelope, originally introduced from an area near Thika, north of Nairobi, also occur here, as well as elephant, buffalo, zebra, common waterbuck, lion and leopard. The birdlife is varied; among the more interesting species that can be seen here are the palm-nut vulture, southern-banded snake eagle, grasshopper buzzard, trumpeter and silvery-cheeked hornbill, carmine bee-eater and Fischer's turaco.

Funzi Island ✦✦✦

Southwards of Diani, all the glitz of modern hotels is soon left behind as the road passes through cashew, coconut and sugar plantations, and the sleepy villages of the Digo people. Approximately 72km (45 miles) from Mombasa is the village of Ramisi. A left turn here leads to the village of Bodo which faces Funzi Island, a private tropical paradise. A short 15-minute boat ride takes you to this delightful hideaway whose only tourists are migrating birds.

A special camp is run by Tony and Robina Duckworth of the **Funzi Island Club**. It is the perfect place for anyone wanting to get away from

> **A CHILLY TALE**
>
> Gazi, a village south of Diani, has a house that once belonged to Sheikh Mbaruk bin Rashid. A local story tells of the sheikh having a special room in the house where he would confine unfaithful wives and disobedient servants, forcing them to inhale burning hot peppers until they saw the error of their ways.

Below: *a weathered working catamaran beached at Diani, some 35km (22 miles) south of Mombasa. Diani, a popular coastal resort area, is noted for its tourist hotels, its palms and giant baobab trees, and for its historic Kongo Mosque.*

Right: *the enchanting Mtwapa Creek, just north of Mombasa. Until fairly recently travellers crossed the water by hand-hauled rope ferry; today they do so over the Japanese-built suspension bridge.*
Opposite: *the pool area of the Flamingo Hotel in Mombasa.*

the crowds. Bird-watching and creek fishing are a speciality, as is the magic of going on a dhow cruise, which often combines a visit to a marine park where guests snorkel or dive, and a superb meal.

Shimoni ✦✦✦

About 60km (37 miles) along the main road from Mombasa, a sandy turnoff to the left takes you to Shimoni, on the **Pemba Channel**. Meaning 'place of the hole' after an enormous cave which is thought to stretch for 15km (9 miles), Shimoni was once the headquarters of Sir William Mackinnon's Imperial British East Africa. A series of caves, besides the main one, exists; according to legend, slaves were held here until they were transported to Arabia. Some local historians discount this theory, however, claiming they were used by the local people as hiding places when hostile tribes raided the area.

Shimoni is Kenya's deep-sea fishing centre. This sport can be pursued almost all year round except for May, June and sometimes July.

You can also sail on a dhow to the delightful **Wasini** and **Kisite islands**. Some of the best diving and snorkelling in the Indian Ocean is to be experienced here. The islands are dotted around in the Kisite and **Mpunguti** marine national parks and the **Mpunguti National Reserve**, a combined marine area of 21km²

DEEP SEA FISHING

This is a very popular sport off Kenya's coast, available for nine months of the year, although the period from **August to March** is the prime season as the sea is very calm and rich in nutrients, therefore rich in fish. Sailfish are the most highly prized catch, alongside marlin. Tunny, bonito, wahoo, kingfish, broadbill and mako sharks also provide fishermen with a thrill. A new, preferred method being taken seriously in Kenya is that of tagging the fish once it has been caught and then releasing it. The fisherman is rewarded with a photograph and an impressive certificate to remind him of the occasion.

(8 sq miles). The variety and the colours of the coral and fish are astounding. Most of the divers and snorkellers who join an organized visit to this wonderful spot will enjoy an excellent seafood lunch at the restaurant on Wasini Island. One particular company, Shimoni Aqua Ventures, provides lunch on an uninhabited, secluded island or on board their dhow, the *Pilli Pipa*, while anchored in a remote spot.

NORTH COAST

Leaving Mombasa Island for the north coast by way of the new Nyali Toll Bridge which spans Tudor Creek, the road passes the turn-off for **Freretown**, which was established in 1875 by Sir Bartle Frere as a sanctuary for escaped and emancipated slaves. Just through Freretown is the well-known **Tamarind Restaurant** and the **Krapf Monument**. The monument marks the spot where the first Christian missionary to the area, Dr Krapf, made his pledge to attempt to convert the African continent to Christianity; it is also the burial site of Mrs Krapf and her children. Dr Krapf's wife unfortunately died just four months after arriving in Kenya with her husband.

The road then enters **Nyali**, an elegant suburb and expensive residential area in which the well-known **Nyali Beach Hotel** is situated. Continuing northwards, the road passes the **Bamburi cement work**s. A Swiss ecologist, Rene Haller, was employed by the Bamburi Portland Cement Company to rehabilitate the huge quarries that had been dug by the company over the years, and a wonderful job has certainly been done to hide the quarry scars. Haller has transformed

MAMBA CROCODILE FARM

A popular tourist attraction, Mamba Village has been established near Bamburi, north of Mombasa. *Mamba* means 'crocodile' in Swahili, thus the village is a successful crocodile farm. It is these reptiles – especially when it's feeding time at 17:00 – that most visitors come to see. The village also has a tropical marine aquarium and a botanical garden. Horse and camel riding is on offer, and the popular restaurant serves crocodile meat, zebra, gazelle, buffalo and seafood.

Right: *the ruins of Jumba la Mtwana, or slave master's house, hidden among the trees at the water's edge. The structure, together with the neighbouring mosques, houses and cemetery, was part of a once-flourishing settlement which the Arabs deserted half a millenium ago.*

the area into a wooded wildlife sanctuary containing fish ponds, nature trails and a nonprofit-making farm which is now a major tourist attraction.

The **Mombasa Marine National Park** is situated offshore, and the major concentration of Kenya's coastal hotels occurs along Bamburi Beach.

The road continues northwards over **Mtwapa Creek**, where a number of marinas offers water-skiing and deep-sea fishing. After crossing the creek and turning off immediately to the right, you will find **Kenya Marine Land and Snake Park** (which also organizes dhow trips). Just further on, another road to the right leads to an ancient monument, **Jumba la Mtwana** (slave master's house), which forms part of an ancient city that was abandoned some time between the 14th and 15th centuries. The atmospheric ruins, which have been declared a national monument, are set at the edge of the beach among baobab trees and consist of four mosques (one of which is gently subsiding into the sands), some houses and a cemetery.

Leaving Mtwapa, one passes through farmland, cashew and sisal plantations dotted with huge baobabs. There is a good chance of seeing the most strikingly beautiful of all the bee-eater family, the carmine bee-eater, in this area as it usually perches on the sisal and roadside telephone wires. Yet another coastal hotel area, Kikambala Beach, can be seen on the right. Before arriving at Kilifi, roughly halfway between Mombasa and Malindi, the road passes through territory belonging to the Giriama people, and on through the large Vipingo Sisal Estate.

Kilifi

For many years **Kilifi Creek** was crossed by ferry, which has been replaced with a new toll bridge. Kilifi is best known as the home of the **Mnarani Club**, famous for its big game-fishing competitions; the club can be seen on the right of the road before crossing the new bridge. The creek is a favourite anchorage for ocean-going yachts and is very popular for water-skiing and wind-surfing.

Before crossing the creek, there is a turn-off on the left of the road for the **Mnarani Ruins**, sprawled on a bluff

CARMINE BEE-EATERS

Kilifi Creek is lined with mangrove trees. From November to April they are home to thousands of carmine bee-eaters, which create one of the most incredible sights imaginable as they fly into the trees at sunset to roost, flashing their brilliant plumage. These birds nest in the north of Kenya, in areas close to Lake Turkana, and spend their nonbreeding time along the Kenyan coast where most of them roost (they certainly don't breed, as some travel guides will tell you) in the mangroves of both Kilifi and the nearby Mida Creek.

Left: *printed fabrics in vibrant colours on sale on Jadini Beach along the south coast.*

Above: fishing craft off Malindi. The port was a major Arab trading centre until the arrival of the Portuguese navigators at the end of the 15th century.

overlooking the water. The ruins include a group of tombs – one of them a pillar tomb – two mosques and a deep well. They were occupied between the 14th and 17th centuries; pillaged by the warring Galla tribe that swept down from Somalia, the ruined town was only uncovered two centuries later.

Leaving Kilifi, the road passes small, romantic coastal villages shaded by rustling palms, and runs along the edge of the **Arabuko-Sokoke** forest (*see* panel); at one point a glimpse of **Mida Creek** can be seen before arriving at the turn-off for the famous **Gedi Ruins** and the village of **Watamu**.

Watamu

Primarily a small beach resort on **Turtle Bay**, Watamu has on its doorstep its own marine national park. The park and adjacent national reserve, together with the **Malindi Marine National Park and Reserve** (the latter having a combined area of 219km² (84 sq miles) form one of Kenya's biosphere reserves.

The three caves at the entrance to **Mida Creek** are the most attractive feature of the marine park, and are home to a number of giant 1.8m-long (6ft) grouper fish weighing 200kg (440lb). The park wardens protect the caves, limiting the number of visitors to them. Along the beach are a number of hotels, among them **Ocean Sports** and **Hemingways** (famous for their deep-sea fishing).

Mida Creek ✦✦✦

At the southern end of Turtle Bay and guarded by **Whale Island** is the entrance to Mida Creek, mangrove-lined tidal mud flats. Mida is famous for its migrant birds which concentrate around the creek's food-rich mud from March to April, before flying northwards. Most of the birds are of the sandpiper and plover families, but there is also usually a flock of greater flamingos in residence, adding a splash of colour to this wonderful place. Mida is also the best place to see the unusual and uncommon crab plover, resident here from September to April. Other notable birds are the carmine and Madagascar bee-eaters, and various species of tern. From June to September roseate and bridled terns breed on Whale Island. Most of the Watamu Hotels organize dhow or motorboat trips in the creek, but the best way to see the birds closely is to drive down one of the many sandy tracks off the main Mombasa–Malindi road that lead to the creek's mangrove-fringed shore.

Gedi Ruins ∗∗

Sixteen kilometres (10 miles) south of Malindi, the ruins of an old Arab town set in the midst of the coastal forest combine to provide an atmospheric reminder of the past.

Gedi was founded in the 14th century; it flourished during the late 14th and 15th centuries, but was abandoned in the early 17th century, probably because of increased pressure from the warlike Galla tribe as they moved southwards. The word 'Gedi', or more correctly 'Gede', is a Galla word meaning 'precious'; it is also a personal name. Gedi was originally surrounded by a 2.7m-high (9ft) wall which had at least three gates. The north-west part of the town has been excavated and covers an area of 18ha (44 acres).

Among the excavated ruins are the **Great Mosque**, origin-

> **A THREATENED FOREST**
>
> Parallel to the coast just inland from Malindi and Watamu is the largest remaining stand of indigenous coastal forest in Kenya. Called the Arabuko-Sokoke, this forest reserve covers an area of 372km² (144 sq miles) and is internationally known for its unique endangered bird species, the Sokoke scops owl and Clarke's weaver, and two lesser-known endemic mammals, the Sokoke four-toed mongoose and the golden-rumped elephant shrew. A number of wide drivable tracks enables visitors to travel deep into the forest. Look out for the primitive giant tree ferns. Visitors must call in at the forest station along the Malindi–Mombasa road to arrange for a guide to accompany them.

Below: *the ruins of Gedi, a town founded by Arab traders centuries ago.*

BIRDERS' PARADISE

Bird-watchers will not want to miss visiting the mouth of the Sabaki River where, at times, there are thousands of migrant wading birds, including broad-billed sand-pipers (the area is the only place in Kenya where this rare migrant is seen regularly). Other special birds found at the mouth of the Sabaki are the Madagascar pratincoles (the Sabaki is virtually the only place other than Madagascar where they can be seen); the rare and localized Malindi pipit too can be spotted – with dili-gence – in the sand dunes along the river banks.

ally constructed in the 15th century and rebuilt 100 years later, the **Palace**, the **Dated Tomb** inscribed with its Arabic date AH802 (1399) and the **Pillar Tomb**. A number of wells are now the home of barn owls.

Interesting birds can be seen at Gedi, among them the lizard buzzard, palm-nut vulture, trumpeter hornbill, Narina's trogon and black-breasted glossy starling. Blue monkeys and red-tailed squirrels also live among the ruins. Gedi is administered by The National Museums of Kenya and is open to the public daily from 07:00 to 18:00.

Malindi ••

North of Watamu, Kenya's most famous resort town, Malindi, sits in an attractive bay south of the Sabaki River. For centuries Malindi was an important Arab trading centre. Portuguese explorer Vasco da Gama landed here in 1498 and in the following year erected a cross to commemorate the occasion. Carved from Lisbon limestone and inscribed with the Portuguese coat of arms, the cross was originally erected at the site of the Sheikh of Malindi's palace, but was later taken down and re-erected at Vasco da Gama Point.

Malindi became Portugal's most northerly territory in East Africa, reverting to Omani rule during the 17th century, before being taken over by the Galla people.

Nowadays Malindi swarms with foreign tourists, mainly Italians and Germans on package holidays, and there are few signs of those blissfully tranquil former days.

The **Vasco da Gama cross** and **church**, built in 1541, are accessible to the public, and Sheikh Hassan's 15th-century **pillar tomb**, standing beside a 19th-century pillar tomb, can be seen on the waterfront next to the mosque.

Below: *Malindi's Pillar Tomb, which contains the mortal remains of Sheikh Abdul Hassan, and the graceful Jumah Mosque.*

Unfortunately, due to poor farming practices upstream of the Sabaki River, tons of silt are washed into Malindi Bay every year. The beach hotels that were once right on the seashore are now set well back and the silt often stains the once blue water, and is killing the coral in the vicinity of the river. Malindi is a deep-sea fishing centre and the home port of a number of commercial fishing boats.

The Malindi Marine National Park and Reserve, 219km² (84 sq miles) in area, extends from Malindi southwards to Watamu. The southern section of the park embraces beautiful coral gardens, and is popular for divers and snorkellers, and visitors in glass-bottomed boats.

LAMU ARCHIPELAGO

An exciting 25-minute flight to the north of Malindi, affording breathtaking views down into a turquoise sea, brings one to the famous Lamu Archipelago, comprising the islands of **Lamu**, **Manda** and **Pate**. The only mode of transport here is the sailboat and charismatic dhow.

> ### THE LAMU *MAULIDI*
>
> *Maulidi-Idd Milad ul Nabi* is a religious festival celebrating the Prophet Mohammed's birth on the 12th day of the 3rd Islamic month, *Rabi al-Awal*. On Lamu Island this festival has become a major celebration. Religious ceremonies continue throughout the month, reaching a climax on the last Thursday when the main event, the reading of the *Maulidi*, takes place in the Riyadha Mosque. During the last week of celebrations the people of the town are joined by Muslims from all over East Africa, and from places as far away as Pakistan and Morocco.

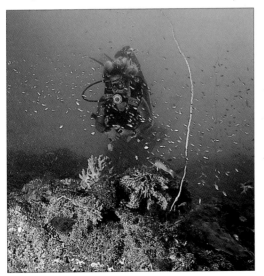

Left: *the coral reefs offshore of Malindi and the Lamu Archipelago to the north serve as a mecca for scuba divers and snorkellers. Visitors can also experience trips in a glass-bottomed boat.*

Lamu Island ***

No matter whether one arrives by road or by air, the only way to get to 19km-long (12 miles) Lamu Island is by diesel-powered dhow. Visitors arriving by air land on **Manda Island**; a five-minute walk takes them to **Mkandi Channel**, where they can cross the strait aboard a dhow to Lamu Town or on to **Peponi's Hotel**. Those arriving by road will have to leave their vehicles on the mainland at **Mokowe** and take a dhow from the town's jetty.

Visiting Lamu Town is a journey back in time; here life goes on much as it has done for hundreds of years. The town itself has been in existence since at least the 9th century, although most of its dwellings date from the 19th century. In the 1500s Lamu was a thriving port exporting slaves, ivory, rhino horn and mangrove poles. Now, except for the continued export of a few mangrove poles, its main business is tourism.

The town is a maze of narrow streets and small flower-filled courtyards enclosed by walls, its houses made of coral rag, many of which feature ornately carved wooden doors and lintels. Most of the streets remain undisturbed by motor vehicles, as donkeys alone find enough room to navigate them. There is only one vehicle on Lamu Island, owned by the district governor.

The people of Lamu are orthodox Muslims and wear the traditional white *kanzu* and an embroidered cap (*kofia*); women wear brightly coloured *khangas* but cover up in a black cloth, called a *bui-bui*, when they go outdoors. Of Lamu's mosques, none is remarkable as each differs little in appearance from nearby homes.

The **Old Fort**, built by the Omani Arabs in 1812 and until recently a prison, is worth a visit; so is the museum. Otherwise the visitor can soak up the atmosphere by taking a slow stroll through the streets. The museum was

---

TROPICAL ISLAND PARADISE

Northeast of Pate Island, the Kiunga Marine Reserve stretches from the Somali border down to Oseni; adjacent to this coastal village lies Kiwaiyu Island, a long, narrow, strip of sand. Kenya's most exclusive and expensive getaway, Kiwaiyu Lodge, is situated on the mainland in a beautiful bay opposite the island's northern tip. The lodge (if one can call it that) consists of a few small thatch-built chalets perched on the beach. All types of watersports are on offer (sailing, water-skiing, diving) and the food is legendary. Kiwaiyu Lodge is accessible only by air or boat.

once the home of the British district officer and has many interesting exhibits, among them the reconstruction of a traditional Swahili home, and models of various types of dhow and canoe. There are also some very good displays of carved wooden doors, and two examples of carved ivory *siwas* – wind instruments which are still used today on special occasions such as the Maulidi celebration (this takes place after the Prophet's birthday).

The village of **Shela** is a 40-minute walk along the shore. Popular among visitors to Lamu Island, the village has a lovely dune-lined beach. The interesting **Friday Mosque** in the village has a rocket-like tower.

Manda Island **

Close to Lamu, across the narrow Mkandi Channel, is the mystery-shrouded Manda Island with its extensive ruins of the old Swahili city, **Takwa**, which flourished between the 15th and 17th centuries before being inexplicably abandoned. The ruins sprawl over an area of 5ha (12 acres) and include a tomb dated 1681. All of the buildings and the mosque face north towards Mecca.

Pate Island **

A two-hour boat ride to the north of Manda Island takes one to Pate Island, which has some of the most impressive ruins in Kenya. Among these is the recently excavated Shanga, an ancient Swahili city state that is at least 1200 years old. The ruins cover an area of 8ha (20 acres), and were uncovered with the help of members of the Operation Drake Team.

> **MAULIDI CELEBRATION**
>
> All of Lamu's mosques participate in this Muslim celebration (the exact date varies so it is best to check with the Lamu Museum), which continues for several days each year. Sheikh Habib Salih, Lamu's patron during the late 19th century, brought fame to the small town for introducing the prophet's birthday celebration and turning the occasion into a major annual festival. Muslims from across East Africa are drawn to these festivities, which include singing and dancing.

Opposite: *elegant dhows off Lamu Island.*
Below: *the Dhow Palace Hotel on Lamu.*

The Coral Coast at a Glance

BEST TIMES TO VISIT

The prime time for fishermen, snorkellers and scuba divers is **August to March** when seas are calm and the water clear. Over April and May, and into June, many hotels close, but visitors are sure to find a hotel open during that time.

GETTING THERE

Major **car-hire** companies are represented at Moi International Airport, and at most bigger coastal hotels. The best way to get to Lamu is **by air** from Mombasa or Malindi, contact Malindi Air Services, tel: (011) 433061 or 434325, fax: 434264, or Eagle Air, tel: (011) 434502/4/5 (Mombasa), or (0123) 31006 (Malindi). They also offer visits by air (one- or two-day excursions) to national parks and reserves. Visits to Tsavo National Park and Shimba Hills National Reserve can be arranged through **Galu Safaris**, tel: (011) 229524 or 209057, and other safari companies.

WHERE TO STAY

Mombasa Town
Royal Court, tel: (011) 312389/312398, fax: 312398.
Safire Hotel, tel: (011) 494841/494893, fax: 495280.
New Outrigger Hotel, Ras Liwatoni: tel: (011) 220822.

South Coast
Shimba Hills Lodge in Shimba National Reserve: tree top game-viewing lodge, book through Block Hotels.

Indian Ocean Beach Club: new hotel resembling Swahili village, on Diani Beach, book through Block Hotels.
Diani House: secluded home, book through Bush Homes.
Jadini Beach Hotel: one of original beach hotels, book through Alliance Hotels.
Chale Island, 12km (7 miles) south of Diani Beach: 25 luxury bungalows and tents on the beach, write to Chale Paradise Island, PO Box 4, Ukunda; tel: (0127) 3477 or 3235, fax: 3319/20.
The Samawati House, Msambweni Beach: Arab-style house with sweeping beach-front, book through Safaris Unlimited (Africa).
Funzi Island Club, 72km (45 miles) south of Mombasa: luxury camp set on secluded island, birdlife superb, call Sargas, tel: (02) 212763 (Nairobi) or tel: (0127) 317179 (Diani), tel: 2396.
Pemba Channel Inn, Pemba Channel: mainly for fishermen as no beach here, but ideal base for visits to nearby marine national park and reserve; contact Pemba Channel Fishing Club Ltd, tel: (011) 313749, fax: 316875.

North Coast
Tamarind Village, Nyali: fully equipped, self-catering or room service, write to The Tamarind Village, PO Box 95805, Mombasa; tel: (011) 471729, fax: 472106.
Nyali Beach Hotel: book through Block Hotels.

Mombasa Beach Hotel, Nyali: write to PO Box 90414, Mombasa; tel: (011) 471861.
Whitesands, Bamburi Beach: book through Sarova Hotels.
Severin Sea Lodge, Bamburi Beach: write to PO Box 90173, Mombasa; tel: (011) 485001.
Serena Beach Hotel, Shanzu Beach: built in style of Swahili village, contact Serena Hotels.

Kilifi
Takaungu House: on beach, for six guests, book through Bush Homes of East Africa.
Mnarani Club: book direct, PO Box 1008, Kilifi, tel: (0125) 22320, fax: 22200.

Watamu
Hemingways: highly recommended, write to PO Box 267, Watamu; tel: (0122) 32624, fax: 32256.
Turtle Bay Beach Hotel: write to PO Box 22309, Nairobi; tel: (0122) 32226 or 32080, fax: 32268.
Ocean Sports: write to PO Box 100, Watamu; tel: (0122) 32008 or 32288, fax: 32266.

Malindi
Indian Ocean Lodge: book direct, PO Box 171, Malindi, tel: (0123) 30736.
Che-Shale, 20km (12 miles) north of Malindi: small super-luxury lodge among sand dunes: write to PO Box 857, Malindi; tel: (0123) 20676.

Lamu Archipelago
Lamu Palace Hotel, on waterfront: all rooms air-

The Coral Coast at a Glance

conditioned, write to the hotel at PO Box 86, Lamu; tel: (0121) 33272, fax: 33104.
Petley's Inn in Lamu town: first hotel on the island, write to PO Box 4, Lamu; tel: (0121) 33107, fax: 33378.
Peponi Hotel, Shela village: at water's edge; write to PO Box 24, Lamu; tel: (0121) 33421/23, fax: 33029.
Blue Safari Club, Manda Island: small *bandas* on beach (excellent), book direct, Havambee St, Lamu, tel: (0121) 33205.
Kiwaiyu Safari Village, Kiwaiyu: very exclusive, Kenya's top beach accommodation, write to PO Box 55343, Nairobi; tel: (02) 503030, fax: 503149.

WHERE TO EAT

Dhow lunch cruise (on *Pilli Pipa*) or a five-course meal on a 'desert' island, very highly recommended, call **Shimoni Aqua Ventures**, tel: (0127) 2401.
Tamarind Restaurant, Mombasa: Moorish-styled seafood restaurant overlooking Mombasa Old Harbour; dhow offers lunch or dinner cruises, tel: (011) 474600/1/2, fax: 472106.
Hemingways, highly recommended, tel: (0122) 32624.
Le Pichet, north of Nyali bridge: French gourmet cuisine, tel: (011) 485785/881.
Ali Barbour's, popular seafood restaurant set in coral cave on Diani Beach, tel: (0127) 2033.

Wasini Island Restaurant: seafood restaurant, dhows stop here for lunch; reservations at Wasini Island booking office in Jadini Beach Hotel, tel: (0127) 3200, fax: 3154.
Driftwood Beachclub in Malindi, international and seafood cuisine, tel: (0123) 20155 or 20406.

ACTIVITIES AND EXCURSIONS

Deep-sea fishing: Hemingways, Watamu, tel: (0122) 32624; Kingfisher Lodge, Malindi, tel: (0123) 21168; Hall Mark Enterprises, Mtwapa Creek, tel: (011) 485680; Pat Hemphill's Sea Adventures, tel: Shimoni 12 or 13; Pemba Channel Fishing Club, Mombasa, tel: (011) 313749.
Diving: Shimoni Aqua Ventures, tel: (0127) 2401; Ocean Sports Hotel, Watamu, tel: (0122) 32008 or 32288.
Dhow cruises: Shimoni Aqua Ventures, tel: (0127) 2401; Kisiti Dhow Tours (lunch at Wasini Island), contact Wasini Island Hotel, tel: (0127) 3200; Tamarind, Mombasa, tel: (011) 471747, 474600/1; Ocean Sports, Watamu, tel: (0122) 32008; Peponi Hotel, Lamu, tel: (0121) 33421/23, fax: 33029; Jahazi Marine Ltd, Mombasa, tel and fax: (011) 472414.

USEFUL ADDRESSES

Safari companies
Galu Safaris Ltd, tel: (011) 229524, fax: (02) 314226.
Kingfisher Safaris, tel: (0123) 20031 (Malindi).
Pollman's Tours and Safaris, tel: (011) 316733 (Mombasa), fax: 312245, 228935.
Southern Cross Safaris, tel: (011) 229520-6, 220737, fax: (02) 314082/314226.

Booking agencies
Alliance Hotels Ltd, PO Box 49839, Nairobi; tel: (02) 337501, fax: 219212.
Block Hotels, PO Box 47557, Nairobi; tel: (02) 335807, fax: 340541.
Bush Homes of East Africa Ltd, PO Box 56923, Nairobi; tel: (02) 571647/571649, fax: 571665.
Safaris Unlimited (Africa) Ltd, PO Box 24181, Nairobi; tel: (02) 891168, fax: 891113.
Savannah Camps and Lodges, PO Box 48019, Nairobi; tel: (02) 331191, fax: 330698.
Sarova Hotels, PO Box 30680, Nairobi; tel: (02) 333248, fax: 211472.
Serena Hotels, PO Box 48690, Nairobi; tel: (02) 711077, fax: 718103.

MOMBASA	J	F	M	A	M	J	J	A	S	O	N	D
AVERAGE TEMP. °F	81	82	82	81	79	77	75	75	77	79	81	82
AVERAGE TEMP. °C	27	28	28	27	26	25	24	24	25	26	27	28
Hours of Sun Daily	8	9	9	7	6	7	7	8	8	9	9	8
RAINFALL ins	1	0	1	4	6	2	1	2	2	2	3	1
RAINFALL mm	18	10	29	109	150	53	35	48	45	62	64	33
Days of Rainfall	11	1	2	11	15	13	12	8	9	8	7	6

Travel Tips

Tourist Information

The Kenya Tourist Board has offices in the UK (London), the USA (New York and Beverly Hills), France (Paris), Germany (Frankfurt), Hong Kong, Japan (Tokyo), Sweden (Stockholm) and Switzerland (Zürich). There are also information offices in Nairobi, tel: (02) 604246/5, fax: 501096, in Mombasa, tel: (011) 224365, and in Malindi, tel: (0123) 20747.

Safari companies: There are many safari companies in Kenya whose price and service vary tremendously. You are advised to use only ones that are members of KATO (Kenya Association of Tour Operators). If in doubt, do not hesitate to contact the KATO Office, 5th Floor, Jubilee Exchange Building, Mama Ngina Street, Nairobi, tel: (02) 225570, fax: (02) 188402.

Entry documents

Every visitor must have a valid passport; visa requirements vary from time to time, so you are strongly advised to check the latest requirements at the airline or the nearest Kenya Tourist Board Office, Embassy or High Commission. Visitors with a valid passport may obtain a visitor's pass on arrival if in possession of an onward or return airline ticket. A visitor's pass is normally valid for three months.

Customs

Although there is no import duty on photographic equipment, you may be asked to pay. If asked, refuse and request a senior official. You may also be asked to record the serial numbers of your cameras, lens and video camera in your passport – this is a valid requirement.

When leaving the country, travellers are required to report to the customs desk before checking in, where you will be asked the contents of your baggage. The export of rhino horn, ivory and any wildlife items is strictly illegal.

Departure Tax

International departure tax is added to the cost of the ticket by most airlines. There is also a tax of KSh100 charged on all internal flights departing from government airports.

Health requirements

Visitors from, or who have recently passed through, a yellow-fever zone, must have a valid international certificate of vaccination. Rules regarding health change regularly; when planning your trip, therefore, check with your airline for the latest information.

Air travel

The major points of entry into Kenya are Jomo Kenyatta International Airport (JKIA) in Nairobi and Moi International Airport in Mombasa. Wilson Airport is the main airport for charter services. Kenya Airways is Africa's fastest growing airline and operates a fleet of modern aircraft.

Kenya Airways
Flight information and reservations: Nairobi: tel: (02) 29291 or 82288/171; Mombasa: tel: (011) 221251; Kisumu: tel: (035) 4405516; Malindi: tel: (0123) 20237 or 20574.

Air Kenya
Flight information and reservations:
Nairobi: tel: (02) 501421/2/3, fax: 602951;

Mombasa: tel: (011) 229777/ 229106, fax: 224063;
Moi International Airport: tel: (011) 433982, fax: 435235;
Malindi: tel: (0123) 30808, fax: 21229;
Lamu: tel: (0121) 33445, fax: 33063.

Road travel

Kenya has an extensive and well-signposted road network – 8300km (5157 miles) are bitumen and 54,000km (33,555 miles) are earth and gravel. The state of the road surfaces is variable, from well maintained to badly neglected and potholed. The roads in the national park are usually good murram (laterite) surfaces.

In Kenya one drives on the left. The speed limit is 100kph (60mph) on highways, 50kph (30mph) in towns and villages and 30kph (20mph) in national parks. Drivers require a valid driving licence which should be carried at all times. They may use their domestic licences for up to 90 days, providing that they are fully endorsed at the Road Transport Office in Nyayo House, Nairobi.

Car Hire: To rent a car you have to be between 23 and 70 years old. The best-known car-hire companies are:
Kenya Rent a Car (Avis):
Nairobi, tel: (02) 336794;
JKIA, tel: (02) 822090;
Mombasa, tel: (011) 220465;
Malindi, tel: (0123) 20513.
Hertz UTC:
Nairobi, tel: (02) 822339;
Mombasa, tel: (011) 316333;
Malindi, tel: (0123) 2040.
Insurance: Your vehicle must be covered by a third party

insurance policy; if you are hiring a car the rental firm is responsible for making the appropriate arrangements.
Maps: Regional and city maps are available from bookshops. Both Nation Bookshop and Prestige Booksellers in Nairobi have good selections.
Petrol: Cities, towns and main routes are well served by filling stations. In main towns there is a 24-hour service, other stations are open from 06:00 until 18:00. All fuel – super, regular or diesel – is sold in litres. There is no octane rating shown on pumps. Pump attendants see to your needs as there is no self-service in Kenya. Always check that the pump is zeroed prior to filling up.
Automobile Association of Kenya (AAK): Situated at Hurlingham Shopping Centre, PO Box 40087, Nairobi; tel: (02) 714212 or 724378.
Coach Travel: This form of travel (between Nairobi and Mombasa) is for the younger or hardier traveller, and not recommended for the faint-hearted. Do not accept any sweets or other food from fellow travellers as there have been many cases of travellers being drugged and robbed.

Rail Travel

Rail travel is a comfortable and relatively inexpensive method of travel. On a daily basis, Kenya Railways operates services to Mombasa and Kisumu. Each evening two trains leave Nairobi for the 12-hour journey to Mombasa. First-, second- and third-class

tickets are available. First class consists of two-berth compartments with fold-away bunk beds and a washbasin. Second class is similar but has four-berth compartments with fold-away beds, while third class has seats only. Bedding is available at a small extra cost. There is a dining car offering dinner and breakfast at very reasonable prices. For first and second class it is advisable to book a few days in advance; this can be done though a travel agent or directly at the station. Kenya Railways, enquiries and reservations:
Nairobi, tel: (02) 221211, fax: 340049;
Mombasa, tel: (011) 312221;
Kisumu, tel: (035) 42211.

Boat Travel

Lake steamers: Kenya Railways operates ferries that connect Kisumu with Kendu Bay, Homa Bay, Mfangano Island and Mbita Point, tel: (035) 42271.
Dhows: It is possible to travel by dhow from Mombasa to Malindi and Lamu, and it is also possible to travel by dhow to Dar es Salaam and the islands of Pemba. There is no set schedule for dhow trips and the visitor must enquire on the spot.

Money Matters

The Kenya currency unit is the shilling, which is divided into 100 cents. Coins are issued in denominations of 5, 10 and 50 cents and 1 and 5 shillings. Notes are issued in denominations of 5, 10, 20, 50, 100, 200 and 500 shillings. Foreign currency regulations are being slowly revised; at the time of writing foreign currency does not have to be declared on arrival or departure. The importation and exportation of Kenyan currency is not allowed. All foreign currency must be exchanged at banks or licensed exchange facilities such as major hotels and safari lodges. On arrival in Nairobi or Mombasa visitors are advised to change the bulk of their foreign currency or traveller's cheques at the airport or at the hotel. Safari lodges often have a shortage of cash, so queuing and long delays waiting for cash are very often the case. Banks in towns other than Nairobi or Mombasa will change foreign currency and traveller's cheques but are very slow – 45 minutes or more is not at all unusual – which can make you somewhat unpopular with your fellow travellers. Do not be tempted by black-market dealers who are prevalent in Nairobi streets.

Banks operate a 24-hour service at Jomo Kenyatta International Airport in Nairobi and at Moi Inter-national Airport in Mombasa. Banking hours in the bigger cities and towns are: 09:00 to 14:00 Monday to Friday, and 09:00 to 11:00 on Saturdays. Traveller's cheques are accepted at hotels, lodges, restaurants and shops, includ-ing roadside curio dealers. However, they are not usually accepted at the smaller places such as petrol service stations.

Value Added Tax: VAT of 16% is levied on most goods and services, and cannot be reclaimed by visitors.

Tipping: Tipping is usual to those giving a good service. Ten per cent is acceptable at hotels and restaurants even though there is frequently a service charge on your bill. There is also a training levy on restaurant bills. It is usual to tip your tour driver or guide, at least KSh100 per day.

Measurements

Kenya uses the metric system.

Accommodation

Although there is a grading system ranging from one to five stars it is seldom used. The best hotels in Nairobi, the best beach hotels at the coast and the top safari lodges are of international standard. Major groups are Serena Hotels, Sarova Hotels, Hilton Hotels, Block Hotels, Lonrho Hotels and Musiara Ltd. Many ranches and private homes will accept visitors; these are highly recommended for those who are interested in something different or who would like

to get away from the crowds. In a number of the national parks there is self-catering accommodation. This tends to be very basic and the visitor is advised to take food and bedding, crockery, cutlery and cooking utensils as well as a stove; although cooking gas and bedding should be available, they often are not. Make sure that you are well prepared, as national parks' rules forbid you to drive to the nearest lodge for food and drinks after dark. (Ol Tukai Lodge in Amboseli is possibly the only exception but check on arrival if you intend to visit the nearby Amboseli Lodge.)

Clothes: What to Pack

Kenya enjoys warm to hot dry seasons and cool to chilly rainy seasons. Nights can be surprisingly cold, especially in the highland areas. Dress is informal, though after dark 'smart casual' is worn. Some restaurants do not allow blue-jeans in the evening and a few require jacket and tie for gentlemen and a similar standard of dress for ladies. Mount Kenya Safari Club

CONVERSION CHART		
FROM	**TO**	**MULTIPLY BY**
Millimetres	Inches	0.0394
Metres	Yards	1.0936
Metres	Feet	3.281
Kilometres	Miles	0.6214
Hectares	Acres	2.471
Litres	Pints	1.760
Kilograms	Pounds	2.205
Tonnes	Tons	0.984
To convert Celsius to Fahrenheit: x 9 ÷ 5 + 32		

requires jacket and tie for gentlemen, and ladies are not allowed to wear trousers in the evening, except for traditional costume. Casual wear is usual at the coast and on safari in the game parks. Beach wear is only to be worn at the pool or beach. Please note that nude bathing is not allowed and any offender will be prosecuted. Year-round clothing should be quite lightweight and a hat is a must. A light jacket is necessary all year round, and a warm sweater is advisable for the months of the cool season – June to August.

Business Hours

Businesses generally operate from 09:00 to 18:00 Monday to Friday with a break for one hour at lunch time, usually from 13:00 to 14:00. Some businesses, such as travel agencies, are open on Saturdays from 09:00 to 13:00. Most shops and stores will not open for business until 09:00 but will remain open over the lunch hour and close at 18:00. Some of the larger supermarkets and modern shopping complexes remain open at weekends and on public holidays. In Mombasa some businesses open at 07:00 but may close between 12:30 and 15:30 or 16:00. However, they will remain open until well after dark. City bars and nightclubs remain open until 03:00.

Telephones

The country code is 254. International and local direct dialling is available from Nairobi and Mombasa and most other towns in Kenya. Telephone directories list the dialling codes. If you have any telephone enquiries, dial 991 for assistance.

Facsimile transmission: Facilities are available in most larger hotels and also in some safari lodges. Be warned that hotels and lodges make a heavy surcharge for telephone and fax service.

Electricity

The power system is 240 volts AC. Plugs are usually 13-amp square pins. The bedrooms in all the larger hotels and lodges are equipped with electrical outlet sockets, and

---

PUBLIC HOLIDAYS

New Year's Day 1 January
Good Friday
Easter Monday
Labour Day 1 May
Madaraka Day 1 June
(anniversary of self-government)
Idd ul Fitr, a Muslim holiday timed for the sighting of the new moon after Ramadan (this holiday is taken by both the Muslim and non-Muslim communities)
Nyayo Day 10 October
Kenyatta Day (Kenyatta's birthday) 20 October
Jamhuri (Independence Day) 12 December
Christmas Day 25 December
Boxing Day 26 December
Those holidays falling on a Sunday include the following Monday as a public holiday.

---

even smaller hotels are able and willing to recharge guest's video camera batteries in the reception area.

Time

Kenya is three hours ahead of Greenwich Mean Time (GMT).

Medical Services

Visitors are responsible for their own medical arrangements and are advised to take out medical insurance before departure. Nairobi and Mombasa have several good private hospitals. There are also a number of physicians and surgeons of international reputation. Good dentists and opticians are also available. Visitors can have temporary membership of the Flying Doctor Service, as, in the event of an accident or illness, emergency evacuation to Nairobi may be necessary. There are also some private insurance companies who will evacuate visitors (check with your safari company for details). The African Medical & Research Foundation (AMREF) has a flying doctor service, the telephone number of which is (02) 501301; emergency numbers are: (02) 501280/ 997/331 and 336886. The Flying Doctor's Society is a private company with which you can buy temporary membership for US$50 for 30 days' coverage; PO Box 30125, tel: (02) 501301.

There are many chemists or drugstores in Nairobi and Mombasa, staffed by well-qualified pharmacists. Most drugs are available but often listed under a different brand name. Although most chemists are closed over weekends and during public holidays, there is always one open at these times. The name of the chemist open is usually posted on the door of those that are closed, or it can be obtained from the local hospital. Visitors who are taking regular medication should ensure they bring an adequate supply of their drugs with them.

Health Hazards

Malaria: All visitors to Kenya should be taking anti-malarial prophylactics on arrival in the country, throughout their stay and for a designated time after leaving as malaria is endemic in most areas of Kenya. It is important that these tablets are taken between 18:00 and 19:00 and not in the morning. Some people find that they have to take their anti-malarial tablets with a meal, otherwise they feel unwell. Avoidance of the malaria-carrying mosquito is also very important. As it usually feeds after dark, from about 21:00 onwards, the following is suggested: always sleep under a mosquito net if one is provided; wear long clothing after dark, keeping the ankles covered; and make use of mosquito repellents. (This advice is especially important to remember when sitting around the traditional safari camp fire.) When leaving your room or tent after dark do not leave any lights on inside. However, whatever

you do, you may still contract malaria. At the first sign of illness, consult a doctor (this is particularly important if you fall ill after you have returned home), making it known that you have been in a malaria area. Insist that a blood test be taken. Early diagnosis and treatment will result in your being cured.

Bilharzia: Also known as schistosomiasis, bilharzia is a debilitating waterborne disease caused by a parasitical worm. The worm lives in a small water snail which is usually found in shallow water along the edges of lakes, dams and slow-moving rivers and streams. Bilharzia is not known to occur in either Lake Naivasha or in the area adjacent to the three tourist resorts on Lake Victoria. Before swimming in any water be sure to ask whether it is free of bilharzia.

Aids: The risk of contracting Aids is no greater in Kenya than elsewhere, providing that the usual, well-publicized precautions are taken.

Creepy crawlies: Although snakes, scorpions and spiders are certainly not uncommon in Kenya, they are seldom seen. Even so, when visiting the toilet at night it is still advisable to wear shoes, and where there is no electrical power to use a torch to ensure that you are not about to step on anything nasty! When walking in the bush avoid long grass whenever possible, wear long pants or apply a liberal amount of insect repellent for protection

against ticks. Although ticks in Kenya do not carry Lyme disease, there is still a very slight chance of contracting tick fever.

Drinking water: Most hotels and lodges provide flasks of filtered and boiled water in their guest rooms. Bottled water is available from most hotels and lodges but is expensive. If possible, buy it at a supermarket in Nairobi or Mombasa or at a *duka* (shop) in a small town that you may pass through on your way to the wildlife areas.

Emergencies

The national emergency telephone number is 999 or 0 for operator assistance. Although there is no reliable national ambulance service, there are a number of private ambulance services for insured people. Cover can be bought before commencing your safari and, of course, there is also the Flying Doctor Service. Some safari companies enlist their clients in temporary membership of the service. Almost all safari lodges and camps are in radio contact with the Flying Doctor Service at their base in Nairobi.

Security

Nairobi and Mombasa are as safe for visitors as any major city or town in the world. Avoid deserted streets and beaches, especially if you are alone, and at night take a taxi if you need to leave your hotel. Do not wear expensive-looking jewellery or watches

FEROCIOUS

PHIL

ROSS

FITNESS

A FIGHTER'S PROVEN ACTION PLAN TO DEVELOP BLAZING POWER, ANIMALISTIC STRENGTH AND KILLER CONDITIONING

 ★ with **MARTY GALLAGHER** ★

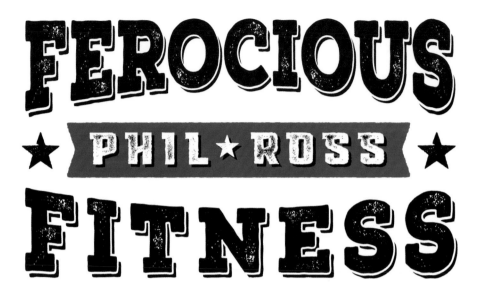

ISBN 13: 978-1-942812-08-1

This edition first published in November 2016

Printed in China

BOOK DESIGN: Derek Brigham • www.dbrigham.com • bigd@dbrigham.com

PHOTOGRAPHY: Michael Polito

— TABLE OF CONTENTS —

ACKNOWLEDGEMENTS.. V

FOREWORD BY BRIAN EBERSOLE.. VII

WHY FIGHTERS SHOULD PAY ATTENTION TO PHIL ROSS...........................1
BY MARTY GALLAGHER

INTRODUCTION 5

CHAPTER 1: ROOTS...7

CHAPTER 2: WHAT I BRING TO THE PARTY 15

CHAPTER 3: CATASTROPHIC INJURY 17

CHAPTER 4: GREATNESS:
THE COMPONENTS OF A SUCCESSFUL FIGHTER 23

CHAPTER 5: WHY ALL FIGHTERS NEED
TO TRAIN FOR STRENGTH AND POWER 27

CHAPTER 6: PHIL'S PHILOSOPHY OF FIGHT TRAINING............................ 35

CHAPTER 7: THE EXERCISES.. 37

CHAPTER 8: FIGHTER NUTRITION: COSMO'S CREDO 69

CHAPTER 9: DIET AND WEIGHT CLASSES 75

CHAPTER 10: HOW POWER SAVED MY LIFE 81

CHAPTER 11: FRANK "THE LEGEND" SHAMROCK 83

CHAPTER 12: KO POWER PROTOCOLS 87

CHAPTER 13: TALKING SMACK... 93

CHAPTER 14: TOP 10 BADASS FIGHTERS 95

CHAPTER 15: TIME FOR TALK IS OVER 99

CHAPTER 16: TRAINING ROUTINES 105

CHAPTER 16: FIGHT CAMP! 125

DRAGON DOOR PRESENTS

THE MAIN EVENT

FEROCIOUS

PHIL

ROSS

FITNESS

ACKNOWLEDGEMENTS

I would like to thank all of my students, wrestlers and fighters over the many years of my training and coaching. There are far too many to name individually—but, you know who you are. Thank you for placing your trust in me, my methods and philosophy and thank you for giving it your all in combat while representing my teams and American Eagle MMA.

I would like to thank my parents, Patricia and Phil, for their endless support and for instilling a strong work ethic and solid foundation of integrity in me. Special thanks goes out to my grandfather, my "Poppy", who introduced me to the world of fighting and provided me with an incredible base. I just wish that my father and grandfather were still with us to read this book, but they did get to see me grow up to become a man, for that I am thankful.

Thanks goes out to Marty Gallagher for all of the time he spent with me, coaxing me to relay some of my stories and helping me to discover my "writing voice." I felt as if Marty were actually in my head during our collaboration.

Thank you John Du Cane, for all of your continued belief and support of me as a person, trainer, coach, athlete and now author. I appreciate all of your insight and friendship. This book, its title, and the knowledge for martial artists and combat athletes would never have come to fruition if not for your inspiration. Your ability to see in others what they do not see in themselves is one of the many reasons that I love you and your vision. I am indebted to you and am honored to be a leader of an elite group, the RKC!

FOREWORD
BY
BRIAN EBERSOLE

When I was first asked to write the foreword for this book, I nearly asked, "What's the book about?" But, for some reason, I paused. With that short moment to consider that this book was penned by Phil Ross, I stated, "You've written a kettlebell/strength and conditioning book, haven't you?". Of course he had! And who better to do so...

I've known Phil since 2005, when he made the trek from New Jersey out to California to visit Frank Shamrock's Martial Arts Academy. At the time, I was training for a San Shou (Kickboxing-style) bout vs. Cung Le, who was the star and champion of that sport, and who later transitioned into MMA, competing for both StrikeForce and the UFC.

So here there I was, young, fit, and ferocious; going through one of the harder training camps of my career. And in saunters Mr. Phil Ross, stocky, bald, coming off of an injury, older than I had thought he was, and jumping at Frank's invitation into the ring for rounds of sparring.

So, Phil punched me a few times, upon first meeting me, and yet I've kept in regular contact with him for the past decade. That seems to be a common theme, with my friendships! I was only given a glimpse into Phil's background, during this first visit to California. He obviously had some training, as he was confident enough to walk into a gym and spar with athletes at a renowned gym, with little warning or notice.

During the next few training sessions, we traded stories of high school wrestling, kickboxing fights (his past bouts, and my upcoming debut), and I learned that he owned his own school back in New Jersey . Over the course of the next two or three years, I would come to know Phil as the "Kettlebell Guy", as he passionately embarked on his journey toward becoming an RKC (Russian Kettlebell Certified). Now, he is an RKC Master, and I commonly refer to Phil as the Kettlebell Guru!

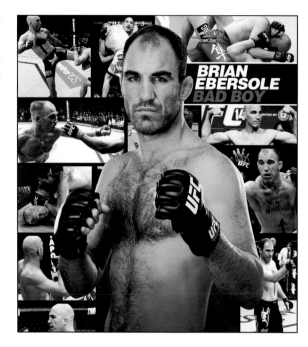

That's why it was easy for me to predict, with fair certainty, the topic of Phil's book. He's proven great at two things, the martial arts and kettlebell training. Phil has worked a long time to gain insight into the workings of the human body, how it adapts to stress/work (training), and how to best program/plan for strength/fitness, and even mobility improvements. He's gained a unique personal insight through many styles and strategies of training; as he's competed in the sports of bodybuilding, wrestling, kickboxing, Jiu Jitsu, and others.

A lifetime of athletic training leaves you with a certain level of knowledge. Coaching only adds to that. Coaching brings a depth and validation to the knowledge you'd gained as an athlete, as you can break down why things work, and see them from another perspective. Personally, I've changed a few of my favorite techniques and strategies; offering them to my students a bit differently than I'd used them myself—only because as a coach (bystander) I could see weaknesses or flaws that I couldn't see as an athlete, whilst I was moving at 100 mph.

Phil has been a lifelong athlete, and a long-time coach. But what sets Phil apart is the fact he has continually sought out science through continued education and certification. He's combined years of anecdotal evidence & personal observations/feedback with the observations and conclusions of the scientific-academic community, and that's both unique and powerful!

When it comes to training, Phil has "seen it all". If there are pitfalls, Phil has seen them. If there are shortcuts, Phil has tried them. If there's a new way of doing it, Phil's looked into it. If there's a Fountain of Youth, Phil has found it and drank his weight's worth! And finally, he's sharing his experiences and proven methods with the rest of us.

There's a lot to be gleaned from Phil's *Ferocious Fitness*. I only wish I could have had this book in my travel bag over the last seven years. I've spent those last seven years traveling the world (for training and competition), and this book would have surely simplified and amplified my fitness efforts. Heck, I'd rather have been able to pack Phil himself in my check-in luggage!

I hope you'll enjoy Ferocious Fitness as much as I have. It offers an interesting perspective on the development of a fantastic athlete and coach, as well as the distilled knowledge acquired over a lifetime of experience and education. May it add to your understanding of human optimization and offer you an enjoyable set of challenges—from within the programs and routines outlined in the book's final section. Happy reading and safe training!

Brain Ebersole
UFC Fighter, Division 1 Wrestler, Coach

★ WHY FIGHTERS SHOULD PAY ATTENTION TO PHIL ROSS ★

BY
MARTY GALLAGHER

COMBAT GUMBO

esults and athletic credentials need to count for something.

In our politically correct age of lockstep fitness orthodoxy, unless you have a PhD and cite twenty-seven footnoted sources to justify a chin-up variant, your opinion is ignored or discounted. Real world experience is relegated into irrelevancy with the cute, unchallenged contention that combat experience doing what the academics are discussing is somehow irrelevant. "Anecdotal empirical experience" is the dismissive rejoinder when asked about the role of real world results.

Thus, the academics are able to discount and dismiss, by mutual consent (within their echo chamber/mutual admiration society) factual, actual, real world results. This type of pompous arrogance brings to mind a story I once heard about the head of the Eastern Studies department at a major university lecturing senior Zen monks—on Zen. The ludicrous academic was chock-full of lofty thoughts and profound conclusions about Zen, which he graciously and unceasingly shared with the two monks—who had a combined 100 + years of hardcore Zazen under their robes. The academic was dismissing deep insight as "anecdotal and irrelevant."

When a guy like Phil Ross decides to get his strategies, modes and methods down on paper—that's the guy I want to learn from.

Phil walks the walk, having won over 300 fights in a mind-blowing array of martial disciplines. He has fought in karate, kickboxing, Taekwondo, wrestling and submission fighting. He competed successfully in different disciplines on the national level from 1979 through 2010.

Phil took a silver medal at the 1979 AAU Eastern National Greco-Roman Wrestling Championship; he won the bronze medal in 1992 at the AAU Taekwondo National Championship. In 1995, Phil was the Free Fighting National Champion and in 2010 won the NAGA No-Gi submission fighting title, becoming the Expert Level Champion. Phil is an eight-time gold medalist at the New Jersey Garden State Games in their karate championships. Phil was named MVP at the 1996 NJ vs. NY Karate Challenge. He was team captain of the 1994 World Champion Karate Union team. Phil is a Black Belt Hall of Fame martial artist.

Phil won the Brooklyn New York's Big Apple Challenge and was the 1989 Black Belt Kumite Champion. Phil holds black belts from the East/West Martial Alliance along with black belts in combat Jiu Jitsu, Bando, Black Belt in Brazilian Jiu Jitsu and Taekwondo. Phil is certified to teach CDT, Arnis and Shamrock Submission Fighting. Phil operated at a high level as a competitive bodybuilder when in 1981 he won the Mr. Wilkes Bodybuilding Championship. In 1983 he took 3rd in the Mr. D.C. Bodybuilding Championship. In 1982 he was the University of Maryland Olympic Weightlifting Champion. In 1987 Phil squatted 525, bench-pressed 370 pounds and deadlifted 505 at a 180 pound bodyweight to become the Reebok Challenge Powerlifting Champion.

Along the way he became a RKC Certified Kettlebell Instructor, a Master Personal Trainer, a Functional Movement Specialist and a Certified Specialist in Bodyweight Strength. Phil has been a high school wrestling coach and a professional bodyguard. Phil made a series of self-defense videos (called S.A.V.E.) that were rated #1 by two separate nationally recognized martial video reviewers. Phil's *Advanced Russian Kettlebell* video is ranked in the Top 10 of kettlebell workout videos. His Kettlebell Basics Workshop (and manual) was one of the first kettlebell training courses approved by the National Academy of Sports Medicine for continuing education credits. This guy has an incredible fighting and training resume; he is extremely bright and articulate; he holds a master's degree.

Oh, and he obtains dramatic results for his students: those results are in direct proportion to their degree of adherence to his modes and methods. He walks the walk. Of this there can be no doubt. Yet the orthodox academics would be quick to dismiss Phil's decades of high level, hardcore experience as "incidental" or "not relevant" or "inappropriate."

Personally, I'd rather talk to a martial Zen master like Phil about all things fight-related than a PhD strength and conditioning coach expressing reflected knowledge. Phil knows where the landmines are planted; he's stepped on all of them at one time in his forty-years of combat immersion. He can show you, the reader, all the productive shortcuts and just as importantly, all the unproductive dead-ends.

In real world, where Phil lives, experience is hard won. Experience is everything in a world where factual, tangible, measurable (objective, not subjective) results are the only things that matter. His system obtains dramatic results for disciplined adherents. The report card on any method, eventually comes down to a lone question: Does your approach, regardless of its sophistication or barbarity, obtain actual, measurable, objective results for those that religiously adhere–yes or no? Period.

Guess what? Much to the dismay of those that dismiss real results as overrated, Phil Ross has a brain (not all fighters end up like punch-drunk Mountain Rivera in the movie *Requiem for a Heavyweight*.) Phil is a crystal clear thinker and he speaks plainly and concisely. He has taught martial arts for decades and over that time has become adept and polished in verbally instructing groups of people.

When he turned his full attention to getting his philosophy down on paper, he found that if he wrote as he spoke, no one had any trouble understanding exactly what he was saying. Phil found his "writer's voice" immediately; his manuscript read as if he were in the room talking to you.

I jumped at the opportunity to work with Phil (and John) on this project. One cursory glance at Phil's book and you could see that it "wrote itself." The logic of the prose propels you along, from start to finish; there are no dead spots or sections of impenetrable ambiguity. All I needed to do was add some spice and seasoning to Phil's plain vanilla, unambiguous prose.

He had zero problems communicating clearly on any topic he selected—I would iron out some of the passive sentences (alpha males only speak in declarative sentences!) I added the herbs, spices and seasoning to his combat gumbo.

I relished the idea of helping introduce this martial legend to a wider audience. His approach is battle-tested and track-proven. And yes that does matter, a lot. Frankly, combat credentials are the first thing I would look for in a fighter. If I had a son or grandson wanting to become a fighter, Phil would be who I would take them to. I can't think of a higher compliment or endorsement.

—**Marty Gallagher,** author of ***The Purposeful Primitive***, co-author of ***Strong Medicine*** and ***CrossCore HardCore***

INTRODUCTION

I love MMA, martial arts, wrestling, boxing, sambo, kickboxing, jiu jitsu, judo and virtually every other combat art. The combat arts not only build character, but they also reveal it. How will you react when adversity slams you in the face? What will happen when you have no other teammates to depend on and success or failure is 100% up to you? The combat arts tell us a great deal about ourselves and force us to face our shortfalls and improve—or perish. The combat arts have given me the strength and self-awareness to flourish when others would have cracked under the pressure only to be vanquished. It is my strongest desire to share this knowledge with others so they may also benefit from the combat arts. MMA (Mixed Martial Arts) has become extremely popular and I want to contribute to making it better, stronger, and more widespread. I truly believe that the world would be a better place if more people would adopt the tenets of martial discipline: respect and reverence for their fellow humans. The true warrior knows the consequences of war, so he does his best to avoid it.

All cultures—no matter how primitive or sophisticated—have some form of combat and have been formed by war and conflict. Nations spend billions upon billions in defense to protect and enforce their interests. Essentially, *fighting solves everything.* Combat is ingrained in our DNA, which also probably accounts for the ever-growing popularity of MMA.

Why are some fighters better than others? It all boils down to preparation. Fail to prepare? Prepare to fail! Proper preparation is imperative for a combat athlete—being conditioned and skilled are essential. Strict adherence to a training regimen, diet, and adopting the proper mindset are the keys to being a successful fighter.

Fighters, wrestlers, boxers and other martial artists must be able to use explosive strength over a sustained period of time. A bout or encounter may last ten seconds, ten minutes or ten rounds. Your body will need to process lactic acid, deal with the adrenalin dump and maintain muscular endurance without sacrificing the explosive power necessary to execute a throw, deliver a knockout punch or apply a finishing hold for the duration of the contest.

Attaining *and* maintaining strength while staying within a particular weight class or while losing weight is particularly challenging. Fighters are faced with the task of maximizing their strength while increasing flexibility, athletic prowess, reflexive power, cardiovascular conditioning as well as developing essential core stabilizers.

The practice of "cutting weight" has both short and long term adverse effects. Too many fighters and wrestlers diet poorly in the off-season, and then struggle to make weight or even miss it. When I was the promoter and match maker for the UCC, a professional MMA League, I would come down hard on the fighters that missed weight. Not only was it a pet peeve of mine, missing weight carries risks of organ damage, susceptibility to concussions, tissue damage and poor performance, particularly in the later rounds.

As with actual combat, focus, concentration and intensity are required for a Ferocious Fitness workout. We are not just conditioning the body, but are also forging a mindset for success in the combat arena.

Many of my students are martial artists, wrestlers and fighters. Many of my students have competed successfully in such venues as the UFC, Bellator, NCAA and high school wrestling, Brazilian jiu jitsu, kickboxing, taekwondo, karate as well as in amateur MMA shows. Their strength, conditioning and flexibility have increased dramatically with our training system and it enables them cope with—and reduce the incidence of—injuries while participating in some of the toughest sports on the planet.

There are many other clients who also benefit from the methods employed with training the fighters. Not only do they benefit physically, but they like knowing they are doing the same workout as a professional fighter. They become empowered!

ROOTS

I was born in Paterson, New Jersey on October 22nd, 1962. We lived in the neighboring town of Fair Lawn. My parents and I lived with my grandparents until I was 7 when we moved to Ridgewood, New Jersey. I have always been physical and I have always had an innate urge to improve my physique and my athletic performance. I have had this intense motivation since I was six years old. It stems from my small stature. Compared to other kids my age I was short, skinny and unimposing.

I was hyperactive and always competing with myself to better myself; I found great satisfaction in trying to better my previous best efforts in push-ups, chin-ups, pull-ups, sit-ups, sprinting, climbing, leaping, jumping...I was the poster child for hyperactive males. I ran everywhere or biked and was a continual ball of frenetic energy. Luckily I was born in 1962 because if I'd have been born nowadays I am quite sure the authorities would be dosing me and medicating me and

Phil at age 20: bodybuilding got Phil lean; he dropped bodybuilding, kept the leanness

subjecting me to every politically-correct "behavior modification" tactic available in order to break me of that manic, boy-energy and smooth the rough edges off of me.

Even at the tender age of 6, I felt compelled to do something about my size and stature. Luckily I had someone that told me exactly what I needed to do if I wanted to morph from tiny to towering and from frail into herculean. Imagine this: when I was 7 years old I developed a list of twenty exercises that I did every morning religiously; I believed that doing these exercise and getting really good at them would enable me to morph into a muscular giant. I derived terrific satisfaction from doing these exercises and I always had a "current best or improve upon my current record. Plus I was being goaded, guided and led on by my first mentor: at age seven I had a fight coach.

Cosmo Ferro with teeny little Phil.

My grandfather was a character. He was an old school, hardcore New Jersey Italian named Cosmo Ferro. My granddad was a boxing coach; a trainer at Paul Cavalier's famed boxing gym in Paterson. Starting at age 8, my grandfather, with my excited collaboration, worked me like a fighter: I learned to box from professionals, I learned about hard effective training from professionals, and I learned at an astoundingly young age. Boxing, punching, using my hands to strike, I have been doing it for so long that it is part of my DNA. My grandfather impressed upon me the fact that I had to "be in condition".

Cosmo goaded me and taunted me and lured me and challenged me and made me better. He taught me how to hit a heavy bag hard and right; he taught me how to build up my abdominals around my solar plexus; he'd have me hanging backwards off of a folding chair to do his torturous version of ab crunches; he taught me how to skip rope and impressed upon me why rope skipping is important, not just for cardio but for agility, speed, precision of movement and grace. I leaned that skipping rope, in the hands of a master, is a beautiful thing to look at–rhythmically mesmerizing, skillful and beneficial.

Much of Cosmo's Old School approach lives on through me today; a hell of a lot of those ancient lessons he taught me still ring true and I still use them and teach them. The men of that era did not baby themselves; they felt fighting, real fighting, was a brutal thing and ergo, the training needed to be brutal so as to prepare the fighter for the brutal realities of a real fight. Not that they purposefully hurt each other, however their PT (physical training) always took it right to the limit of pain and injury and their sparring was real as real could be. I try to keep that ancient flavor in my modern strategies.

I learned the psychology of coaching from that old man and use it to this day on my clients and students. Call it "elementary child psychology" or whatever, but I learned that doable challenges are important. The fact that someone is paying real close attention to your efforts is also real important. Cosmo's approach was, is, and remains a spectacular way to coax clients into exceeding personal bests. As all good coaches know, the true gains lie in getting students to exceed their current capacities.

At home, all the males—grandpa, dad, and uncles—were genuine elite alpha-male athletes. As a child I idolized tough guys and fighters. My father was an All Metropolitan football player and former Marine. He wasn't tall, but he was stout, thick, big and very powerful. I was tiny. I hated that. I intuitively sensed that intense physical exercise would enable me to transform from insignificant into a gargantuan super hero.

> AS ALL GOOD COACHES KNOW, THE TRUE GAINS LIE IN GETTING STUDENTS TO EXCEED THEIR CURRENT CAPACITIES.

No one ever needed to push me in sports, training or any physical task or challenge. I was *driven*–I wanted to be bigger, stronger and I wanted to be invincible. I HATED being small and skinny. I was actually picked on in junior high school. At age 12 I weighed 77 pounds and got bullied a lot by a kid who weighed 170 pounds. I actually wound up beating him up in the lunchroom; wailing the hell out of him in front of 150 students eating lunch when he pushed me too far. It must have appeared to have been a scene out of the horror movie *Leprechaun in the 'Hood*. I punched him in the groin, thus doubling him over and all 77-pounds of me jumped all over him like a crazed screeching monkey. I proceeded to land about 50 blows on his big head with my tiny little fists before I was pulled off. He was in shock. Needless to say, he never bothered me again.

I went on to have four more major fights in 8th grade, despite weighing no more than 98 pounds at my heaviest. I won all of them; I was a savage dwarf. I became a pretty good wrestler in my freshman year of high school and by now I was up to 108 pounds. When I got involved in high school wrestling I was a holy terror. That's when people started giving me respect; after all, the crazed dwarf had ripped apart five full-sized bad asses, all while weighing less than 100 pounds. I was killing it on the mats. Now I was starting to grow.

It was good to beat people up legally and have them call it "wrestling." I had despised feeling inferior and weak; beating up five bullies made me feel good about myself. I changed my inferiority complex through fighting. Beating the piss out of schoolyard bullies turned my frown upside down.

My Father was a former Marine and All Metro Football Player. When he saw I was serious about strength and sports, he gave me his old weight set. He also passed along his Joe Weider "Triple Threat" weight training manual. I hung my heavy bag and put my weights in the basement. I would train with my friends, but it seemed that I was rotating through friends, and that I was the only one who really stuck to the program throughout high school.

I played football, wrestled and ran track during my freshman year, and football and wrestling in my sophomore year. In my junior year I broke three bones in my back during our first football scrimmage. I was out for a full year—I missed a whole year of sports.

I really got into lifting during this "no sports" period. I lifted, ate, rested, and all of a sudden I picked up twenty pounds of pure, solid muscle. In my high school sophomore year, I wrestled weighing 129 pounds. We lived in a very sports competitive area, so I faced some tough competition. I was always either stronger or a good deal fitter and a lot more aggressive than any wrestling opponents my size. Whatever edge I had, I used it. But I did take my lumps as a younger guy challenging myself to face the older, tougher guys in the off-season tournaments.

After I recovered from injury, I decided to train for the Freestyle Wrestling State Qualifiers. I went from the 129-pound class to wrestling at 154, but with new found muscle. I made the cut and secured a berth at the Freestyle and Greco-Roman National Qualifier. Prior to my senior year of high school, I wound up taking 2nd place in the Eastern Region National AAU Wrestling Tournament: I weighed 154 pounds. I learned what an advantage brute power was in combat. Yes, we need skills, and yes we need to work the hell out of our techniques, regardless the martial discipline—however, regardless the discipline, school, technique or tactic, explosive power is a decided advantage for a fighter.

Now I had wrestling: it was organized mayhem and I was good at wrestling right away— and why not? I was strong as hell for my size and my cardio conditioning was off the charts; I had a nasty attitude and was extremely combative and competitive. I was a natural! I graduated from Ridgewood High School, and was the captain of our wrestling team.

My father was very supportive but realistic; I was, by the way, an honor roll student from a good high school. My parents did not really fully support my fighting career until my dad saw me beat six guys in a row at the Empire State Game Karate Competition in 1981. Things changed after I came home with a big trophy. However, my folks still were never

100% behind my full-contact karate, kickboxing and boxing aspirations, even though I won a great deal of tournaments and scheduled bouts.

By the time I graduated from high school, I had my full height and weighed a rock-hard, ultra-lean 170 pounds. You can imagine the psychological changes a boy goes through when he adds 50% to his body weight in just three years. When a kid goes from108 pounds to 170 pounds—in just 36 months it changes his perspective. Now while I might have been 98 pounds, I was *never* a 98-pound-*weakling*. I overcame my adolescent smallness by always being super-fit and super strong for my age and size. Always. Any age, at any size, I was always fit and I was always strong. I also ate food as if I were continually starving to death.

> ## WHEN SKILLS ARE EQUAL BETWEEN FIGHTERS, THE STRONGER, FITTER FIGHTER WILL PREVAIL.

When skills are equal between fighters, the stronger, fitter fighter will prevail. I learned that early by having that decided advantage over my equally-skilled high school wrestling opponents. It was an "ah ha!" moment for me way back then. It is a message that still resonates with me to this day: increasing power and conditioning should be a continual part of the ongoing quest to be the best possible fighter I can be.

MY "FUTURE FRAME OF REFERENCE" WAS FORMED IN 1978.

Real fighting is very brutal. That sounds trite and ridiculous, but you would be stunned at how many wannabe fighters are shocked to their core and quit after getting smashed in the face with a fist, suplexed onto their head, punched in the throat, choked out or knocked freaking unconscious.

There was a very smart line in one of Clint Eastwood's *Filo Betto* fighter movies where his opponent says, "You are dangerous because you like the pain." In a weird way that is right on the money, though I would modify it slightly and say, "Real fighters take pride in how much pain they can absorb". I always have prided myself on my ability to take a beating.

In the movie, *Raging Bull*, Martin Scorsese presented a great portrayal of the superb Ray Robinson. "Sugar Ray" was the prototypical athlete-fighter that represents an opponent who is stronger, faster, more agile and has better reflexes than you. In the movie (and factually), Jake LaMotta, being beaten stupid, yet somehow was still standing, taunts Ray, his destroyer, "Can't knock me down Ray! *Can't knock me down!*" This to me encapsulates the Samurai/Bushido code I strive to emulate.

I have always had tremendous pride in my LaMotta streak, "I can take *anything* you can dish out and bounce back up and get right back in your freaking face! When I was a kid the Timex watch company had a corporate phrase, "Takes a licking and keeps on ticking." Amen to that.

My ability to take it has always endeared me to my mentors at every stage and at every age. In any and every martial discipline I have practiced, my pain tolerance and ability to always bounce back from some devastating blow or gruesome lock has always been one of my strengths as a fighter.

Is this "ability" a gift? Can it be attained? That depends on the individual.

I first became aware I possessed the gift of being able to "take it," when I was 16 years old and was thrown into the midst of some of the greatest wrestlers on the face of the planet. Seriously, these guys went to the Olympics, were World Class competitors and won national championships; these were grown men who did not give a good goddamn about me or my situation, this was not "mentoring" troubled teens or helping out as a big brother at the YMCA. I was a training partner to be used and abused as they sought fit.

In 1978, I heard about a gym in my area that had a bunch of high-level wrestlers as members. The gym was a commercial facility open to the public, but they also had wrestling mats and a bunch of topflight wrestlers trained there. I considered myself a wrestler, in the truest sense, and the idea of "rolling" with champions fired me up.

So as a high school junior, I headed to Dave Pruzansky's Nautilus Gym. Dave was a Pan Am champion, a deadly wrestler who also was the national champion in judo. His partner in the gym was Steve Strellner, one of the best wrestlers Iowa ever produced. Steve was the longtime head wrestling coach at Montclair State and was a collegiate champion and Olympic team alternate. Those were the owners; the members were twice as credentialed.

Kenny Mallory was there too, and wrestled for Coach Strellner, who everyone called "Strapper." Ken was so good he had a signature wrestling move; it was named after him, "The Mallory." Ken was the first-ever Division III national champion to win the Division I NCAA wrestling title. Before Ken, no Division III wrestler had ever won a Division I title.

In addition to these incredible wrestlers, the most decorated heavyweight freestyle wrestler this country has ever produced, Bruce Baumgartner, trained at Dave's gym. Bruce would win three world titles, seventeen national titles, three Pan-Am titles, eight World Cup wins and was the only American wrestler to ever win four Olympic Medals.

And then there were the Cataffo brothers...

Chris and Tim Cataffo were two of the baddest mofos I have ever crossed paths with, before or since. And trust me when I say I have seen more than my fair share of genuine badass fighters. These guys were savages; first to each other, then to the rest of the world. Chris was the youngest. He went to the Olympic Games as a Greco-Roman wrestler and was a Pan American Champion.

Tim Cataffo was big and very brutal. He was truly one of the best fighters I have ever encountered: he had the technique, he had the cardio, he had the pain tolerance and he was able to amp himself up like a beast during a fight. Both men gave the word "intensity" new meaning.

Tim possessed an ungodly explosive power that rocked opponents. He tossed topflight wrestlers around like they were 6-year-old children. He was operating at an entirely different strength and power level than the rest of us. He could pick you up and pile-drive you, hip throw you halfway across the room, and then land on top of you with his full bodyweight. Both men were feared and both had a reputation for being brutal. They would typically dis-locate the arms and shoulders of opponents.

Tim later went on to fight in the earliest versions of MMA in the early 1990s. There were very few rules then. The Japanese loved him and gave him his nickname, *Obake*, which means Monster. He was that and then some. I should know, I was on the receiving end of his power moves. Man, did I take my lumps!

I was a 150-pound high school kid yet these guys took a shine to me, especially the Cataffo brothers. I was game and scrappy and I kept coming back and they kept beating me up—but I still showed up three times a week. I trained at this gym from the April of my junior year in high school until I left for college the following fall. When the guys went back to college, my friend Dave O'Hanna—an accomplished high school and Division 3 wrestler and a member of the US Army 82nd Airborne—and I would meet to train at the gym. There'd always be some high-level wrestler around to train with.

The Cataffo Brothers and Dave Prizansky taught me how to throw my opponents, which earned me a second place in the 1979 AAU Eastern National Greco-Roman Wrestling Tournament. I learned a great deal during my time there: toughness, perseverance and how to be nasty.

I never feared *anyone* on the mat, ever. I knew that anyone that I faced wouldn't be as good as these guys.

WHAT I BRING TO THE PARTY...

So do we *really* need another fighter training book? The world is flooded with fighter training styles and strategies, so what do I, Phil Ross, bring to the fighter party that is new, improved or different? Why should the serious fighter take the time to understand and incorporate my protocols into their training template?

I can increase your striking power to a significant degree and I can significantly elevate your cardio conditioning. To put a finer point on both attribute acquisitions, I can provide the fighter a particular type, kind and flavor of strength that is particularly applicable to fighting; I can provide my fighters a particular type, kind and flavor of cardio conditioning most applicable for the peculiarities of fighting.

What I offer the modern martial artist is a new and extremely effective approach towards the age-old problem: how does a fighter increase and improve—to a dramatic degree—their current level of power, strength and conditioning? How does a fighter increase and improve—to a dramatic degree—their level of cardio conditioning?

Note that I make a point to say I can offer you dramatic improvement: any new training program taken up by a serious fighter/athlete will likely yield some short-term instantaneous results due to the newness of the protocols. These gains are quick and insignificant.

My protocols are unlike anything the athlete has ever been subjected to and the results obtained are both dramatic and sustained. Why? My protocols are progressive; as soon as the athlete adeptly performs one of my drills, there are other drills of greater complexity and severity. We never run out of room to run because there is always another progress-boosting protocol to rotate in.

After 30 years of fighting and training fighters, I have built up an arsenal of effective protocols and workouts, from mild to wild, from tame to insane. This has been my life's work; fighting is my art. I have been immersed in fighting since and fight training since age 7, I am now 53 years old; you do the math.

My protocols are all designed to create a type of strength and conditioning applicable for fighters. We seek to create a certain type of strength. We seek a certain type of cardio conditioning. There are different degrees and shades of strength and conditioning, and I intend to share with you which specific type of strength you should seek, what type of cardio conditioning you need to attain—and I will show you *exactly* how to acquire exactly what you seek.

We fighters need explosive power that translates into knockout blows; we need hercu- lean power that enables us to manhandle opponents. Real power shocks and rocks, real power is the most frightening attribute a skilled opponent can possess. Fighter strength is expressed by blows that render people unconscious, and fighter strength is expressed when the strong man exerts his will and turns a routine clinch or a simple lock into a sub- mission.

Fighter power is the coordinated ballet wherein muscles groups work in harmonious synchronization to deliver a ferocious punch, a bone-breaking kick or to perform a devas- tating throw or apply a simple joint lock. Power is about imposing your will on the oppo- nent: truly powerful people are also adept at absorbing blows and avoiding injury. Strength training makes you bulletproof.

We fighters need a particular and specific style of cardio conditioning: the modern fighter must be adept at exerting a high level of energy output for protracted periods of time. MMA fighters must possess the type of stamina that allows them to continue to make extreme muscular contractions while deep in an aerobic zone.

It is not enough for the fighter to be able to perform steady-state cardio, that flavor of aerobic conditioning is better suited for a marathon than an MMA fight where the ath- lete must push, shove, punch, kick, throw, clinch, grapple and dodge—all of which require *intense* and *instantaneous* muscular contractions. Muscular contractions require oxygen and lots of contractions require lots of oxygen.

The ability to put out a high volume of high intensity muscular contractions late in a fight is the hallmark of a truly great fighter. My training is designed to provide "fighter strength" and "fighter cardio".

I use three tools: a kettlebell, a jump rope and bodyweight. I have thirteen core exercises. When you take into account the variations possible within each of our core thirteen exer- cises (seven, kettlebell: six, bodyweight) and further examine the possible exercise combi- nations (adding the variable of sets, reps, pacing, duration and rep speed), you will see that we can create unlimited variety and variation possibilities.

Dealing with Catastrophic Injury:
One Tale Worth Retelling

Real fighters get injured. It comes with the territory. Fighting isn't tennis or bowling; we punch and kick one another in training and in competition; we accidently butt heads, twist joints, land wrong and hurt ourselves and our sparring partners. Hell, the goal of fighting is to inflict injury on the opponent and anyone who says differently is not a real fighter. When we compete, regardless the fighting format, the idea, the goal, is to decimate the opponent.

In wrestling, jujitsu, sambo and the grappling arts, the goal is to submit the opponent; in Muay Thai, boxing and karate, the goal is to knock the opponent unconscious. Hurting your opponent breaks their spirit and changes their mindset. Inflicting pain makes it easier to defeat your opponent and impose your will. Is it any wonder that injury and dealing with injuries is an integral part of the fight game?

In 2010, right before my 48th birthday, I got a wild-haired idea and decided to enter the NAGA Battle at the Beach Brazilian Jiu Jitsu and Submission Fighting Competition. I entered two divisions at Light Heavyweight (179.9-199), Expert No-Gi, 40-49-years-old and since I have only trained Gi BJJ for 3 months prior, I went white belt level, but fought in the 18-29-year-old division.

There were 49 competitors and since I was the oldest and the lightest (184 lbs), I was awarded a bye in the first round. I had five fights during the day-long tournament and went undefeated. I didn't give up one point in any match. I had a great day; from a fighting perspective it could not have gone better. The competition was of a really high caliber, and at age 48—literally twice the average age of the competition—I not only won, I dominated. I got a lot of attention for this dominating performance and consider it one of the highlights of a long fight career. Little did I know that it'd be my last...

A good friend of mine, Ryan Ciotoli, was the head trainer and manager for a MMA fight school called The Bomb Squad. Based in Ithaca, NY, this club was rightly considered one of the best MMA fighter prep outfits in the country. Ryan coached and trained many fighters that competed and won in the WEC, Bellator, Ring of Combat and the UFC. The best MMA fighter of the last decade (with the possible exception of Anderson Silva) Jon "Bones" Jones was "discovered" and mentored by Ryan before he went to Greg Jackson's Camp. Anyway, after my dominant performance at the Battle of the Beach, which Ryan witnessed, he suggested something I hadn't really considered: he wanted me to become an MMA fighter for The Bomb Squad.

Wow. What a huge compliment from a guy who knew MMA inside and out and would NOT waste his time, effort or energy on any fighter that he did not feel capable of entering the biggest, richest, most competitive fight venue in the world (excepting a very few pro boxers). I was intrigued. Ryan explained that he felt my balance—I was a grappler and a striker—my conditioning, and my power would make me a formidable MMA fighter. I was stoked! Hey, coaching the fighters is fun and I am really good at it, but training to fight in the cage at my age fired me up like I hadn't been fired up in decades! This was purely incredible.

We had quite a few tough cage fighting pros at my gym at that time. These guys were in the UFC and Bellator (think of Bellator as college football, and UFC as pro football). I stepped up my training dramatically and increased the frequency and intensity of my MMA. I trained with a vigor and intensity that I didn't know I had. I was determined to put myself in the best shape and condition of my entire life. I trained like a demon and everything was on track: I was determined to blow some MMA minds.

During one of our heavy Thursday night sparring sessions in October of 2011, I took a hard hook shot to my head. I heard a crack, saw a flash of light and experienced an incredible burning sensation from my neck down into my right hand. I'd been hit harder in my life (though, truth be told, this was the worst blow I'd taken in years) and I did not think much of it. I went home.

The next morning, I did my usual warm-ups and went to hit the heavy bag, my first serious drill of the day. When my fist impacted the bag I experienced what might be compared to an electrical shock. I hit the bag once and dropped to one knee in pain: I had no control of my right hand. I couldn't clench it to make a fist and I saw my MMA dreams fly away. I knew injury and I knew how to differentiate between a nagging injury, a serious injury and a catastrophic injury.

This injury was potentially a career-ender. I steeled my mind for the worst eventuality and went to see a doctor.

My doctor ordered an MRI. I had what he called "severe stenosis," the single blow to my skull, added to years of abuse, had herniated two discs completely and created five bulging discs. The bad news got worse when it was determined I also had an "osteophyte on the inside of my spinal vertebra that was causing edema to form on my spinal cord." In other words, the impact from the blow caused a calcium deposit to smash into my spinal cord. I had a permanent spinal scar and irreparable damage. My body had lost the "signal" to my thenar muscle—permanently.

It was determined that I would need surgery and the outcome was a 50/50 chance of ever returning to "normal."

During the time between my injury and my eventual operation, I continued to train "around the injury". That is, while I could not engage in any training that aggravated the damaged body parts, I could work the rest of my body. I trained the body parts that I could like a maniac. I was so screwed up that I could not press a 22-pound kettlebell with my right arm. My hand was so pathetically weak. I still worked hard, primarily with calisthenics. I had no hand strength and things got positively scary when my hand began to whither away.

I met with my doctors and we scheduled my operation for December 22nd, 2011. I trained what I could train even harder. My mind was racing and my emotions were high. I never let on to anyone that for one of the few times in my life, I was scared. I was losing everything I had worked my whole life to attain. I felt my livelihood could be at risk: so much of what I do depends on me demonstrating what is expected and if I suddenly could not perform the drills I expected others to perform, I didn't see how I would be able to teach.

> I NEVER LET ON TO ANYONE THAT FOR ONE OF THE FEW TIMES IN MY LIFE, I WAS SCARED. I WAS LOSING EVERYTHING I HAD WORKED MY WHOLE LIFE TO ATTAIN. I FELT MY LIVELIHOOD COULD BE AT RISK.

I underwent a four-hour surgery. The surgeons worked on my injured vertebra but decided against spinal fusion or any "trimming" of my discs. In technical terms I had to undergo a "frenectomy" and "laminectomy" on four of my vertebra: C6, C7, C8 and T1. They had to alleviate the pressure on my nerves by removing the lamina and cutting windows in my vertebra.

When I awoke, it felt as if I had 100% of the power back in my right hand. I was ecstatic! In fact, I had less than 50% of my pre-injury arm strength—but 50% was 100% improvement over 0%!

Now the real work began.

I was laid up at home for a little over a week and went back to work on January 2nd of 2012. One of my surgeons, Dr. Arnold Crisitiello, was a member of my gym. He saw me training in the immediate aftermath of the surgery and expressed his concerns: if I came back too fast too hard I could really screw things up. He asked me if I was still taking the prescribed painkillers. I told him that I stopped taking them two days after the operation. He told me that regular people take six weeks off from work after undergoing the type of injury I had incurred (which usually happens in auto accidents involving head trauma). He repeatedly cautioned me to "be patient." But I didn't listen.

I started rehabbing myself with push-ups and planks at twenty days post-surgery. I tried to do a pull-up. I heard a snap and felt a sharp pain in my neck. I had ripped one of the sutures and "disconnected" muscles from insertion points. I now have a little hole in the back of my neck and will have it forever. Chastened and more than a little relieved that I had dodged a bullet, I now I took Doc Arnold's advice to heart and became patient with the process. I waited six weeks until the doctors determined I fully healed before I resumed my rehab training.

Six weeks after my surgery and after getting the medical sign-off, I began training again. I began with planks and push-ups and I was past pathetic. Five rep sets of push-ups were kicking my ass. I like challenges but I didn't like this one. I was 49-years old and I felt 49. This was a first because up until this catastrophic injury, I have always looked, felt and acted 20 years younger than my actual age. I was old, felt old and hated it: I was determined to regain what I had lost but had to make haste slowly. I had dodged one bullet trying to come back too soon and I sure as hell did not want a repeat performance.

I began doing a great deal of grip work for the withered hand. I did plank pull-ups and got my push-ups back up from 5 to 20 full reps per set. Once I was able to perform 20 reps of hip level plank pull-ups, I progressed to full, (no thumb) tactical pull-ups. I was able to do one rep. By April of 2012 I felt I had recovered to a significant degree. I was set to begin work on a project I had contemplated for a decade: I wanted to create a filmed "encyclo-pedia" of kettlebell exercises; I called the project "The Kettlebell Workout Library" and started filming in May of 2012. Naturally I wanted to be in tiptop shape, yet knew I could not go buck-wild. I was NOT going to reinjure myself.

By the end of April, I was able to do sets of 12 pull-ups and virtually all of my kettlebell exercises. I started to add weight to all the exercises and worked on getting my strength back. I was able to do a set of five bottoms-up kettlebell presses using a 44-pound kettlebell. This was with the formerly withered hand.

SEVEN MONTHS AFTER THE OPERATION, I WAS ABLE TO COMPLETE THE GRUEL-
ING "SECRET SERVICE SNATCH TEST". THIS REQUIRED SNATCHING A 53-POUND
KETTLEBELL FOR 200 REPETITIONS IN 10 MINUTES OR LESS.

Seven months after the operation, I was able to complete the grueling "Secret Service Snatch Test". This required snatching a 53-pound kettlebell for 200 repetitions in 10 minutes or less. I finished my 200 snatches (without pain) in 8:48. This was a real turning point and made me feel like I was finally successfully mounting a comeback.

While this was being written, I regained approximately 80-85% of the strength in my right hand. I think that I may be topped out, but I'm still working on it. On good days I can hang in an L-sit position holding onto the chin bar with only my damaged right hand. I've hit 20 reps in the tactical pull-up on more than one occasion.

The doctor who handled the neural section of my operation is named Dr. Pat Roth; he is the author of the best-selling book, *The End of Back Pain.* He told me that most likely I would need a neck operation at some point in my life due to a genetic condition called "congenital stenosis." Like many other people, I have a narrow spinal canal, more narrow than normal. It's something that you're born with.

The blow to the head simply accelerated everything. I had noticed for years prior to my surgery that my right arm was getting weaker. I also experienced shoulder and neck pain that I attributed to the normal aches and pain associated with hard training. I can't tell you how many times when sparring or grappling that I'd get a "burner," a shot of pain that ran down my arm. I would see a flash of light, pain, and numbness but shrugged it off. It all made sense now.

While part of me feels cheated out of my late-in-life MMA dream, another part of me is thankful that I was able to recover from a catastrophic, potentially career-ending and livelihood-ending injury. Still, I really think that if I had not gotten injured, I would have been able to enter the cage and would have shocked some folks. On the other hand, I peered into the abyss of total body destruction and was able to stay in the game.

I thank my lucky stars that I was able—barely—to dodge permanent debilitating injury. Had things gone slightly differently, I would be a cripple walking around with a worthless hand attached to a withered arm or have been paralyzed.

GREATNESS
⚡ THE ⚡
COMPONENTS

OF A
SUCCESSFUL
★ FIGHTER ★

Becoming a Great Fighter is one of the coolest things on the planet! Let's consider what ingredients it takes to become successful. Some people are born with these attributes, yet others develop them over time through their training and determination.

DRIVE AND DESIRE

To become a Great Fighter, you must have the drive and desire for greatness. This is the willingness to put our body, soul and comfort to the side and accept the pain and sacrifice that is required to prepare your self for—and to engage in—combat.

DISCIPLINE

Discipline is the most important component for success in any field and one of the major reasons that West Point puts out more millionaires than any other college. This attribute goes hand in hand with Drive and Desire. Discipline is often the differentiator between two otherwise equally matched opponents. Do you stick to your training, eating and sleeping schedule? Do you perform tasks that you absolutely hate, but know are good for you? Discipline will enable you to stick to your fight plan while under fire. Discipline forges an Iron Will.

TOUGHNESS

You have to be tough. You may have the desire, but can you take the punishment? The body and spirit get tested, often. Do you have what it takes to come back from a potentially career ending injury? Can you withstand the abuse? Will you be able to handle the lack of support from your friends and family? The loneliness associated with your training regiment? Getting kicked and punched in the head, resisting a submission attempt, coming back from being down in a fight to score a knockout or submission? This all takes toughness. You have to be tough to be a successful fighter.

NASTINESS

Nasty. Yes, NASTY! You have to want to hurt people and impose your will. When you see someone on the ropes, you need to posses the bloodlust to finish them off without any hesitation whatsoever. When you hit, you hit hard. When you apply a lock, it's with your whole body. Wanting to see your foe lying defeated on the ground in front of you is important. Not stopping until you've achieved is more important.

ATHLETICISM

Being a great athlete does not make you a great fighter, but athleticism helps. I've seen some incredible athletes get destroyed in a fight by a guy who looks like he just raided a doughnut shop! Possessing athleticism makes you more in tune with and in control of your body. This facet helps immensely with movement and application of technique. Natural athletes flow better from one move to the next and tend to absorb concepts more readily.

HATRED OF LOSING

Everyone likes to win, but you NEED to hate to lose. You must hate losing so very much, that you will do anything not to be defeated. This comes from your training. Pick something that you hate to do. Take roadwork for example. If you hate to run, make sure that you do it on a regular basis. If you detest stretching, do it every day. Whatever it is that you dislike doing most, make it part of your training routine. This will evoke the strong emotion of disdain when you are confronted with adversity during a contest. Do not allow yourself to lose to someone that you trained so hard and sacrificed so much to beat in your preparation.

CHANNELING OF FEAR

I don't care who you are, there is a point, albeit a short period of time, that you question yourself. No matter how many fights I had, there was always some point that I would question what I was doing and why I felt the need to hit, throw or choke someone. This would usually happen right before I entered the ring or mat. I wouldn't have it while training or even while warming up, but it would hit me right before I was about to go. Then the feeling would completely disappear at the time of contact. I had similar feelings playing football. The "butterflies" (the pre-game sensation in your stomach) would go away when my pads crashed into the opposing team member's pads while flying down the field on the kick-off.

I have seen guys get so worked up and so nervous that the fight doctor has had to call the fight due to dangerously high blood pressure. There have been many instances when guys have simply left the building before their fight. They "lost their nerve." I had one student who had incredible athletic ability as well as technique. This all went good, as long as he was winning. He lost at a Jiu Jitsu tourney and at the next competition he feigned a stomach illness right before his division and pulled out. Obviously, he's not cut out for competition. He's no longer a member of my school either.

The Successful Fighter knows how to bend the fear to his advantage. Channel the adrenalin dump and harness the fear as he directs the energy toward his opponent.

STRENGTH, POWER AND CONDITIONING

This is where we come in and something that you, the fighter, coach, instructor, athlete or martial artist are in full control of, your strength, power and conditioning.

Some people are born with better genetics and are naturally stronger than others, at the onset. However, how many times have the more gifted athletes fallen by the wayside as others with drive, discipline, desire and a succinct training protocol surpass the more gifted? I've seen this far too many times in my life to discount a superior training regiment. The best thing about this is that your training is 100% in your control!

WHY ALL FIGHTERS ★ NEED TO TRAIN ★

FOR

STRENGTH & POWER

Have you ever wondered why we have weight classes in fighting? Seriously, let us take a minute and explore this: the short answer to the rhetorical question is, "We have weight classes in fighting because a big skilled fighter will crush a small skilled fighter". When we examine what we mean by "big" really what we mean is "strong" and "powerful" not "big".

The power and strength that a big man has makes fighting a smaller fighter unfair. Why would it be a mismatch to have BJ Penn battle his good friend Mark Coleman? The Hammer would be the first one to say, BJ is simply a better fighter: he is faster, and has better submissions than Coleman. BJ is in better condition and trumps Coleman in every definable fight category except one: raw human strength.

At 6'2" and a shredded 245 pounds, Coleman would simply manhandle the 145 pound Penn like a stern father scooping up a 6-year-old throwing a tantrum. Now, if Penn were facing a "normal" 245-pound male "civilian", he would easily whip the untrained person, despite his 100 pound size difference. Pure power makes Coleman versus Penn man-slaughter.

For that matter, why separate men and women by gender? Why is it so ridiculous to have 135 pound Ronda Rousey fight 135 pound TJ Dillashaw? Ronda may have better fighter credentials than TJ, but he would be too much for her to handle. Why would Tyson versus Sugar Ray Leonard be a massacre?

Two words: power and strength! But what *kind* or strength? A fighter needs strength, but strength combined with speed; a fighter needs strength that is combined with velocity to produce power. The slow strength of a giant clumsy person is of no use to a fighter. We seek "shock power" for our punches and kicks. Our shock-power is apparent when we grab an opponent or in the ease of which we muscle an opponent around. With shock power, we effortlessly dominate in clinches and when grappling.

The question then becomes: can a fighter increase his raw quotient of power? Can a fighter find a protocol that infuses him or her with a dramatic increase in usable athletic muscle, strength and power?

- *This book is a handbook for using kettlebells and bodyweight exercises to dramatically increase any fighter's current levels of power, strength and overall conditioning. I offer specific techniques and specific training protocols designed to lift the fighter's shock-power to the next level.*

- *This book is a handbook for using kettlebells and bodyweight exercises to dramatically increase a fighter's current degree of conditioning. By purposefully injecting intense physical effort into our cardio training, we "build a bigger gas tank," we increase the type and kind of cardio most needed for fighting.*

Martial artists need the ability to employ explosive strength over a sustained period of time. A flurry, scramble, clinch or submission attempt might last ten seconds or four minutes. We teach the body how best to process lactic acid, how best to deal with the adrenalin dump, how best to maintain and prolong muscular endurance without burning out, without gassing out, without sacrificing the explosive power necessary to execute that crushing throw, deliver the knockout punch or apply a bone-busting finishing hold. We build power and we build endurance—those are two awesome attributes for a fighter to possess.

I can show you how to improve your raw power and I can show you how to improve your cardio: I can give you the kind of power needed to overpower an opponent and I can give you that particular flavor of cardio peculiar to fighting.

Fighting isn't a weightlifting contest and fighting isn't running a marathon: the weightlifter's slow strength is fine for picking stuff up, but for fighting our strength needs to be expressed fast, quick, snappy and with shock-power in the hands and legs. The marathon runner's cardio is fantastic for gliding 26.2 miles. But that type of cardio does the fighter no good when Brock Lesnar is attempting to kill you with a neck-crank. We fighters need a specific brand of power and we need a specific type of cardio.

I am not a personal trainer or a fitness expert inventing a training program to capture a new sales market. I am a fighter. Period. Always have been, always will be. I am an elder tribe member at this stage of my career, having fought competitively for over thirty years. Now my focus has shifted toward making others become better, faster and stronger.

I look at any and all training through the eyes of a fighter. Will this tactic, will this exercise, will this set and rep scheme, will this frequency improve me as a fighter? Yes or no.

I have been doing this for the entire time I have trained. I trained with a purpose: to be a better, stronger, more successful fighter. I adapted movements to be more purposeful for fighting. I give new ideas a serious tryout using myself as the laboratory. I test them dispassionately. After a reasonable period of time, I come to a conclusion about the tactic or technique: did it work? If it did, I add it to the lineup. I will also pass it along to students.

All the techniques and tactics we discuss and recommend, all the training plans and routines, have been tested and passed the test: all are battle-proven.

Prolonged practice in the combat arts not only builds character, but reveals character. Martial training better prepares a person for when adversity strikes. Martial arts immersion forces the athlete to confront their weak points, and face their short-comings in order to improve.

It is my desire to share my accumulated knowledge with the larger martial arts community so that others may benefit from the hard and often profound lessons I have learned. I want to contribute in some small way. I truly believe that the world would be a better place if people everywhere would adopt the tenets we teach and demand of our students: discipline, work ethic, truthfulness, respect for others, and reverence for the martial traditions passed to us, that we in turn pass along to you.

TOOLS AND MODES...

Hardstyle kettlebell training lends itself to sport and combat fighting. We need explosive, kinetic energy powering our strikes and blows. The optimal blow is the perfect combination of mass, acceleration and force: when a massive object is propelled with tremendous velocity, it impacts explosively and causes maximum damage.

At the other extreme is an "arm punch." An arm punch is unconnected to the torso: the arm extends and because there is no packed shoulder, no engaged lat, no leg and no explosiveness, the impact is insignificant. A 240-pound man with a 500-pound bench press that arm punches, causes far less damage than getting hit by a 140-pound lightweight boxer who hits with tremendous kinetic energy and explosive power.

The arm puncher simply extends their arm. My fighter training protocols for kettlebells and using bodyweight teach shoulder-packing and lat-engagement; these are strategies designed to develop and improve applicable power. Conscientious kettlebell and bodyweight training will make you faster, far more powerful, and able to transmit pure power from the soles of your feet to the fist or foot, shin or elbow that you deliver the blow with.

The COG or center of gravity of the kettlebell changes throughout the movements, and that is a good thing. When in the white-hot heat of battle against an opponent, the body must compensate for shifts in weight during movement. We need the ability to apply our power from a variety of angles and awkward positions. Explosiveness is a learned skill and using the kettlebell or your bodyweight in the fashion I recommend will result in a tremendous increase in your raw power and stamina.

CIRCUITS, GROUPINGS AND STRATEGIES

Once you have a working knowledge of the exercises which I champion, and once you are aware of the techniques required, then it is time to train. Generally speaking, we do sets and repetitions, that is, once we select a movement, we will have a predetermined rep target and a predetermined number of sets.

In kettlebell training, we employ several different types of circuits. A circuit groups various exercises together to elicit a specific effect. The dynamics of groupings and multiple sets and sequences will yield different results. In other words, do a movement solely, completely, properly and with the correct amount of intensity and reap a certain result: perform the identical movement in the identical way as part of a group of movements and elicit a different physiological response.

A word on technique: we worship at the altar of correct technique, be that the technique of slinging a kettlebell or grinding out a high intensity set of push-ups or chins-ups. If and when your technique starts to break down as you perform an exercise, curtail that set! Injuries occur when we continue when fatigue sets in. We'll tell you when to be a hero, but being a hero at the wrong time can cause a career-ending catastrophic injury.

SUPERSET

Superset is a term that I borrowed from bodybuilding. To superset is to alternate—take two movements and perform them in a row without resting. If you were super setting pull-ups with push-ups, the superset strategy is a set of pull-ups followed immediately by a set of push-ups, then rest. If you were doing three supersets the format would be: 1, 2, rest, 1, 2, rest, 1, 2, rest... I like to superset pushes with pulls. Combine a kettlebell press with a row, for example.

POWER COMPLEX OR GIANT-CHAINS

We string together sequences of 3-4 exercises, again without pause between the exercises. The rest periods happen at the end of each chain. One typical complex: narrow-grip push-up, hanging leg raise, kettlebell row and goblet squat. Note that although four movements were selected, none "conflicted".

The push-ups hit triceps and pecs, leg raises attack abs, and the rows zero in on the lats and mid-back, while squats hit the thighs. You could also seek the opposite effect and use four exercises in a row that all hit the same muscle group. The choice is yours, but must be predetermined depending on the result you seek.

CARDIO CHAINS

If we seek to improve our muscular endurance or strength endurance, we can use the chain complex strategy for cardio development by simply performing high reps. A power chain might consist of goblet squats, double kettlebell rows, and double overhead kettlebell press. A chain can be done for power and strength by using heavy poundage that taxes the athlete in ten or fewer reps.

To convert a power chain to a cardio chain, keep the exercises, keep the sequences, but kick the reps upward to 20-100 per set. Increase cardio density by performing lots of cardio chains.

TABATAS

Professor Izumi Tabata developed a protocol for Olympic speed skaters that I use. Blast as hard as possible for 20 seconds. This is followed by 10 seconds rest. Every 30 seconds you complete one "Tabata cycle". The Tabata protocol is to keep this up for 8 cycles of either 12 minutes, three exercises or 20 minutes of five movements. I will use this approach, though I will alter the session length, depending on what is being sought after and worked on. Needless to say, this is a lung-burning, incredibly intense and demanding protocol.

WARRIOR'S CHALLENGE

This is a cardio method used by combat athletes to "build a bigger cardio gas tank". Think of the Warrior's Challenge as a Tabata on steroids. Select 8 to 10 movements, link them together in a cardio giant chain. While Tabata had his athletes go all out for 20 seconds, the Warrior's Challenge demands 30 seconds per burst. The athlete is allowed 15 seconds rest between bursts and we will repeat the 8-10 exercise long chain for three or

SCRAMBLED EGGS

This is another cardio or strength-endurance workout. The idea is simple: you either use high repetitions or you forget about counting reps and simply see how many reps you can do in the allotted time. String together a bunch of exercises, and there is no rest until the total circuit is complete. A typical Scrambled Eggs circuit might be 8 to 10 exercises long, and all are done in succession with no rest until the last rep of the 10th exercise is complete. The net cardio impact of this type of training is profound: those who can embrace this difficult type of training acquire incredible muscular endurance.

Bad to the Bone: Phil dressed up and ready for some self-inflicted body trauma

PHIL'S
PHILOSOPHY
OF FIGHTING

All I need to train myself (or you) as a fighter is a kettlebell, a jump rope, a chin-up bar and somewhere to do the drills and roadwork. I am simple and direct when it comes to my philosophy of fighting: we need to train our fight skills and we need to train the body. A better body makes for a better fighter. A smart fighter breaks down the quest to become a better fighter into two parts: skills and attributes.

- **Skills** differentiate one fighting style from another. Want to become a better Brazilian jujitsu fighter? Learn the fight style, the techniques, the skills specific to BJJ under the auspices of a master. Each fighting style will have a skill-set unique to it. Nowadays, mixed martial artists incorporate a wide range of skills gleaned from different fighting styles. We separate learning the skills that define a fighting art from improving the athletic attributes that give us better bodies.

- **Attributes** are identifiable physical characteristics, physical and psychological abilities and capacities that we identify then train to improve. We seek ways by which to improve our body and our performance. If we are able to become leaner, faster, and stronger, if we are able to have better endurance, to leap higher, to jump further, if we improve our reflexes and develop a higher pain tolerance, then we improve as fighter. If we can identify an attribute, we can devise a training protocol to improve upon it.

This book is about identifying and then improving the attributes needed to make you a better fighter. Regardless if you are a 10th degree master or a white belt beginner, if you are able to significantly improve on certain physical attributes, then that automatically translates into improved fight performance. What fighter, regardless of age, skill or rank, does not become a better fighter if they dramatically increase their endurance and/or their strength?

I have developed an arsenal of exercises and protocols that improve the body and improve the body's capacities, capabilities and performance. You need to work on your martial skills in your own way. My job is to provide you with a system for improving a long list of identifiable physical attributes.

I have devised a streamlined system for training fighters that allows us to improve across the board in a very broad, methodical and e ective fashion. My system improves the human body emphasizing the traits, characteristics and attributes needed to become a better ghter. I use a deceptively simplistic system that uses a bare minimum of tools.

THE EXERCISES

Be critical. When looking to improve or revise your training, you should always ask yourself, "Why am I doing this exercise? To what end? What is the expected result?" Every exercise I recommend has an exacting technique and this technique needs to be closely adhered to if we expect to obtain the desired results.

Bruce Lee's training partner Ted Wong famously limited himself to four punches and four kicks—that was his entire martial repertoire. He explained his approach as "fewer things done better". He spent all his time mastering the important kicks and punches; he was extremely exclusive, and so am I. Seek to become extremely proficient in the few exercises I use and recommend.

I have pared down and reduced my menu of exercises. Like Bruce Lee and Ted Wong, I want to limit the exercises. It's better to master a few than be familiar with dozens. I have selected seven kettlebell exercises and six bodyweight exercises—keep in mind that each of our thirteen exercises will have numerous subtle and overt technical variations.

CONCENTRATE ON THE BASICS

Not all kettlebell exercises are created equal. I use a very limited number of key, critical kettlebell exercises. With these seven kettlebell movements, I am able to achieve any training effect I care to strive for. While there are an almost infinite variety of kettlebell exercises, many are variations of the core seven movements I use.

For each movement, I have developed a special technique designed to squeeze all the results possible out of that particular exercise. Various exercises can be grouped or paired differently. Sets, reps, frequency and duration can be tweaked, modified or manipulated to obtain a specific result.

After a few decades of fight training, I have learned what exercises work and what exercises are redundant or a complete waste of time. Also keep in mind that first and foremost, this book is about making you a better fighter. I am not here to make you a better kettlebell lifter. That is not the goal. It just so happens that becoming a better kettlebell lifter also happens to make you a better fighter. It is a coincidence we use to our advantage.

You need to learn these lifts and do them in the way they are supposed to be done. Sloppy technique will get you hurt. Make haste slowly: learn the technique using light poundage: drill hard, long, and repeatedly, always looking to hone and improve exercise technique. Do the exercises as often and as hard as is recommended.

THE
KETTLEBELL
LUCKY
SEVEN

1. THE SWING

The kettlebell swing is the mother of all kettlebell exercises. A fighter needs a tremendously strong hip-hinge and no tool strengthens the hip-hinge like a proper "pop and lock" swing. The kettlebell swing is an essential exercise for any fighter.

The kettlebell swing is unique and demanding—and the power it builds is completely applicable for grappling or dirty boxing. The swing can be used to build power: swing a big heavy bell for low reps. The swing can be used to build cardio: swing a light weight for high reps. Each swing needs to be crisp and accurate.

When technique starts to disintegrate, end the set. Swing technique is honed and refined over time. Synchronize the exhalation breath with each exertion.

FEROCIOUS FITNESS

2. THE GOBLET SQUAT

No fight training is complete without leg training. Elite strikers know that powerhouse punching comes from powerhouse legs. Knockout power is initially generated in the legs then travels to the torso and upper back before being sent down the arm ending at the fist.

The kettlebell goblet squat builds leg strength to a degree comparable to the traditional back squat—and is far lighter, far safer and far easier to learn and master.

A proper goblet squat is deep and upright, and when done correctly builds incredible leg power. Higher rep goblet squats can be used to increase cardio: a high rep set of 50 to 100 reps will challenge the most conditioned of fighters.

Mastery of the goblet squat is the key to developing leg power and punching power.

3. THE CLEAN

The kettlebell clean is performed by pulling one or two kettlebells set at your feet to the shoulder(s) in one fluid motion. The kettlebell held at the shoulder is in the "racked" position.

Once we rack a clean, the kettlebell lifter can press the bell overhead, bent press it overhead, or return it to the floor for repetition kettlebell cleans.

The clean, done as an exercise, is the finest upper back strengthener. A powerful upper back is useful for grappling and power punching. High rep cleans, both single and with two kettlebells, can be made into a grueling cardio exercise; a heart-exploding aerobic gas-tank builder of the first magnitude.

Cleans also build a powerful grip, a huge advantage in grappling. Sloppy cleans will get you hurt.

4. THE PRESS

The kettlebell overhead press is an exercise that is without rival when it comes to building shoulder and arm strength. More awkward than a dumbbell, pushing a 55-pound kettlebell overhead is a hell of a lot harder than pushing a 55-pound dumbbell overhead. Why? The kettlebell payload is "off-set", it's not all centered and nice. Purposefully inefficient, the awkward kettlebell causes more muscle fiber stimulation than an identically weighted dumbbell.

The single or double overhead kettlebell press strengthens the deltoids, triceps, upper chest and upper back. I insist on a very specific type of pressing: from a "cocked and loaded" racked position, the kettlebell is then fired overhead to a full and complete lockout. No half reps or sloppy reps—every single press rep needs to be perfection.

5. THE TURKISH GET-UP

The Turkish get-up with a single kettlebell is unique: in my thirty-plus years as a fighter, fight trainer and student of the game, I have never come across an exercise like the Turkish get-up. The trainee lies on their back on the floor and proceeds to arise while holding a single kettlebell on a locked arm. There are no less than seventeen performance points to be adhered to in a single get-up.

The technique is exacting and demanding, but the payoff is huge. Mobility, stability, the ability to travel through planes, flexibility, "in-between" strength, tension mastery and above all else, balance, are all highlighted, isolated and improved with conscientious practice of proper get-ups. This is a skill lift that improves with time and practice.

Ferocious Fitness

6. THE SNATCH

The kettlebell snatch is performed by simply pulling a kettlebell set at your feet all the way overhead, then catching the kettlebell or kettlebells on fully locked arms. The snatch is a mighty back builder and a developer of explosive power—exactly the type and kind of coiled explosiveness a fighter needs. We need to strike with speed. A slow, telegraphed punch, no matter how powerful, is easily avoided. We seek lightning speed—coupled with power.

The snatch develops explosiveness; the snatch demands explosiveness! The snatch is my personal all-time favorite kettlebell exercise. Snatches build my explosive power and my muscular endurance. I can use snatches for straight cardio conditioning. A proper set of snatches causes full body engagement.

FEROCIOUS FITNESS

Using two kettlebells for alternating double-bell snatches.

7. THE KETTLEBELL ROW

I love the kettlebell row. I have always gotten great results from doing them and have had great success teaching effective kettlebell rows to others. A lot of people do not get good results from rowing. Optimally, rowing is a back exercise. The muscles of the upper and lower lats, the teres, rhomboids, and rear delts all have to contract to pull the kettlebell to the body.

Unfortunately, a large majority of trainees "arm pull" their rows. They use their biceps instead of their back to pull the weight to the body, thereby turning an incredible back exercise into a mediocre arm exercise. The idea is to keep the arms out of the rows; I have a very specific way to row and strongly advise you to do them my way!

TOOL VERSATILITY

I have been slinging kettlebells for over a decade, and one of the most marvelous aspects is the sheer versatility of the tool. I am truly limited only by my imagination. Competitive fighters need to peak for scheduled fights: the kettlebell can be used in such a way that the degree of difficulty can increase exponentially as the fight grows nearer. I can tailor my kettlebell workouts to elicit the training effect I seek and desire. If I need to work on my pure power, no problem, I up the sheer poundage of the kettlebells and hoist them for low reps, grinding and imposing my will on them.

Conversely, if I want to work on my pure cardio, no problem, I select a lighter kettlebell and toss it ballistically for hundreds of reps. Other times I might split the difference for a "strength/endurance" workout where I use moderately heavy kettlebells for sets of 25 or less.

Do I need to work on my grip strength because in the clinches I am getting bullied-around? How about heavy rows with a thick-handled kettlebell. Or just pick up two monster kettlebells and see how far you can walk with them before they pry your fingers open—now, that is a real grip exercise!

I have tried every possible kettlebell exercise known to man at one time or another. This was and is my passion—I *love* discovering new and different, exciting kettlebell exercises that deliver on whatever they promise. It is magical to find a new exercise, use the right technique, and sync it up with an optimal set, rep, duration and frequency protocol to get fantastic results.

Most exercises are dead ends, unable to deliver on their promised results and, ergo a waste of time. I can show you which exercises don't work, but more importantly, I can show you which exercises do work. Certain exercises done in very specific ways deliver extraordinary results: fighters that practice my protocols become faster, stronger, improve their endurance, increase their agility, become leaner and more muscular—you name the athletic attribute and I can show you an exercise that will improve that attribute.

THE SIX CRITICAL BODYWEIGHT EXERCISES

I have done bodyweight exercises my entire life. Starting with push-ups and chin-ups as a preteen, bodyweight exercises have been the eternal cornerstone of my fighter training. I find it amusing and gratifying that the "bodyweight" movement took off and got commercial traction when Paul Wade wrote **Convict Conditioning.** That book started a revolution: the idea of "progressive calisthenics" was born and nowadays bodyweight training seminars by Al and Danny Kavadlo are packed to the rafters. The public is finally catching on to how effective bodyweight exercises can be.

Not all bodyweight exercises are created equal. I have tried every bodyweight exercise you can name and of all the infinite number of movements I have used over the years, I use six on a continual and repeating basis. So should you. As Yip Man pointed out, "Better to *master* a few select movements, than be acquainted with a dozens yet the master of none".

Do yourself a favor; spend all your available bodyweight exercise training time mastering these six fundamental exercises. Each of these six core movements will have variations, creating a wide variety of choices.

1. THE BRIDGE

I love to bridge. I have done bridges since I was a kid and I am very comfortable doing them. To me, since I started so young, bridging is natural and seems second nature. For most people, arching the spine backwards and to a significant degree, is unnatural. It takes time, patience and practice, it takes reps and tenacity to become adept at bridging. Fortunately, we have incremental steps towards being able to bridge in dramatic fashion.

Why bridge? A lot of reasons: proper bridging builds powerhouse neck muscles; there is no better neck building exercise. Spinal erectors get worked as they power the bridge upward to completion. Flexibility, mobility and power are all improved by bridging.

Weighted bridging while having an opponent lie across the chest or while gripping a heavy bag, is the greatest neck strengthener ever devised. The famed Russian wrestler George Hackenschmidt once did a complete bridge with 440 pounds on his chest. Bridge mastery is critical.

2. HANGING ABDOMINAL RAISES

To me, the most natural thing in the world is to grab onto a pull-up bar and perform some type of abdominal exercise. Exercises such as the frog kick, where you raise your knees to your chin, bent leg style; straight-leg leg raises, straight-leg leg raises with the feet raised over the head; side-twist leg raise where the feet are raised to each side on each rep, thereby activating the external oblique side muscles.

I might mix these different variations within the same set: 10 reps of frog kicks followed immediately by 10 reps of hanging leg raises (feet lifted above the head), ending with 10 side-twist leg raises to each side. This is a 40-rep uninterrupted set of high intensity ab work, with four distinct exercises, 10-reps each.

Master the various types of hanging abdominal exercises and strengthen the entire abdominal region. Intense ab work also increases flexibility and enhances thoracic mobility.

3. SINGLE-LEG (PISTOL) SQUATS

In my experience, single-leg squats, when done correctly, are the most beneficial of all leg exercises. The single-leg squat, known as a "pistol" squat, has to be done with a very specific technique. If you cheat on the depth, how deep you go on each squat rep, you reduce the benefits associated with doing the movement. It takes time and practice just to master lowering all the way down without toppling over. I will suggest that people just learning how to do a pistol hang onto a pole or door jamb for balance.

First learn the goblet squat. Once you've built up your leg power, try the twice-as-difficult pistol squat. When rising out of the lowest position of the pistol, I insist the fighter maintain proper pistol technique. Contorting, jerking or rebounding while doing pistols will get you hurt. We learn to power through the pistol sticking points, all while maintaining perfect technique. From butt to heel, pistol mastery builds balance, trunk stability, incredible leg strength and leg endurance.

4. HANDSTANDS

I love various types of handstands and include them in my key bodyweight exercises. Most of us need to do our handstands against a wall. Position your hands next to a wall, then flip your feet overhead until the heels lightly touch the wall. You are now upside down on locked arms. Just holding this position is extremely beneficial: shoulders and triceps muscles are maximally stressed. The athletic elite are able to do a handstand without the wall. This takes muscle stress levels to a whole other level.

Once the athlete becomes comfortable with wall handstands, or for a few, no-wall handstands, you may attempt the super-difficult handstand press. The handstand press against the wall is essentially a partial press with bodyweight for reps. If a man weighs 170 pounds, in the handstand press he is pressing his full bodyweight from forehead to lockout. The super-elite are able to do handstand presses without needing the wall for balance. Handstand presses provide the ultimate in shoulder and punching power.

5. THE PULL-UP/CHIN-UP

Another couple of my favorite movements. The number of potential variations makes it impossible to grow bored with pull-ups or chin-ups: wide and narrow grip widths, palms forward, palms facing you, straight bar pull-ups, uneven pull-ups, towel pull-ups, pinch-grip pull-ups, weighted pull-ups and chins...the variations are limitless. Chin-up and pull-up mastery strengthens the shoulders and upper back muscles. The chin-up grip works the hell out of the biceps and upper lats.

I am a stickler for chin-up and pull-up technique: I want my fighters to use a full and complete range-of-motion—all the way down and all the way up on each and every rep. Half-reps and incomplete reps yield half results and incomplete results.

It's not coincidental that every person who has mastered pull-ups has a defined six pack. The movement tightens ab muscles while a low body fat percentage makes it easier for a person to chin or perform a pull-up. I think 20 pristine pull-ups represent a true benchmark in upper body strength.

6. THE PUSH-UP

Push-up variations are as numerous as stars in the sky: regular hand spacing, super-narrow hand spacing stressing the triceps, wide hand spacing making the pectorals do all the work, do them slowly at grind speed, do them explosively.

Push-ups not only work all the front torso muscles, they also strengthen and condition your abdominals. A push-up is done from a "plank" position and doing lots of push-ups reinforces total body tensioning. Push-ups can be done anywhere that there is a floor. Another benefit of push-ups is the important "de-loading effect" they have on your forearms. Kettlebell training and fighting requires a great deal of gripping and clenched fists. Be sure to do yourself a favor and avoid inflammation and tendonitis by making de-loading exercises a regular part of your training regimen.

I consider all forms of "planking" to be push-up variations. Proper planking is the prerequisite for performing perfect push-ups. Avoid doing push-ups on your knees. I have never found them to translate into the ability to perform regular push-ups. You are much better off working on creating tension with your planks. Forget knee push-ups and hold planks at different levels. Plank holding will enable you to execute push-ups properly.

I also include parallel bar dips in the extended push-up family. When you dip, keep your chin down and your feet forward.

FIGHTER NUTRITION

COSMO'S CREDO

When I graduated from the University of Maryland in 1984, I was 22 years old and weighed 188-pounds at a 10% body fat percentage. Fast forward to 2015 and at 53 years of age, I weigh 188 at a 10% body fat percentage. A lot of fitness types dismiss a guy like me, attributing my late-in-life high degree of conditioning and leanness to "genetics".

In my experience, anytime an armchair fitness expert wants to dismiss someone else's ideas, conclusions or strategies the cute little verbal technique is to be snide and dismissive while saying, "His late-in-life leanness is completely attributable to superior genetics; ignore his consultation and advice because you don't have his genes and could never hope to duplicate his results. He's an anomaly." Naturally this "expert" also has a system that *will* work for you—for three easy payments of $99.99, MasterCard and Visa accepted.

If you are unable to get real results as a trainer and if that incompetent trainer is competing against a real trainer who gets real results, the way to torpedo that effectiveness and steal the client is to woo and lure them by attributing those real results to genes. Most folks want to believe the "expert" as opposed to a guy like me, because I tell people the hard truth about leaning out and getting into shape. Real results are dependent on hard ass work—and that work needs to be multiplied with consistency and discipline. That's a damn tough sell.

But the hard truth always is a damn tough sell. People would prefer to believe that the system, tool or strategy promoted by "the expert" can and will deliver all the desired results acquired by hard-ass work but without the hard-ass work. My favorite fake fitness expert strategy is to tell the client—who is wondering why they have spent six months and six thousand dollars and are wearing the same pants size, dress size and a have lost less than 10 pounds—that they "are the same body weight but are exchanging muscle for body fat".

In other words, when you started with "the expert", you stood 5'5", weighed 200 pounds, and wore size 40 pants—now, half a year later, you weigh 196 and still wear size 40 pants. However, because I have lost 15 pounds of fat while adding 15 pounds of muscle, the bathroom scale says you weigh the same. Who are you going to believe? The male-model-looking expert with dyed hair, perfect teeth and a dazzling smile or your own lying eyes? The fraudulent expert has no problem selling you a system, tool or protocol that he flat-out knows doesn't work. That is how he makes his beach condo and Porsche payments.

I hear a lot of semi-smack talk about genetics directed in my direction and wanted to take a New Jersey minute to set this shit straight: The inconvenient truth is my father stood 5'8, weighed 285 pounds and died of a heart attack (his third) at age 66.

I am a hardcore Italian-American and our culture revolves around food. Delicious food. Fattening food. I was brought up in a house where every meal had red sauce "gravy", loaves of bread slathered in real butter, cheese galore, super sugary deserts, wine by the gallon. So, stop with all the genetic bull.

Let's get real: nutrition is a critical component for a fighter. A lean physique is optimal for maximizing cardio capacity. A lean body is faster and more mobile than that same body hauling around 30 extra pounds of body fat. A lean, muscled-up man carrying a 10% body fat percentage makes a formidable opponent—even if he doesn't know jack about fighting, he's going to have great cardio and be strong as hell.

Being lean maximizes explosive power and promotes quickness; the lean athlete carrying a 10% body fat percentage can strike much faster and strike way more often. The lean fighter can hit much harder and last much longer than the same fighter packing a 20% body fat percentage.

In the real world, this would be the difference between a 170-pound fighter with 10% body fat (163 pounds of lean body mass) and that same fighter, the guy with 163 pounds of lean mass, now having to drag around 34 pounds of body fat while weighing 187 pounds and saddled with a 20% body fat percentage.

Pick up a 35-pound barbell plate and imagine the dramatic difference in performance shedding that much body fat would have. I have used a very specific approach towards food and nutrition for decades. My students have also used this commonsense approach towards body composition manipulation and all have gotten terrific results. My leanness strategy is based on a subtle balance between *fuel* (food/drink) and *activity*. I combined a savage, unrelenting work ethic with a *portion control strategy*.

There are no lightweights in my family. Both my younger brother and sister have to work at keeping their weight down; they have to work at maintaining their good physical condition. I trained both of them for quite a few years. My grandfather, Cosmo, was also heavy, but he was all about "being in condition." He was a staunch proponent of old-school conditioning and would tell me stories, parables, about how he had to push his fighters to get into shape and stay in shape. He was a huge proponent of roadwork. Cosmo stressed cardio—above all else, he wouldn't tolerate a fighter "gassing out", to use the modern definition.

Cosmo was remarkable in a lot of ways. He taught me solid boxing basics, and showed me what fighters needed to do (other than box) to improve: road work, jump rope, double-end bag and heavy bag. He showed me how every one of these tools can be used to improve fighter stamina and endurance. In addition to exposing me to his old-school fight trainer approach, he also had a really effective way for keeping his fighters lean. In his gruff way, he would emphasize his approach to eating: portion control. Literally, regulating the volume of food and drink you consume.

His advice was common sense all the time in every way; he was an old-school genius dispensing bunkhouse logic. When he worked fighters, he would instruct them at each meal to limit their food intake to one plateful of food. How much trouble can you get into if at each meal you never eat more than one plateful? Oh, and no drinks that contained calories: no sodas, fruit juice, beer, hard liquor or milk for fighters. None. Eat smart. Eat less. This advice was from a guy who had a tough life of hard labor, yet lived a vital life until the ripe old age of 94. I'm convinced he would have made 100 if he had not fallen down a flight of stairs. I have used Cosmo's portion control strategy for decades.

- Use portion control to establish a nutritional toehold: become consistent and disciplined about eating no more than one plateful of food—ever.

- Once we have food *volume* under control, then we can start playing with the *content* of the food selections. First conquer volume, then attack content.

Initially, when you are getting serious about training and nutrition, just eat what you eat, good or bad, but limit the volume to one plateful. Once we get the volume consistency down, it makes perfect sense to start "switching out" bad foods for good ones...

- **PROTEIN:** Fighters love protein; there is nothing better for healing and regenerating a body that was beat up in training than by dousing it with protein. Favor the leaner protein sources; though don't get stupid about it. If I'm at a steakhouse, I eat steak and I am not counting fat grams that night! On the other hand, generally speaking, leaner is cleaner and lean protein gets digested and processed faster.

- **FIBROUS CARBS:** Green stuff is great, the perfect complement for an athlete who purposefully eats a lot of protein. Greens beans, bell peppers, broccoli, asparagus, salad greens...the more of these vegetables you can consume, the better. Just don't fall into the trap of loading them up with butter, oil, rich salad dressing or cheese.

- **STARCHY CARBS:** Fighters really need to be careful about starchy carbs; when you do eat them, make them natural starchy carbs, i.e. rice or potatoes. I have found that starch needs to be monitored carefully. Some starchy carbs are great for energy, but if your bodyweight starts heading the wrong direction, look to reduce starchy carbs right away.

- **SATURATED FAT:** I think some dietary fat is good for recovery, joint lubrication and healing. Too much fat overwhelms the body and excess fat (at 9 calories per gram!) gets shuttled into body fat fast. So let's keep the saturated fat down, not crazy down, just try and eat lean protein. If some saturated fat sneaks in, it's no problem whatsoever.

- **REFINED CARBS, ARTIFICIAL FOOD, SUGAR, ALCOHOL: BANNED!** There's no room for them. This is the disciplined part—you *cannot* get lean eating pizza, drinking beer and having ice cream for dessert. Sugar is a real problem; refined carbs are a real problem; booze is a real problem. To be the best fighter you can be, you must let them go. Man up. Get over it.

A DAY IN THE LIFE...

It is a continual challenge for me to adhere to proper nutrition during my busy day. I usually get up around 5:30 or 6:00, depending on what kind of day I have ahead. My daily caloric intake is between 2000 to 2500 calories, hardly starvation eating for a guy weighing 188 pounds. I actually used to eat a lot more, but as I've gotten older I have cut back on the overall volume. Still, I hardly starve to stay lean and have a pretty good latitude and looseness about what I eat. Here is what I typically eat and when...

Breakfast	6:30AM	Eggs with yolks or yogurt and fruit
Snack	11:00AM	Nuts, fruit or a protein bar
Lunch	2:00 pm	Turkey, tuna or fish with raw and/or cooked vegetables
Snack	6:00 pm	Nuts, fruit or a protein bar
Dinner	9:30 pm	Chicken or sushi, green vegetables and/or salad

They say the devil is in the details: first off, I believe in breakfast and have come to rely on this first meal of the day as my fuel for long, active days filled with motion, exertion and activity. I like eggs and I eat a lot of them. I am a guy that cooks; I feel comfortable in the kitchen and I am pretty good at preparing my favorite foods.

On most occasions, I make lunch for myself at home. I will pair a protein with whatever is handy at home—a salad, leftover vegetables, fruit or a small portion of potato or rice. I might have a protein muffin. If I don't make lunch that day, I grab a wrap or a salad with meat at one of the fine little local eateries. The food that the places in my neighborhood crank out is exceptionally good—and surprisingly healthy.

In the morning, I will take a vitamin supplement along with some liquid minerals. I drink an aloe drink with glucosamine and chondroitin; I also take probiotics and DHEA. I used to make and take a protein shake every morning, but I've gotten away from that over the past ten years or so. However, I like to eat a protein bar (mainly due to their convenience) if I start to bonk during the day. I save the protein bar trick for when and if my energy levels start to nosedive.

Every time I go to put something in my mouth, I try to be mindful: is this food or drink going to add muscle, aid my energy, or help me repair my blasted body? Or, on the other hand, is this bite/mouthful of food/drink going to end up as body fat? Now I am not saying that I attain and retain perfect mindfulness for every minute of every day, however I have programmed my brain to ask that question at least once a day. I have found that this simple act of self-reflection is a powerful antidote to mindless eating.

I am not so much a sweets guy and I don't crave or eat very many desserts. My particular guilty pleasure is those baked chips and crunchy, salty stuff...I have never been a fan of greasy foods. I try to stay away from processed carbs, especially at night.

My dinner will usually consist of chicken or fish with some type of green vegetable and a salad. I eat a great deal of salad and a great deal of chicken. I will have sushi carryout (I *love* really good sushi!) a couple times a week, and I'll have red meat once.

The shocker is that each week I'll also have some pasta or pizza. I am a believer in the "reward meal" strategy: stay dead-on and rigid in my eating 6.5 days a week, and for one meal per week I can eat or drink *anything*. I don't drink a great deal of alcohol and generally I'll only have two or three drinks tops, one night per week. If I drink more one weekend, then I'll skip the next one. There are periods that I go a month or so with no alcohol at all. It's mostly for my mental discipline. Now, it is only natural that for that one meal that might include pizza, pasta or bread to throw in a couple of drinks...then get back in the saddle the next morning.

One of the major contributors to my ability to maintain a low body fat percentage is the amount of sheer energy I expend during my workday. First off, being an American entrepreneur, I work seven days a week and I am in near continuous motion.

I start my day by walking my dogs. After that, I head to work. My classes generally begin at 7:00AM, though some days I start even earlier. I will engage in strength training early in the morning four times per week with my training partner and fellow RKC, Zoe Georgiades. Our training focuses on kettlebells and bodyweight exercises. I also travel across the county to train jujitsu at Jay Hayes' school once a week. I practice boxing at our studio with Coach Joe Rubino, a former member of Gleason's Fight Team in NY, national boxing and kickboxing champion. In the mornings I will do my roadwork, practice various martial arts skills and hit the heavy bag.

Depending on the size of my martial arts class, I may train with the class and/or spar. Unless I'm at my desk, I am on the floor, training students in martial arts or kettlebells. We offer over 40 classes per week and I have about a dozen personal training clients. I'm moving and expending energy throughout my entire day. I lead the warm-ups for most of the classes and I am constantly picking up various sized kettlebells and demonstrating. I also demonstrate throws, kicks and grappling techniques in every single class. My energy level is always high. I average over two hours per day, six days a week for my own improvement. Not all of the training is high intensity; I work on my martial skills and sequences when I'm alone.

I don't take much in the way of nutritional supplements. Generally speaking, I strive for a nutrient balance of 45% protein, 40% carbs and 15% fats. Again, it all ties back to Cosmo's credo: limit portion size. Concentrate on reducing caloric volume; once the volume is under control, then refine the food choices!

Diet and Weight Classes

FIGHT AT YOUR PROPER WEIGHT

Most people have a weight where they will perform at their best. It may take some time to discover what this weight is and it may also change as the fighter gets older and more mature. Through training and diet, you have the ability to alter your natural design to fit into a different or more desirable weight class. For example, if you are a Light Heavyweight (205 pounds) and having issues making weight, you may want to put on some mass and grow into the Heavyweight Division. Proper nutrition, training and a sensible weight gain plan will get you there.

Here's a slice of little personal history for you. During my senior in high school I wrestled at the 148-pound weight class. It was OK for me in the beginning of the season, but I was young for my grade, starting my senior year at age 16 and I was still growing. I actually grew until I was almost 20. By the end of the year, I had a measured body fat of less than 3%. That amount is barely enough to sustain your internal organs, never mind engaging in physical contests. Well, I began to break down a few weeks prior to the end of the season tournaments. I was an Honor Roll Wrestler was predicted to go to the State Tournament.

I subsequently tore my calf away from my shin bone while cutting weight. I almost missed weight for the only time in my life and lost 6-5 in the semi-final round to a guy that I had handily beaten by a margin of 10-1 approximately a month prior. I wound up taking 3rd Place and back then, the Bronze Medal gave you a pat on the back, not a trip to the next level. I had to sit there and watch guys that I pinned and handily beat move on. I was a "Power Wrestler", but after dropping all of that weight, my strength eluded me.

I continued to wrestle in the spring and into the summer that year. I allowed myself to go up to the 170-pound weight class, two levels up from only the month prior. I was unstoppable, beating Regional Champs and State Place winners. One wrestler I pinned was from Blair Academy and had taken 2nd in the Prep School States.

You would have thought that I learned my lesson, but I didn't. My sophomore year in college, I dropped down to 158-pound weight class to try to break the line-up. We had a couple of studs at 167 and 177 and I wasn't able to beat them. I wound up making weight and during the third match of the first tournament; I tore the ligaments in my ankle and popped out my knee. I couldn't do anything but eat and lift, so that's what I did. In less than 2 months, I was 202 pounds. My College Wrestling career was over.

I vowed that I would never "suck weight" again, but I didn't allow myself to get fat. I wound up settling in at between 185-190 pounds. That is the weight I'm at today. I began to fight in Karate and do kickboxing, often fighting at Light Heavyweight and even Heavyweight as opposed to losing weight. My last competition was in 2010. I weighed in at 184 pounds. Even though the next weight down was 179.9 and weigh-ins were the night before, I didn't care. I fought Light Heavyweight and competed with guys that weighed up to 200 pounds. I went in two divisions and won all five of my fights, without giving up a point. It was a good way to end my competitive career.

Let us consider a couple of UFC Welterweights. They are two, completely different cases. In one, the fighter just gets too darn heavy between fights. In the other, he's simply too big for the weight class.

The dethroned UFC Champion Johny Hendricks. Hendricks reportedly cuts 40 to 50 pounds for each fight. He utilizes a "designer weight cut" method and dehydration to make the trip from 220 pounds to the 170-pound weight limit. When he defeated Robbie Lawler, he sustained a nasty biceps tendon tear. I will make the assertion that his tendons were dehydrated and brittle from the weight cut. The 24-hour time period between the weigh in and the fight did not allow sufficient time for the rehydration to reach the tendons and ligaments to restore maximum pliability prior to being subject to the rigors of the battle in the Octagon.

Seven months later, after surgery and rehabilitation, he faced Lawler once again and suffered a loss. He later spoke about his weight cut and how it had drained him, made him weak, and how he will now stay below 195. Unfortunately, Johny only stuck to this plan for one fight. He showed up grossly overweight at 183 pounds the day before the weigh-ins for a scheduled bout with Tyron Woodley at 170 pounds. Johny wound up in the hospital as a result of the weight cut\—and the fight got cancelled. He subsequently lost his next fight. He's a great talent and I wish him luck in getting his weight under control and back to his winning ways.

Anthony "Rumble" Johnson is a BEAST at 205 pounds (Light Heavyweight). At 170, he would typically miss weight and fizzle out during the later rounds of his fights. The guy is HUGE and I have no idea why his trainers had him fighting at Welterweight. I sat next to him on the UFC bus in Brazil during UFC 142. During this fight, he was fighting Vitor Belfort at Middleweight, 185 pounds (186 with the one-pound allowance). Johnson was thick and powerful; he also missed weight by 11 pounds, weighing in at 197 for the bout. This action, coupled with his loss, caused the UFC to cut him from their roster. He was then picked up by another promotion and went on to fight at 205 pounds, Light Heavyweight and even one bout at Heavyweight, 265-pound limit. He won 11 of his last 12 bouts, got re-signed by the UFC and steam rolled his way toward a second UFC Light Heavyweight Title Shot. Johnson is my pick; I wish him only the best in his quest! He's one of my favorite fighters.

There are several other fighters that come to mind, Frankie Edgar and Anthony Pettis. They do not lose a substantial amount of weight, yet they have both been UFC World Champions, even though their "Walking Around Weight" is quite a bit lower than most of their adversaries.

We've seen some real life examples of fighters being at the wrong weight class. It's an easy trap to fall into; I fell prey to the weight cutting while wrestling. Had I gone up in weight class, as I eventually did, I performed much better. You think that you will be stronger and have an advantage at the lower weight class. Not necessarily true. Let us exam some pitfalls.

The major issue that I see is fighters "cutting" weight through starvation and dehydration prior to a fight. Let us look at the drawbacks of this method.

- **LOSS OF STRENGTH:** No matter who you are, if you dehydrate yourself, your energy will be sapped. Your muscles are comprised of 79% water. Denying your muscles of their main ingredient will do nothing good for you. You will have no choice but to lose strength. This fact, coupled with the sugar reduction (or elimination) will also rob your muscles of much needed energy reserves.

- **CLOUDED THOUGHT:** Your brain operates on fats and sugar and is surrounded by cerebral fluid. If you are cutting a great deal of weight, the chances are you have significantly reduced your carbohydrates and your fats. By denying your brain of these, your thoughts and even your vision will be affected.

- **SUSCEPTIBLE TO KNOCKOUT:** We have established that our brains are surrounded by fluid. When we become dehydrated, the cushion of fluid around the brain becomes diminished. This leaves us more susceptible to knockout or even death due to the bruising of the brain.

- **TENDON AND LIGAMENT DAMAGE:** Your tendons and ligaments also require moisture to slide and operate at full capacity. If they are subject to dehydration, they will become brittle, opening you up to injury when they are stressed during combat.

- **FOCUS ON FIGHTING:** The best wrestler ever was Dan Gable. He set the bar for all others after him. He never cut weight. I have been involved in camps where the whole focus of the last 2 weeks was making weight. It is far more prudent to be focused on your training and fight preparation than it is to have your mind preoccupied with losing weight. Look at what Bernard Hopkins' take on cutting weight is. He is one of the longest lasting boxers in history and always stays in condition and very close to weight. Depending on your weight class, 15 to 25 pounds is all that you should allow yourself to gain after a fight.

Again, the poundage described is dependent on your weight class. Once you start training again, you'll lose from 5 to 10 pounds of water weight. You clean up your diet and you're there. Please bear in mind that you should not feel like you have to walk around "on weight" or be "on weight" during your fight camp. It's good to have 5 to 7 pounds to work off during the last week or so of Fight Camp. Less for amateurs because you weigh in 3 hours before the event. Professionals are given 24 hours to eat and rehydrate.

Here's another point. Let us consider that you fight at 170 pounds (MMA Welterweight) and post-fight you balloon up to 210 pounds. What have you been doing? Either you are fighting at a weight class that is too low for you or you are not training properly and not exercising proper dietary discipline.

Post-fight, take a couple of weeks off. Unless of course you sustain an injury, then you will be required to heal, rehab and whatever is necessary to get you back to training. But if you are medically OK, two weeks off is sufficient. Get back to work. This is the time that you use to address the deficiencies from your last fight and to either expand on or enhance your current repertoire of fighting skills. Also use this time to improve your flexibility and gain strength.

If you are a full time, professional fighter your training should be consistent and then ramped up during fight camp. It's tough to improve if you simply train during your camp. For starters, you will not be in good shape. Then you need to work on the fight strategy for your particular opponent. How will you be able to focus on improving your fighting techniques and gaining strength? Another thing to consider, there are many "last minute" opportunities to fight as a replacement. I've seen this make and break careers. If you are in shape and you get a call to fight in two or three weeks, your chances of performing are much better. However, if you are 30 pounds overweight, you will need to cut down fast and therefore increase your chances of "gassing out" after the first round of the fight. You may have blown an opportunity to shine and boost your career. You will have blown it because you haven't maintained your training regiment.

Being called to fight as a replacement is a true reality. When I promoted fights, I'd typically start with 18 to 21 bouts and wind up with 8 to 10 fights by the time Fight Night arrived. I'd spend the last three weeks prior to the show scrambling around making last minute bouts to fill the card and secure fights. Don't miss out on an opportunity just because you are not in shape.

If you are not in a fight camp, you should still be training approximately three hours per day. You will want to work on your cardiovascular endurance, strength, flexibility and mobility. This type of training will enhance your performance and lessen the incident and/ or severity of injury.

There needs to be time spent on your striking (Boxing and Kickboxing/Muay Thai), Wrestling (Takedowns, Scrambles, Top Control), Submissions (Brazilian Jiu Jitsu, Catch Wrestling) and then the synergy between the disciplines. The aforementioned Martial Disciplines are simply examples. There are various other arts of striking and grappling that have merit in the sport Mixed Martial Arts competition. It's an imperative to have seamless transitions from Stand-up, to takedowns and submissions. The aspects require being trained first separately and then with transitions to develop them in a synergistic fashion. Drilling, drilling and more drilling. You must drill and do so with purpose. Offensive and defensive maneuvers, combinations and working one range of fighting to the next. There must also be a great deal of time for live rolls (grappling) and sparring (stand-up). Three hours a day gets eaten up very quickly when you add in all of the aspects needed for success in MMA.

In 1983, I worked as a manager of a restaurant-bar in College Park, Maryland. At night I was the last one out the door and would lock up behind myself. Then I would take any cash we had collected during the day and walk it over to a night drop box at our bank a block from the restaurant. One evening, I closed up and, along with a friend, was walking towards the bank when two guys walking in the other direction stopped to ask for a light for a cigarette. They looked a little suspect, so I kept a good distance between them and myself. My friend, however, did not display the same situational awareness.

This was College Park, the epicenter of the University of Maryland, so to have young guys crawling the streets at all hours of the night was no big deal and nothing out of the ordinary. At first, when we were stopped, my sensors went off because these dudes were *definitely* not college material. My suspicions were confirmed instantly when as my friend rooted around in his pocket for a lighter, the smaller of the two guys in front of him lashed out with a savage straight right, and hit him right on the "button". My buddy fell like he'd been pole-axed and hit the ground, already unconscious. This was a robbery.

My training went on autopilot and in the same motion with which I shoved the money bag into the back of my jeans (this is what they were after) I instinctively fired a right kick to my assailant's forward left knee. He had all his weight on his left leg and when my adrenalized body blasted my right shin into the side of this thug's knee, he screamed in pain and was upended by the kick. He fell to the ground clutching his knee and I delivered a downward punch to his head, thus rendering him unconscious. He would later need surgery (in prison) to repair the damage. I leapt back to put some distance between myself and assailant number two.

Being a seasoned professional criminal with a lengthy prison record, assailant number two reached to pull out his six-inch combat knife and was going to stab me—just as he'd stabbed numerous victims and enemies before. Thank God this was in the "pre-gun" era, nowadays any self-respecting thug packs a gun. Back then, the crime tended to be physical or with a knife or club. Chances are, I would have been dead had he been strapped. He was to the left of his fallen comrade and had to jump over and around him to get to me.

The brief instant where he had to maneuver a bit allowed me to set and drop when he cleared his pal. As he got set with his knife in hand, I seized the opportunity and launched a straight right; I was much shorter than him and had squatted down. I drove upwards with every ounce of leg power I had. My fist impacted his chin and shattered his jaw. I stooped to attend to my semi-conscious friend.

One powerful cut kick and two blows from my right hand had dropped two professional muggers.

This is the type of stopping power and brute force my type of training bestows on the fighters who follow my protocols. Light, fast, peppery blows would not have stopped these two thugs; getting into a wrestling match or grappling with one would allow the other to join in. The only way to stop this deadly situation was to hit them hard enough, one time each, one punch to each, and only one kick, but with so much power that it literally stopped them dead in their criminal tracks.

My friend was fine and the police told us that this DC duo was responsible for a rash of strong-arm robberies, including two stabbings. They had apparently been casing me, studying my movements, studying my managerial habits, and thought ripping me off would be about as easy as taking candy from a baby. Wrong baby, boys. I believe the knife-wielder is still incarcerated.

FRANK
"THE LEGEND"
SHAMROCK

Back in December of 1997, I saw the famed cage fighter, Frank Shamrock fight Olympic Gold Medal Freestyle Wrestler Kevin Jackson. Jackson was the reigning UFC Champion. I had seen him wrestle and win the Olympics, but had never seen Frank Shamrock fight yet. Frank was taken down and immediately slapped an armbar on Jackson, submitting Jackson in a mere 0:16 seconds (it was actually a bit faster, but that's what the records show). I was an instant fan.

In 2004, Frank Shamrock was putting on a seminar about two hours from my house. Now I don't go to too many seminars, but Frank Shamrock, Five Time UFC Champion? That was a different story. This guy was a proven fighter and someone I wanted to learn from. He submitted MMA Legend Dan Henderson in a Grappling Match back in 1998 and beat the "Huntington Beach Bad Boy", Tito Ortiz into submission via tap out from strikes in Round four of their UFC Unification Bout in 1999. There was no way that I was going to miss this.

Frank, "The Legend", is the brother of Ken Shamrock, "The World's Most Dangerous Man" and the Hall-of-Fame, multi-time UFC and Pancrase World Champion and a genuine bad ass. Ken Shamrock was prototypical in that he was the perfect personification of a certain type of fighter that has always existed and always will: the perfectly trained, muscled-up jock with off-the-charts endurance and a 440-pound bench press. Ken was a savage; he was stronger then any opponent, he had better cardio than any of his opponents, he had a higher pain tolerance than any of his opponents, he had more muscle, less body fat and a nastier disposition than any opponent he ever fought.

Now, I am speaking of Ken at his glorious peak, when he battled Royce, Severn, Tank Abbott and all the other early greats of the UFC. Shamrock was legendary for the savage work ethic he used at his home fight camp compound, The Lion's Den. Young fighters from around the country would "audition" to become a team member in the Lion's Den stable. One famous audition drill would eliminate two thirds of the guys trying out. Ken would address the new trainees in session one on day one, "Let's start with 500 ass-on-heels squats."

Frank learned his hard lessons about fighting—real fighting—during his years at the Lion's Den. The Lion's Den took pride in their bad-to-the-bone workouts that were far more severe and far more inclusive than any of the fight training going on at that time. Once Frank delved into fighting deeper, he didn't agree with Ken's philosophy 100%, and Ken didn't think that Frank had what it took to be a great MMA Fighter.

Frank had a vision of the complete fighter, so he struck out on his own. Frank took the training to a new level—a more intellectual way of fight training, without abandoning the hard core roots. No one had unlocked the secret of seamless transitions between the different ranges and aspects of fighting. His transitions from striking to take downs to submissions was nothing short of incredible. Frank Shamrock became a tremendous fighter, *Full Contact Magazine's* Fighter of the Year in 1998. So, when I saw he was putting on a seminar in my neck of the woods, I wanted to go and pay my respects to a guy who I admired. I wasn't disappointed. Frank is a smart man, a clear thinker, articulate, humble, with a well-thought-out approach to combat fighting, and no-holds-barred cage fighting.

I was so impressed with the Shamrock approach. He really put a lot of things into perspective: he considered the puzzle of fighting and his view point was consistent with mine—but he had proven it in the cage and I loved that! He had taken the sport of MMA to a new level, one that hadn't been seen before. The degree to which Frank Shamrock *attacked* training was awesome. At the end of this perfect fight seminar, Frank said, "Hey, before we say goodbye, anyone want to roll with the champ?" Naturally, because we are fighters, and fighters fight, every hand in the room went up. Frank chose one guy prior to picking me and submitted him within 30 seconds.

Next it was my turn, and to make a long story short; I took Frank down by surprise with a fireman's carry—but I did not stay on the mat with Frank for I knew his submissions were superior to mine, so I let him up. Having seen him dispatch so many opponents, I wasn't going to stay on the ground with him and become another hapless victim. We went at it with each other for an almost five-minute round. At the end of the day, we were just two good fighters training together—nothing more, nothing less. But I was happy that I was able to "hang" with someone of Frank's caliber. I might add that after our bout, Frank proceeded to decimate every single man that stepped onto that mat as easily as an adult parent disciplining a five-year old.

He was impressed with how I fought. After the seminar, he took me aside to say that he was starting a network of top fighters and fight training professionals and he would like me to join. I told him I would be honored and that started a long friendship with this great, great fighter. I attended Frank Shamrock seminars, acting as his demonstration person and assistant coach for attendees. I soaked up the Shamrock approach like a sponge and credit him with opening my eyes about how formidable a combination extraordinary power and extraordinary cardio capacity are to a fighter. The philosophy might be summed up as: be the strongest, be the leanest—skill and tenacity become the variables.

Frank set the mold for every modern day fighter. His conditioning, strength, seamless transitions, relentless pursuit and high level of competency in each phase of combat, is what current fighters aspire to attain. They (we) owe "The Legend" that level of respect and acknowledgement. Being strong and in condition is easy—provided you are willing to put in the work. You are in full control and possess the ability to become strong and conditioned.

KO
POWER PROTOCOLS

SPEED + STRENGTH = UNCONSCIOUS OPPONENTS!
TYSON POWER: HOW TO GET IT

As I watched the Mayweather versus Pacquiao fight, I was bored out of my mind and wondered why... Both men were fabulous technicians at the top of their game; both men were perfectly conditioned, lean and in shape—so what was missing? Why was this fight so anticlimactic that I actually fell asleep in the sixth round?

What was missing was the element of danger. I never for an instant felt that either man capable of knocking the other out; this would be a chess match instead of a brawl. I find chess boring. So, what was the missing danger element? Neither man had that paralyzing fear that comes from fighting a man with knockout power.

The most feared of all boxers is the power-puncher; if a man hits like a ton of bricks, he can turn any fight to his advantage in an instant. Let your "chess strategy guard" down for one millisecond with Marvin Hagler or Tommy Hearns, Sonny Liston, George Foreman, Rocky Marciano or Mike Tyson, and you will end up unconscious. The power-puncher is feared and gifted.

- *EXPLOSIVE POWER IS THE TRADEMARK OF THE POWER PUNCHER:* knockout power requires a special type of strength. Knockout power is not the slow grinding torque exerted by the powerlifter. KO power is speed and power combined. The faster we can propel a payload, a heavy payload, be it a foot or fist, the greater the devastation. Slow ponderous strength is fine and appropriate in clinch or a grappling situation, but if the goal is to deliver a knockout blow, then our actions need to be explosive and swift.

- *HAND SPEED (ALONE) IS NOT ENOUGH:* both Mayweather and Pacquiao exhibited plenty of pure hand speed—but these speedy blows were without mass, there was no power, no substance or consequence to these hand strikes. Speed without strength is slap-fighting. Any man who fought Marvin Hagler knew what speed combined with power felt like.

- **OUR GOAL IS TO CREATE POWER-PUNCHERS:** I have developed power-puncher protocols that build real speed and real power. To become a power-puncher, you need to explore and master the explosive drills outlined in this book. Our protocols increase hand speed, however they also improve raw power. A significantly stronger fighter with significantly improved hand speed morphs the slap-fighter into a power-puncher.

For the most part, power-punchers, pure punchers, are born, not made. A man like Sonny Liston instinctively and intuitively knew how to punch and punch really hard. Hitting people really hard came naturally and easily to the illiterate ex-con. He was gifted genetically with a powerhouse body—Liston had hands the size of catcher's mitts and the balled up fists at the end of his 18-inch arms were enormous and scarred.

Liston had arguably the greatest left jab in the history of the heavyweight division. One opponent

Bad-to-the-bone: Charles "Sonny" Liston, prototypical power-puncher

described being "shocked" by the severity of Liston's short left jab. "It was like being hit in the face repeatedly with a chunk of concrete." That is different than being hit in the face repeatedly with a pile of feathers.

Liston's jab power originated in his feet. The jab itself was the culmination of a synchronized ballet of muscular integration; Liston exhibited inherent body mastery. He naturally did everything right, insofar as intuitively mastering the subtle mechanics of throwing a power-punch. Now, add that to the fact that he was a physical powerhouse, and you have all the ingredients necessary to construct the ultimate power-puncher.

Sonny Liston was a muscular genetic wonder; he never trained before he was imprisoned and was born with an incredible, thick, lean, muscled-up body carrying low body fat and possessing lightning-fast reflexes. He was blessed, physically, and while he trained (some) his real strength lay in his power.

Liston would start a fight by letting his opponents get a taste of his left jab; when they decided they didn't want to be at arm's length anymore, he'd bore inside and hook to the ribs with vicious bone-crunching blows. He'd look to "shorten" his usually taller opponents with the body shots before ending the fight with sledgehammer blows aimed at the jaw. He was extremely deadly with an overhand right cross.

Because he was so strong and powerful, he could shrug off your punches and had no problem wading through the best his opponents had to offer in return for launching one of his nuclear missile shots to the head or ribs.

Sugar Ray Leonard was another natural puncher. Note that I did not say natural *power*-puncher. Ray was a master puncher and a master boxer but he did not possess "heavy" hands like his murderous opponents: Roberto "Hands of Stone" Duran, Tommy "The Hit Man" Hearns, and Marvelous Marvin. Ray Leonard had light hands, relatively speaking, compared to the heavy hands of his fight opponents.

It is one thing to get hit with an excellent punch thrown by a man weighing 145 pounds, it is quite another to get hit by an equally efficient punch from a power-puncher weighing 220 pounds, like Sonny Liston.

George Forman was a physical giant who, at his awesome peak, likely hit as hard if not harder than any other heavyweight in history. Norman Mailer covered the Rumble in the Jungle and wrote about observing a Foreman training session. He describes what real power—devastating power—looks like up close and personal:

"He (Foreman) was hitting the 100-pound heavy bag. Monstrous, muscular, in amazing physical condition, Foreman, dug in and pounded the bag with alternate hands; his fists created an ever-deeper indentation into the bag until the one section he had targeted was beaten flat and finally split; he pummeled the thick canvas until it ripped apart; my immediate thought was, 'My god, no human alive could be hit with these blows and not crumble or be killed or maimed! The fight should be stopped!' Foreman was beyond human."

In the 1930s, Frank "Farmer" Burns, one of the greatest legitimate wrestlers of all time used to routinely submit opponents using a leg-lock or body clamp with his legs. Burn's leg strength was so incredible he was able to burst a 100-pound burlap sack of grain using a leg clamp. This isometric squeezing of grain sacks was a technique he'd first developed and used as a farm boy. Imagine a man with that level of leg strength clamping onto your waist with legs that powerful?

The question for fighters worldwide becomes: can we devise training that could provide this type of power and strength? Could power be acquired and improved upon?

I have been pondering how to best improve these attributes for decades.

Mike Tyson was a physical powerhouse: thick legs, thick back, arms and chest—a weightlifter's body bestowed by Nature on someone who never lifted weights.

In recent history, Iron Mike Tyson best exemplifies the pure power-puncher. We need demarcate Tyson's career into sections: I refer to the greatest version of Mike Tyson, the Tyson of the early great years while Cus and Jimmy Jacobs were still alive and he was at his most awesome trained-and-honed-to-peak-perfection. Here was a relatively small heavyweight, 5'11" and 219 pounds, consistently chopping down much larger men who were far taller with greater reach; men far more statuesque, athletic and imposing than the short, squat Tyson. Mike Tyson had an almighty equalizer...

Tyson hit so hard (even wearing 12-ounce gloves) that he could knock a man out with a short shot to the ribs. At his power peak, he was frightening. Butch Lewis recounted meeting Tyson backstage in the dressing room prior to the Michael Spinks fight.

"I was Michael Spinks' man and as such went to the opponent's dressing room to watch Tyson get his hands taped, as is customary in boxing. I leave our dressing room and my fighter is down on his knees praying. I walked to Tyson's dressing room and here is this crazed monster punching holes in walls—literally punching through drywall walls with death-blows. I think, my man is praying and this man is punching holes in walls before fighting my man...Oh Lord this is not good!"

And it wasn't good, Tyson destroyed Spinks, knocking him out in the first 90 seconds of round one, annihilating him, and decimating the very best in the world. Tyson was the youngest and most promising heavyweight fighter of all time. Again, keep in mind this is a somewhat undersized heavyweight fighter who overcame and negated his lack of height and lack of reach with off-the-charts punching power: hands that shocked and instilled fear in much larger athletes.

George Foreman was a powerhouse, but he was ponderous and relatively slow, whereas Tyson was a different kettle of fish. At his peak, he was as fast as lightning with locomotive cardio—an unbeatable combination. Here is the question all serious fight trainers need to ask: is there a way to increase current levels of punching power and increase it to a *significant degree* through systematic training?

How much of Nature's genetic gifts can we recreate though conscientious training? My protocols are designed to do exactly that—regardless of your current level of power. By systematically and consistently using my power protocols, over time, the trainee will radically and dramatically increase *how* hard they hit or kick.

While we cannot guarantee that we will infuse you with the power to punch through walls, split open 100-pound heavy bags or burst grain sacks with leg clamps, we can and will guarantee that using these power protocols and strategies in the way in which they are designed, with the diligence and adherence they require—performing them religiously for 90 days—will *dramatically* improve your current levels and capacities.

When it comes to improving pure punching power, we will make you much stronger. We can make you much faster while simultaneously improving "fighter cardio." That sounds like "win, win, win."

TALKING

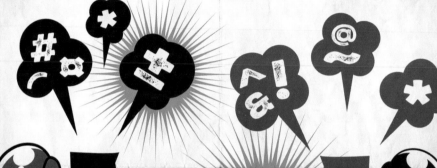

SMACK

I've always hated "talking smack". During and before fights or contests, many people have done it to me, and I just keep my mouth shut. I've always had the attitude of "put up or shut up". All I can say is, thank God for Marty Gallagher. I would have never spoken about my personal triumphs, he brought this out in me. I've always been of the mindset that if you talk too much, it's going to bring you bad karma. So, I just keep quiet and act—when the time is right. People who knew me well, especially back in my fighting days, in the ring and out, knew that I was going to do something when they didn't hear me say anything. I was getting "ready to roll".

As I said before, there have been many incidents, but these two come to mind. One occurred at the Eastern Regional National Greco-Roman Wrestling Championships in 1979 when I was 16. This was the U20 (competitors age 19 and under) division, so there were some college-aged competitors in the tourney.

I was warming up and my little brother was hanging out by the mat. The Ohio State champion told my little brother that he was going to "kick my ass". My brother was six years younger than I was, and he came running to me all upset about what the other wrestler had said to him. I just told my brother not to worry.

The match lasted 0:43 before the guy who proclaimed that he going to kick my ass was taken off the mat on a stretcher. Unlike collegiate wrestling, in Greco-Roman, you get additional points for throwing your opponent so that his feet go over his head. That's just what I did to him. I hit a duck under, got behind him and launched him backward. He landed square on his head as I drove him into the mat.

Another incident occurred at a martial arts tourney in January of 1990. It was the Jersey Shore Championships. I will admit that I have fought in many national and even world competitions, but some of my best fights happened during the local tournaments.

In this particular event, there was supposed to be "limited contact" to the head, but full contact to the body, because we were not wearing any gear—just a mouth piece, groin cup and taped hands. We lined up to match up with our first opponent. There was a "brash" fighter with my same last name in the group. I said, "Hi," and went to shake hands. He looked at my belt and after seeing that he was a 5th degree and that I was 2nd level, said, "Bow to me". My hackles went up immediately. I said, "I'm not bowing to you, you're not my instructor... I'll bow right before we fight".

After the pairings were made, we went to warm-up. As I was getting ready and going through my pre-fight routine, he's over there jumping all over the place, doing all of these fancy kicks and strikes. He's making a lot of noise and running at the mouth. My wife at the time says to me, "That guy looks really good". My reply was, "Everyone looks good, until I hit them".

We both had a couple of fights, then headed into the ring for the semi-final round. He finally got the bow from me that he wanted. Now it was my turn to do what I do best. We started by moving around the ring and he was throwing his "flippy, fancy" stuff... Then I launched my attack, hammering him with a sidekick to the ribs that collapsed him. He hit the ground as I pursued him. The refs stopped me as he lay on the floor writhing in pain. He left the ring on a stretcher with broken ribs.

So much for smack talk.

My "Top Ten" List of Badass Fighters

There is no particular order to this list; though I suppose a psychiatrist would likely suggest the very way in which they appeared in my consciousness as I wrote this is somewhat indicative of my subconscious preference. Of the ten, only one is dead: Frank Gotch.

1. **"JUDO" GENE LEBELL:** My late-in-life role model, Judo Gene, now 83, is revered worldwide as the Godfather of modern MMA. Imagine this: Judo Gene began studying wrestling at age seven under Ed, "Strangler" Lewis, another immortal grappler. Then, at age eleven, he boxed—coached by Sugar Ray Robinson! As a teenager, Gene studied Taekwondo, Shotokan, Kenpo, Greco-Roman and Freestyle wrestling. He moved to Japan to learn Budo from Judokas and Jujutskas. He is also a mentor and trainer of Ronda Rousey. I'll get to her later.

2. **FRANK GOTCH:** Once upon a time, professional wrestling was very real and very big. The two biggest stars were George Hackenschmidt and Frank Gotch. Frank was a superior technical wrestler with tremendous strength and lightning quickness. Frank had a full knowledge of holds, counter-holds, strategy, and was always in the best of condition. Frank Gotch's measurements were taken before his 1911 victory over Hackenschmidt. Age: 33, weight: 204 pounds, height: 5'11", biceps: 17.5", neck: 18", chest: 45", waist: 34", thigh: 22", calf: 18". He was a nasty wrestler that loved to inflict pain.

3. **MIKE TYSON:** He was the youngest ever Heavyweight Champion of the World in boxing. He hit like a truck and had incredible movement and combinations. Tyson was a student of boxing and knew the sweet science like a true expert. There are two Mike Tysons: the Tyson before Cus and Jimmy Jacobs died—and before he fired trainer Kevin Rooney—and the Don King Tyson. The young Tyson was the most fearsome young fighter in history. Toward the end of his reign, Mike abandoned his trademark "relentless aggression" bob-weave-and-uppercut style of fighting Cus and Kevin drilled into him.

4. **BENNY "THE JET" URQUIDEZ:** There were a lot of fake fighters hiding in karate back in the day; the whole "point fighting" concept made sure that no one ever got rocked and created a bunch of dancers masquerading as fighters. Benny was different, his mom had been a pro wrestler and his dad boxed. Benny tore up every type and kind of karate, amassing a 63 and 1 record in kickboxing. He was very much a combat fighter and had a deserved reputation as a fearsome street fighter. His trademarks were power and speed, ergo the nickname; he hit way harder than his size would indicate.

5. **"MARVELOUS" MARVIN HAGLER:** The only other boxer on my top ten list, Hagler was power personified. Marvin was a different kind of power-puncher; most power hitters lack boxing skills, relying and depending on landing a haymaker. Hagler was a boxer who happened to possess some of the heaviest hands in history. Marvin was the complete package—lean, tremendous conditioning, incredibly fast—he was an incredible athlete. 62 professional wins, 52 via KO, two draws and only three career losses—with two of them dripping in controversy. Hagler was frightening and lucky enough to have fantastic opponents like Ray Leonard and Tommy Hearns. Marvin had the freaky ability to shift from southpaw to orthodox stance with no loss in power or precision.

6. **FRANK SHAMROCK:** Frank was the prototypical modern mixed martial artist. The Lion's Den training facility was the first true Mixed Martial Arts training academy and Frank was the first of the early fighters to tie together all the aspects necessary to succeed in MMA. Frank stressed seamless transitions from stand-up to takedown and into submissions. An extremely intelligent and tough fighter, Frank changed the way in which fighters trained. He was a fabulous fighter in his own right and though often overshadowed by his MMA Hall-of-Fame brother, Frank was and is the ultimate authority in my book and he created the Shamrock Submission Fighting system.

7. **ROYCE GRACIE:** The Gracie Family changed the face of martial arts forever and they did it using Royce as their standard bearer. He was sensational. Royce was a slightly built, 175-pound athlete who looked more like a swimmer or a tennis player, yet he beat up, submitted and generally made fools out of physical monsters and giants. Royce had the best heart in the game and for five years no one could solve the riddle that was Gracie jujitsu. The widespread inclusion of "the sprawl," perfected by Chuck Lidell, spelled the end of Gracie dominance. The Gracie approach to submissions is state-of-the-art. The world of martial arts owes this family a huge debt of gratitude—they put the "real" back into fighting.

8. **DAN HENDERSON:** Hendo is the working man's MMA artist. Dan's roots are deep in roughhouse, in-your-face Greco-Roman wrestling. Hendo was an Olympic-level Greco-Roman wrestler who discovered he could hit like a farm mule. His overhand right punch to the nose or jaw is devastating. Like Randy Couture, Dan Severn and Mark Coleman—all in the UFC hall of fame—Hendo never lost his wrestler's taste for grinding opponents down. Over the decade he fought, he continually improved. He actually was at his peak during his years with the Japanese Pride Fighting organization. Hendo had the gas tank, the pain tolerance, the skills, and the tools to accompany his shocking power.

9. **DAN "THE BEAST" SEVERN:** A true American fighter legend, Dan "The Beast" Severn had over 100 professional MMA wins, 102-19-7. He fought professionally for almost 30 years. He started his career as a wrestler at Arizona State. He held the US Collegiate National Record for pins from 1976-1992. He had a controversial loss at the Olympic Trials to the eventual Olympic Champion. Severn was the first "big league" wrestler to become involved with the fledgling UFC. He steamrolled his opponents, and his battles with Ken Shamrock were legendary. He beat the living hell out of Royce Gracie before being choked out with a triangle choke—a move that was unknown outside of jujitsu at the time.

10. **CHUCK ZITO:** Chuck is the only person on the list who is not a well-known MMA fighter. I so respect Zito's skills as a fighter that I included him on my list. I have seen him in action and as a street fighter he is as incredible. Chuck's dad was a professional welterweight boxer and Zito learned to fight at a young age. He is a classic Italian Bad Boy and was the president of the New York City Chapter of the Hells Angels. He was a terrific boxer, an avid martial artist, a professional bodyguard, and a crazed stuntman. He wound up on TV as a regular in the long running cable prison series, OZ, as well as being featured in many movies.

THE TIME FOR TALK IS OVER

Real fighters fight. Pretend fighters talk about fighting. After all the talk is talked, after all the theories are mulled over and pondered, after all the viewpoints are shared, it is time to translate abstract ideas into concrete reality. It is time to train and train hard enough and smart enough to elicit the gains we seek from our training efforts.

Training is sacred. To me, training is everything. Intense training, and effective training need to be sweaty and exhausting. Effective training purposefully pushes us past our current limits and capacities—do we really think we're going to dramatically increase our power or dramatically increase the size of our cardio gas tank without exceeding our present limits, without pushing ourselves past our current capacities? Really?

Maybe in the magical fairy tale fighting world of *Crouching Tiger, Hidden Dragon*, but in the martial fighter universe I inhabit—and have since childhood—results occur as a result of exceeding what we are currently capable of, in some manner or fashion. We get better by working harder, longer, and more often, with ever-increasing degrees of difficulty, attention and focus.

We always have a plan. Most of my students fight competitively in some format, at some level, ergo, we are always either prepping for the next fight or coming off a fight. Both situations require a game plan. I like to get my fighters thinking in terms of goals; obviously if a trainee has an upcoming BJJ match or a karate tournament, that is a goal. I have students set their goals into a timeframe and we work backwards to create an appropriate training template.

My training approach simultaneously addresses strength, explosive power, mobility, flexibility, agility and cardio conditioning. Again, in each of these categories I am 100% biased towards the fighter's unique needs. Everything we do is done with the wants, needs and desires of the true fighter in mind. In our approach, the sagittal, frontal and transverse planes of human motion are all utilized with such precision that our capacities are strengthened.

Our method pays homage to six distinct types, or kinds of training. This allegiance to a half-dozen separate disciplines enables us to build the complete fighter: explosive, powerful, lean, with tremendous strength and the type of stamina and staying power unique to the demands of fighting.

FIGHTER ATTRIBUTE DEVELOPMENT

SPEED: Kettlebell velocity, *plyometric or explosive power drills*

POWER: Grind reps, *slower rep pace*

MOBILITY: Joint drills, *rolling, shoulder and hip "opening"*

BALANCE: Bodyweight exercise, *body awareness and de-loading*

FLEXIBILITY: Pliability drills, *static and active stretching*

ENDURANCE: Cardio conditioning, *muscular endurance and pure cardio*

Any sophisticated and effective fighter training regimen must recognize the value of each of these six invaluable and indispensable fighter characteristics. Once we can identify a valued fighter characteristic, we can then devise a training modality to specifically develop that sought-after characteristic. How does the smart fighter go about getting better?

- Establish a goal
- Place the goal into a timeframe
- Create a workout template
- Work backwards to establish realistic weekly goals
- Hold yourself accountable: log sessions, log results

Once we have a goal, we can create a plan and set the plan into a timeframe. Each week we improve. Here is a hypothetical training template for a competitive fighter. This is just one potential template, every situation, fight and fighter are different, and therefore every fighter template is unique and customized. For illustrative purposes, we show you one particular method we use.

MOVING THROUGH
TIME AND SPACE...

There is nothing like being supremely athletic and being able to effortlessly move your body through time and space in precisely the manner and fashion the situation requires. If you are fighting another person, optimally you seek to impose your will; you seek to maneuver your opponent in a predetermined fashion. How can you expect to move the opponent if you lack self-mastery? Bodyweight training is used as a functionality test: if you are unable to perform the tasks, your strength-to-bodyweight ratio needs to be improved. A high level of thoracic mobility, core strength and tendon and ligament resiliency are required to perform most of the intermediate and advanced bodyweight movements.

KETTLEBELLS AS MARTIAL TOOLS

VARIED BEYOND BELIEF: Often people look at the simple kettlebell and perceive it as limited. But, the variety of movements and exercises, the number and type of protocols that can be enacted and applied using the kettlebell as the tool of choice is truly remarkable. A kettlebell, in the hands of an expert, is a mighty device, capable of providing the fighter with increased power for strikes and that unique locomotive cardio conditioning that kettlebells create.

PRISTINE TECHNIQUE KEEPS US SAFE: We stress correct kettlebell technique over and over—there is a right way and a lot of wrong ways to hoist a kettlebell. Proper technique will keep the kettlebell lifter safe, and sloppy technique will result in injury. We have a technical ideal for every kettlebell exercise. The strategy is to ingrain proper technique using light poundage; once techniques are established and understood, then we can gradually increase the payload—making sure that there is never any degradation in technique. When technique breaks down, we curtail the set. We strive to improve on all of our kettlebell techniques.

LESS CAN BE MORE: We have found that expert use of the kettlebell can provide a dramatic increase in power and strength in just a single hour, three times per week of kettlebell strength training. Unlike cardio, strength training needs to be intense and infrequent; the body needs to recover from the unusual stresses associated with strength training before strength training again. This is not to say that all other types of fighter training cannot be ongoing and continual. The benefits of strength training are optimized when we allow the body to heal, recover and grow before attacking the pulverized body parts again.

UNCONSCIOUS AWARENESS: Our method also addresses proprioception, the internal stimuli of the body's unconscious awareness in relation to the environment. To develop this sensitivity, we take advantage of our proprioceptors. This is the reason we train barefoot or with the thinnest soled shoes. Thick running shoes, for example, prevent us from rooting into the ground and degrades proprioception. Our method of "proprioceptive training" promotes incredible power-to-weight ratios.

BODYBUILDING AND FIGHTING: The bodybuilding notion of isolation exercises and training body parts as in "leg day, chest day, and back and bicep day" has zero translation to fighting. Do we isolate body parts during a fight? How often will you only use your hamstrings or triceps in a fight? The body is used all at once. As in dynamic sports, kettlebells and bodyweight movements require—at least the ones we teach—us to activate our core and use multiple limbs simultaneously.

STAND-ALONE SYSTEM: My method is a "stand alone" system that prepares fighters for the rigors of combat. As a seasoned fighter, I know all about combat fighting. As a stand-alone system for training fighters, I will contend our system offers the most in terms of time efficiency, economy of motion, operating in the transverse plane, strength, flexibility, endurance, durability, hip pop-and-lock and explosive power. All of these attributes are addressed, and all of these components are necessary for success in combat.

KETTLEBELL AND BODYWEIGHT TRAINING: THE PLANES OF MOTION

As a fighter I have come to understand and appreciate the value of thinking in terms of the "planes of motion" and devising methods by which to improve performance within each plane. Sagittal, frontal and transverse planes are all addressed, along with improving function and operation within each plane.

Most weight training exercises only address the sagittal or frontal planes, and do very little within the transverse plane—not coincidentally, this is where most athletic injuries occur. Kettlebell training addresses the planes simultaneously. We create functional strength by recruiting multiple muscle groups to perform the work. Muscle stabilizers are activated to a significant degree, performing the movements in the way we perform them.

The COG (center of gravity) changes dramatically during the explosive movements of kettlebell training. Compound, multi-joint, full range-of-motion movements strengthen the body through each of the different cardinal planes of movement and motion. We seek the recruitment of all the stabilizers and support muscles. Kettlebell training mimics real life, combat fighting, and explosive sports closer than any other type of training.

ALL THE TOOLS I NEED...

I have jump ropes and kettlebells in my studio: no treadmills, no stair-masters, elliptical trainers, or any other hamster-wheel inspired cardio machines. They are not necessary. My kettlebells, a jump rope and my bodyweight are all the tools I need to train. The other simple tools I use are primarily for additional fun and variety.

Your total fitness needs can be met with four pairs of kettlebells, a jump rope, a 6-foot pole and a pull-up bar. Throw in a sledgehammer (or two) and that's all you need. This limited number of tools and limited amount of time allotted for the acquisition of strength and power will allow you more time to spend on developing your fighting skills.

Hardstyle kettlebell training is reliant upon the alternating of tension and relaxation. Just as in sport and life, we move from static, full tension states to complete muscular relaxation. We modulate, back and forth, as the fluidity of the athletic situation demands.

TRAINING

ROUTINES

Before embarking on any of the listed training routines, it's vital to adopt solid warm-up regimens to avoid or at least lessen the severity of injury, increase your ability to move and maximize your strength and power development. Many of the movements listed below are used on a daily basis, not just by fighters and martial artists, but all of my students.

WARM-UP, MOBILITY AND FLEXIBILITY

Following you will find some of my favorite exercises for mobility and flexibility. Being able to move and having a full range of motion is critical to avoiding injury, maximization of power and application of techniques. There should be a good 15 to 20 minutes of these drills built into your workouts. Your body will thank you by responding better to the rigors that you put it through during training. You want to extend your career and augment your performance.

JUMPING ROPE

All sessions should begin with jumping rope. It's the single best aerobic activity for a fighter. The coordination between your foot movement and hands is critical to fighting. It's also a low impact Plyometric exercise.

Jumping rope gives you rhythm and teaches you how to shift your weight from foot to foot while moving. In addition to simply jumping with your feet together or shifting from one foot to the other, there are also some very challenging methods to jump rope. Double Jumps (two rotations of the rope under your feet with one jump), throwing front kicks while you jump, switching your stance front to back, moving forward and backward across the floor and mixing up all of the aforementioned. When I competed, I used to jump rope for 32 minutes straight.

All of my fighters do a warm-up routine. We conduct the warm-up with two different methods. They are either time or repetition based.

TIME BASED: 2 minutes on the rope, 30 seconds of push-ups and abs. We repeat this for 5 rounds of skipping rope and 4 rounds of the calisthenics.

REPETITION BASED: Rounds of 200 hundred skips on the rope with 25 push-ups and 30 abdominals. We perform 5 rounds on the rope to yield 1,000 skips and 4 rounds of the calisthenics garnering 100 push-ups and 120 abdominals. Now we are ready to train. This is also a great workout to do if you have limited time and space. This should never take longer than 15 minutes.

FLEXIBILITY AND MOBILITY

STANDING TWISTS WITH BO STAFF

There are six basic movements with the Bo Staff. You may use any straight stick as a substitute. For the first four, you need to maintain taut buttocks with your hips tilted forward; for the last two, a flat, arched back with straight legs.

1) NEUTRAL SPINE DRILL: Place the staff in a vertical position so that it runs parallel to your spine. Make certain that the staff is in contact with your coccyx, thoracic and the back of your head. Start in the standing position and slightly bend your knees as you pull your hips back while keeping the staff against all three points.

2) SIDE TWISTS: Set your feet about shoulder-width apart with the staff resting comfortably on your shoulders. Keeping your head straight forward, twist approximately 180 degrees to each side. 15 repetitions each side.

3) SIDE BENDS: Maintain the same position and then bend side to side. Keep the staff in line with your body. Do not break the plane. 15 repetitions each side.

4) REACH-BACKS: Keeping the staff and your feet in the same position as the previous exercises, reach upward and back with one end of the staff and low and forward with the other end. The motion is as if you were swimming the backstroke. 15 repetitions each side.

5) BENT OVER SIDE TWISTS: Now arch your low back, as if you were in a "line backer" or "second basemen" stance except that your knees are straight. Head is up and looking forward. Your upper body is parallel with the floor. Begin to twist side to side, rotating around your spine in space. 15 repetitions each side.

6) GOOD MORNINGS: Maintain the same position as previously and go down to parallel with the floor and then up to completely upright. Do 20 repetitions.

X-PRESSES & ELONGATE

Begin with your feet approximately 1 1/2 of your shoulder width apart. Cross your hands in front of you and "push" out to the front and the back as you pivot your feet toward the right side. The palms are flat and the fingers of your right hand are up while the fingers on the left are down. Shift your weight onto the front (right leg). Repeat the process to the left side as you execute deep breaths.

Repeat the movement 3 to 5 times each side.

DOOR JAM STRETCH

This stretch is a great way to reach every part of your back. However, it takes a little experimentation. Find a door jam and start with your left hand. Grip the door jam with your thumb down, your feet a little less than shoulder-width apart and your right foot slightly approximately 18 inches in front of the left. Your right foot should be almost in line with your left hand. Adjust your height and shift your hip to stretch the different areas of your back. Repeat the movement on the opposite side of your body.

CROSS STANCE SQUATS

Stand with your feet close together and your hands overlapping, palm up directly below your navel. Imagine that you have a cup of hot tea in your hands. Spilling it will burn, so you need to keep your body in balance with your nose in direct line with your navel.

Take your left foot and step deeply across and behind your right leg. Both of your feet as well as your body should be facing forward. Bend both knees until the outside of your left knee touches the outside of your right knee. Lower your weight onto the back of your left leg and *be certain to not allow either knee to touch the floor*. Then uncross your legs as you stand up and repeat the process to the other side. Do this 5 times per side.

SHIFTING HAMSTRING STRETCH

Also known as the "Karate Stretch". Stand with your feet approximately 1 1/2 shoulder-width apart and point the toes of your left foot straight forward and the toes of you right foot to the side. Your feet will make an "L". Shift your weight onto your left side by bending your left knee. Maintain a straight back and drop your body low. Flex the right foot and you will feel the stretch in your right hamstring. Place your hands out in front to maintain your balance. Shift to the other side and repeat this movement to both sides three to five times.

BRIDGES

THORACIC BRIDGES

Begin with your hands and feet on the ground, knees flexed so that your feet are almost in line with your hips, but slightly behind. If we were going to the right, post on your left hand, swing your left leg through to the opposite side as you post on your left arm being certain to keep your shoulder packed.

Reach across your body with your right arm and drive your hips toward the ceiling. Your hips should be in a horizontal position to the floor as you drive them toward the ceiling and your shoulders should be vertical. Repeat this process on the other side for 3 to 5 repetitions in both directions.

FLAT BRIDGE

Lie flat on your back and place your arms out to the side at approximately 45-degree angle. Have your knees bent and as close together as possible with your feet flat on the floor. If need be, place a foam roller, small or large ball or another object between your knees to help you create tension. Perform 10 repetitions.

Time under tension is essential. 5 to 30 second holds at the peak of the movement are recommended. When you become more flexible, "walk" your shoulders toward your heels and grab your ankles with your hand to help elevate your bridge even more.

TABLE TOP BRIDGE

Lie flat on your back and bring your feet close to your buttocks. Keep your knees bent and sit up. Place your hands a little behind your hips with your fingers facing your toes. Maintaining a neutral spine, bring your hips up as high as you are able by contracting your buttocks and tightening your core.

Done properly, your body will form a table with your legs and arms at 90 degree angles. Hold for 2, 5 or 10 seconds and then drop your bottom to the ground, touch quickly and come back up. Repeat this movement for 5 to 10 repetitions. Keep your feet, from heel to toe, planted firmly on the floor.

STRAIGHT LEG BRIDGE

Sit on the floor with your legs straight out in front of you. Sit up tall and have your hands on the floor next to your hips with your fingers facing forward. Squeeze your legs together; they will want to come apart. So you'll need to contract your inner thighs and control the motion from your hips all the way down to your metatarsals. Maintain a neutral spine as you drive your hips toward the ceiling. Your head, shoulders, hips and legs should be in a straight line at the top of the movement. Perform 20 to 40 repetitions. Vary the duration of the hold time. This bridge will tax your triceps muscles quite a bit as well.

FULL BACK BRIDGE

Lie flat on your back and bend your knees so that your heels are as close to your buttocks as possible. Invert your hands so that your palms are on the ground with your fingers point-

ing toward you and on either side of your neck. Your elbows should be pointed directly at the ceiling. Feel free to make adjustments and creep your hands and feet closer together as you drive your hips upward. To maximize the effectiveness of this bridge, as well as the others, contract your posterior chain and squeeze your rhomboids together as your hips are raised. Perform 10 to 20 repetitions with 2 to 10 second holds.

FIGURE 8S, LOW HALOS, MID HALOS & HIGH HALOS

FIGURE 8S

Standing with your feet apart, slight bend to your knees, keep your back straight and pass the Kettlebell from hand to hand in a "Figure 8" motion while going between and around your legs. There will a slight up and down motion while you move. Accomplish this by flexing your legs, almost like a shock absorber. Do 10 repetitions in each direction. I always find it best to grasp the corner of the Kettlebell handle.

LOW HALOS

Stand with your legs close together. Knees slightly flexed approximately 20 degrees. Pass the Kettlebell from hand to around your flexed knees. Maintain a straight back. Do 10 repetitions in each direction.

MID HALOS

Stand with your legs close together. Pass the Kettlebell from hand to around your waist. Maintain a straight back. Do 10 repetitions in each direction.

HIGH HALOS

Stand with your feet approximately shoulder-width apart and grasp the Kettlebell by the horns with the bottom of the bell facing upwards. Rotate the Kettlebell around your head with the bottom of the bell pausing at your chin. Try to keep the bell as close to your head as possible. Maintain a straight back. Do 10 repetitions in each direction.

There are 12 Fighting-Based Routines depicted. The first five are geared toward general strength, conditioning, mobility and flexibility for fighters out of fight camp. These routines are designed to lay the foundation and prepare the fighter's body for the rigors of a contest. Our primary focus is on the strength and flexibility development. The secondary aspect addressed is the endurance component. These workouts should be performed three times per week. No other strength training is required. Roadwork and sprints are strongly recommended.

Even though the recommended training routines are built around preparing an MMA Fighter for competition, they may easily be translated to pre-season and in-season training for combat athletes. For example, if a wrestler were using these workouts as a guideline for their strength and conditioning, they would do the pre-fight camp routines as their pre-season workouts. During the season, use the Fight Camp routines. Even the last two weeks of training may be used for an in-season wrestler.

As an in-season wrestler, I used to hit the heavy bag as part of my training regimen. There are many other workouts that I've designed that apply to combat athletes, but contained herein are some of my favorites. For more routines, access **The Kettlebell Workout Library**. This video training system has 104 workouts and a 144-page full color manual and is available on DVD or online.

Embrace the kettlebell and bodyweight techniques and reap the benefits. Treat our strength and conditioning system as an art, for it is. Once attention is paid to the execution of the techniques, you will master them and harness the power of the method. We're not "on a treadmill watching Oprah", we are fully engaged and mentally focused on our task at hand. Detachment has no place in our training method. As with fighting, we are concentrating for the duration of the session; yet another reason that this method is superior for fighters.

"PRE CAMP" RE-ESTABLISHES BASE FITNESS AND STRENGTH LEVELS

The general public might think that a fighter uses "fight camp" to get into shape. Thirty years ago that might have been the case in the traditional boxer fight camp. Nowadays fighters preparing for a fight, be it UFC-style, a boxing match, a BJJ tournament or whatever, are expected to show up to fight camp *in shape*! That way, the first four weeks of camp are not wasted getting an out-of-shape fighter into shape. Ideally, the elite competitor shows up to fight camp in-shape and healthy so that the entire fight camp can be devoted to important technical, tactical and "finishing school" techniques. So how does the serious, seasoned fighter show up to fight camp in shape?

Here are six workouts I have designed over the years specifically to gradually bring the fighter into ever-greater degrees of condition. We want to work hard enough to shape the fighter up, but we don't want to work the athlete so hard that they show up to camp beat up, worn out and injured.

These workouts are ideal if the fighter is coming off of a fight, getting back into shape, or looking to enter his first (or 100th) fight camp. Start off on day one of week one using light kettlebells powered with precise, pristine and powerful techniques. Each successive workout, each successive week we amp up the intensity ever-so-slightly; we make haste slowly but we make haste nonetheless...

HOW TO USE THESE WORKOUTS: Each workout is completely vetted as a result of years of experimentation, mixing and matching different exercises—we tried every possible combination, pacing, order and length. These workouts are assembled the way they are for a reason: don't tamper with them!

FREQUENCY: much depends on your individual "condition" entering this "pre-camp" tune-up. How in-shape or out-of-shape you are determines how frequently you will train. Regardless of your degree of fitness or unfitness, jump in light and easy; too heavy makes it too hard.

PURE POWER ROUTINE #1

This workout features more grinding power and grip strength development, for sustained grinding and controlling an opponent. We use the presses, rows, deadlifts and single-rack squats. Explosive power is developed with the plyometric squats, jump shrugs and bottoms-up cleans. Bottoms-up cleans also taxes the grip quite a bit.

While you are performing your squats, make sure that you have the proper rack position by keeping your elbows in. This will strengthen your lats and core. I also like the unilateral work in this workout. Training one side, especially when it's heavy, forces you to recruit your stabilizers and mimics real sport and combat.

When you are doing your plyometric squats, there is no rest during the set. Hit the bottom of the squat and immediately EXPLODE skyward. The less time that your feet are on the ground, the better the exercise is served. This holds true for the jump shrugs as well.

Plyometric Squats	3 sets, 10 reps
Double Kettlebell, Alternating Static Press	5 sets, 5 reps each arm
Double Kettlebell, Static Bent-Over Row	3 sets, 10 reps each arm
Single Rack Squats	3 sets, 10 reps each side
Bottoms-Up Floor Press	4 sets, 5 reps each side
Dual Kettlebell Deadlifts	5 sets, 5 reps
Sumo Squats	3 sets, 20 reps
Bottoms-Up Cleans	3 sets, 5 reps, 3-second pauses
Double Kettlebell Jump Shrugs	5 sets, 20 reps

INSTRUCTIONS: This routine is done "straight set" style, i.e. perform all three sets of plyometric squats before proceeding to the alternating static press.

FREQUENCY: Two to three times weekly with one to three days rest between sessions.

DURATION: Allow 30-60 seconds rest between sets; this routine takes 45 minutes.

STRENGTH & POWER ROUTINE #2

Again our focus is on sustained grinding strength and explosive power. This time we've added some strength-building bodyweight exercises to the mix to further strengthen our tendons and ligaments for the rigors of combat and provide balance development.

On our pull-ups, there is no "kipping" permitted. Do you punch half-way? If not, then why would you want to perform your reps half-way? While practicing your dips, keep your feet dorsiflexed and forward, as well as your chin down. This will reduce the stress on your shoulder joints. Keep your stomach taut, and work the inner and lower portions of your pectorals.

Bridging with a medicine ball on your hips will add a bit more resistance to the movement. We'll push down on the ball as you bring your hips up to add more pressure. If you touch the top of your foot to the ground on the air lunge, then perform the regression with your foot up on a step or plate instead.

The dead-start swings, push press and ground-up snatches provide INCREDIBLE explosive power. These are some of my all-time favorite explosive power exercises. Be sure to pause with the kettlebell on the ground between each of the reps for the swings and snatches. The resting position for the push press is at the top. Bring the kettlebell down and quickly EXPLODE upward.

Grinding power and grip development come in with our Dual Kettlebell Rows and Dual Bell Single Hand Deadlifts. Not to say that we don't tax our grip on the other movements. These movements also address the strength development of the rhomboids.

Your neck...people are going to want to break it, choke it, grab it and attempt to do any other amount on unimaginable things to it. Make it as strong as possible. I like do the "bite belt" exercise, because it also develops your jaw strength. Chomping down on a karate belt with 35 pounds swinging from it also makes you less susceptible to knock out.

Warm up by jumping rope for three minutes, start off slowly and gradually pick up the pace and finish fast. After jumping rope, perform the "ground-up" stretches and "Egyptians." Now let's go to work...we perform three sets of each exercise, again in "straight set" style—finish all the sets of one exercise before moving on the next exercise. Finish the three sets of bodyweight exercises and then move onto your kettlebells.

BODYWEIGHT
3 SETS OF EACH

Tactical Pull-ups	5 to 10 reps
or	
Plank Pull-ups	20 reps
Dips (weighted or bodyweight only)	15 to 20 reps
Flat Bridge with Medicine Ball	20 reps with 3-second pause
Air Lunges	5 reps each leg

KETTLEBELL

Dead-Start Swings	10 sets, 10 reps
Single Kettlebell Push Press	8 sets, 5 reps each side
Single Kettlebell Rows	3 sets, 10 reps each side
Two Kettlebell One Hand Deadlift	3 sets, 10 reps each side
Bite Belt Neck Training	3 sets, 15 to 20 reps
alternate with	
Hanging Abdominals	3 sets, 10 to 20 reps

INSTRUCTIONS: Another "straight set" style routine. Perform all of the sets of a particular move before going to the next exercise. This will also make it easier for you to increase the weight of your kettlebell during the set grouping.

FREQUENCY: Two to three times weekly with one to three days rest between sessions.

DURATION: Allow 30-60 seconds rest between sets; this routine takes 50 minutes.

"POWERDURE" FOR INTERMEDIATE TRAINEES #3

As a fighter, you not only need power, but also incredible endurance. To meet these needs, a great deal of training revolves around the "PowerDure" workouts which are comprised of both power and endurance. One of the methods to enhance the results lies in the density and intensity of the workout. Challenge yourself with the weight and only allow 30 seconds of rest between your sets. This will tax the muscular and cardiovascular systems as well as train the body to process lactic acid at a more efficient rate.

The ladder circuits increase the number of repetitions as you get deeper in the set. This helps condition the body to process lactic acid more efficiently. This method also prepares the body to deal with the adrenaline dump that occurs in a confrontation or other high stress situation.

We address the thoracic mobility essential for fighters with the scapular push-ups, bridge get-ups and bo staff. The stabilizers of your trunk, abdominals and hips are developed with the contralateral movement supplied with the side planks, single-leg deadlifts and renegade rows. Coordination and grip are built with the swing squats. This is a superior foundation routine.

Warm up by jumping rope for three minutes; increase the speed as you approach the three-minute mark. We now segue into a more advanced warm up: deck squats, side planks and scapular, or straight-arm push-ups. Perform 10 reps of the squats and side planks; 20 reps for the push-ups. Perform these three exercises for two cycles with 60 seconds rest between cycles.

Next we perform ten minutes of stretching with the bo staff and some freehand stretching. Now we are ready to work...

COMBINATION CIRCUIT #1
Swing Squats	20 reps
Single-Leg Deadlifts (soft knee)	10 reps on each side
Perform two cycles	

LADDERS
Ladder 1: Renegade Rows & Push-ups	3 sets of 1, 2, 3, 4, 5 reps
Ladder 2: Snatches	2 sets of 1, 2, 3, 4, 5, 6, 7, 8 reps, each side
Ladder 3: Single Rack Front Squats	3 sets of 1, 2, 3, 4, 5 reps each side
Ladder 4: Flat (Floor) Press	3 sets of 1, 2, 3, 4, 5 reps

Bridge get-up, three sets of 5 reps on each side

INSTRUCTIONS: During the performance of each ladder, keep your hand (or hands) on the kettlebell(s) for the full duration of the set. It's difficult, but very doable. Rest for approximately two minutes before moving to the next ladder.

FREQUENCY: Do this routine once a week or once every other week. It's very taxing. Do not do this workout on a heavy sparring day.

DURATION: This routine, with the warm-up, should take 55 minutes.

TRIPLE SETS OR GIANT SETS
FOR ADVANCED TRAINEES #4

The workout would also fall into the "PowerDure" classification. The ability to implement explosive power on multiple occasions for a prolonged period of time is critical. This is a prerequisite for a fight. There are several advanced movements in this workout, so complete concentration is required to perform the exercises properly and safely.

There is a 30 to 60 rest period allotted between the sets. If you are closer to your fight or if you are focusing more on endurance, use a lighter weight kettlebell and less rest. If you want to concentrate on more power, use heavier kettlebells and longer rest periods.

When performing the one-arm swing with either the same hand or alternating flip, all of the aspects of the one-arm swing are consistent except that you release the handle of the kettlebell so that it completes a full rotation, starting by kicking the handle of the kettlebell forward and toward the ground. Then catch the kettlebell as it completes the rotation. Tremendous concentration and hand quickness is both required and developed through this movement.

On the horizontal toss, your fingers are not involved. Grasp the kettlebell (handle up) at the sides, toss it forward and then catch the kettlebell and bring it back to your chest.

Alternating snatches and alternating cleans require timing and rotational power, both essential to power punching. The timing of your knee bend and lock with the movement of the kettlebell is critical.

On the renegade rows, make certain that your hips and shoulders maintain the same plane. Pushing the kettlebell into the floor as you apply pressure with the adjacent foot will help to stabilize the hips. On the crossing version, you lift the foot on the same side as the hand that has the kettlebell on the floor, switching which side that has the pressure on the floor. For the kettlebell push-ups, place the kettlebells on the floor so that the handles are slightly angled inward. Pull yourself down so that your chest is at least level with the kettlebell handles. These exercises recruit your core, stabilizers and strengthen the wrists.

On the 1/4-turn hop squats, a full range of motion is used to maximize the effectiveness of the movements. Explode upward with your feet leaving the ground. There is no rest during the sets; you will be moving the whole time from one squat to the next until your set is complete.

Renegade lunges require you to pull yourself deep in to the side lunge as you pivot the toes of the bent knee inward. The other leg should be as straight as possible.

Maintain a tight grip and keep your eyes on the kettlebell throughout the full movement of the towel halo. Generate the force from your hips, obliques, serratus, and shoulders.

Finish up with a chain and abdominals to end the session.

The following two workouts contain a complex. The term is applied to selecting a group of exercises, performing the allotted amount of repetitions for each exercise, then immediately moving to the next movement. Rest only when the set of three (in this instance) exercises is completed. You should use this time to stay loose, hydrate, and chalk-up.

Warm up: Jump rope for 3 to 5 minutes.

Below are several suggested stretches. There are many other flexibility increasing regimens that may be employed. I suggest mixing and matching exercises from the various available movements. Variety is important to keep your training fresh and your body continually adapting and responding to the different movements.

1 Set of Low, Middle, High Halos, & Figure 8s

Complex Combination #1: 3 sets, 5, 5 & 10 reps
Same Hand Flips, Alternating Hand Flips, Horizontal Tosses
30 sec. Break

Combination #2: 3 sets, 10 reps
Alternating Snatches, Alternating Cleans, Alternating Presses
30 sec. Break

Combination #3: 3 sets, 5, 5 & 20 reps
Cross Renegade Rows, Renegade Rows, Kettlebell Push-ups
30 sec. Break

Combination #4: 3 sets, 9, 5 & 10 reps
1/4 Turn Hop-Squats, Renegade Side Lunges, Towel Halos
30 sec. Break

Burnout:
Clean, Squat, Single Arm Press: 1 minute each side, 3 sets
Neck Exercises & Gelebart Abs

INSTRUCTIONS: 30 to 60 second rest between the rounds of triple set complexes.

FREQUENCY: Do this routine once a week or once every other week. It's very taxing. Do not do this workout on a heavy sparring day.

DURATION: This routine, with the warm-up, should take 55 minutes.

3 X 3 (4) X 4 COMPLEX #5

Another "PowerDure" workout, this one features both complexes and chains. It's now time to start focusing a little more on muscular endurance with this routine, while still building muscle. I cannot stress enough the importance of clean technique, especially as we become tired while moving at a quick pace.

This workout is to be done in succession. Do one rotation of all four groups of exercises and then repeat three or four times.

Deck Squats & Straight Arm Push-ups: 20 reps, 2 sets

1) Complex: Two-Hand Swings: 20 reps
               One-Hand Swings: 10 reps each hand
               Hand to Hand Swings: 10 reps each hand

2) Chain: Cleans: 5 reps each side
               High Pulls: 5 reps each side
               Snatch: 5 reps each side
               (Change hands & repeat)

3) Complex: Single Rack Lunges: 5 reps
               Single Rack Squats: 10 reps
               Single Rack Renegade Lunges: 5 reps
               (Change hands & repeat)

4) Complex: In-Tight Push-ups, Single Kettlebell: 10 reps
               Single Arm Push Press: 8 reps each side
               Single Arm Row: 10 reps each side
               Do all of the presses and all of the rows on one side.

INSTRUCTIONS: Do all of the exercises in group one, rest 60 seconds and then proceed to the next group. Once you have finished all four groups, repeat. If you are going heavy, do three rounds. If you are going lighter, do four complete rounds.

FREQUENCY: Mix this routine into your regimen once every other week.

DURATION: This routine, including the warm-up, should take 55 minutes.

8 TO 10 WEEK
FIGHT
CAMP

TABATA · WARRIOR
—Phil— · —Ross—
EGGS · PAIN

FIRST 3–5 WEEKS: 3 WORKOUTS
NEXT 3 WEEKS: 2 WORKOUTS
FINAL 2 WEEKS: 2 WORKOUTS

MANUFACTURED IN U.S.A.

These training routines are based on an 8- to 10-week fight camp. If you have less time, make the necessary adjustments in accordance with the time you have allotted to prepare.

THE FIRST 3 TO 5 WEEKS OF FIGHT CAMP

A classic fight camp lasts eight to ten weeks. When I prepare a fighter using my system, for the first three to five weeks, they will train three times a week using the described workouts. If fight camp is a predetermined ten weeks long, then we will work out three times a week for five weeks; if the fighter selects an eight-week long camp, we train thrice weekly for three weeks. Regardless, the last five weeks always have the same template: we cut the workout frequency back to twice a week. If you have less then eight weeks to prepare, make the necessary adjustments in accordance with the time allotted to prepare.

FIGHT CAMP PHASE 1

WARRIOR CIRCUIT: 4 X 9 WORKOUT #1

Pistols	3 sets	5 reps each side
Tactical Pull-ups	3 sets	8 to 12 reps
One-Arm Push-ups	3 sets	2 to 5 reps

The dynamics of a fight are constantly changing. Think of the Warrior Circuit as the Tabata protocol on steroids. Go full tilt for 30 seconds and get your numbers. Attempt to hit (or surpass) the number of repetitions required. Challenge yourself! Working through fatigue is largely mental and 4x9s are when, where and how we teach the mind to control the body.

Swing Squats
Hand-to-Hand Swings
Single Rack Front Squats   Right, Left, Right, Left
Snatch   Left, Right, Left, Right
Dual Kettlebell Rows (feet close)
Renegade Lunges
Dips
Plate Press, Rows, Halos
4-Way Neck (10 seconds each direction. Use a full range of motion applying counter pressure with either one hand on the side of the head or both in the front and back).

30 seconds of work, 15 seconds of rest: Four sets of nine exercises.

Cool down with forearm de-loading and foam rolling concentrated in the thoracic area.

INSTRUCTIONS: Do the bodyweight circuit for three rotations, take a one-minute break and get set for the Warrior Circuit. There is no rest during the circuit except for the 15 second break between movements. Finish the routine with a good cool down.

FREQUENCY: Mix this routine into your regimen once every other week.

DURATION: This routine, including the warm-up, should take 48-50 minutes, the non-stop circuit is 36 minutes.

TABATA: ADVANCED #2

We will combine solid muscular endurance training with an endurance blowout in this routine. After we've done our warm-ups and our strength portion of the session, it's time to go full tilt for 20 minutes with a heart-pumping, muscle-bursting, sweat-producing Tabata. Push the envelope here and hit your numbers. Make certain that you maintain proper form, so choose your kettlebell size(s) wisely.

WARM-UP:
Jump Rope: 3 minutes
Bo Staff Tension:
Above Head: 5 reps, 5 seconds each rep
Behind Back: 5 reps, 5 seconds each rep
Overhead Squat: 5 reps with full tension

CIRCUIT:
Walking Lunges & Bottoms-Up Kettlebell Push-ups: 5 laps (20 steps each leg) and 5 sets of 10 reps of the Push-ups

Bridge Get-ups: 3 reps each side, 2 sets

COMPLEX CIRCUIT: 3 SETS
Alternating Renegade Rows: 5 each side
Dive Bombers: 5 reps
Double Kettlebell Push-ups: 20 reps

TABATA: 20 seconds on, 10 seconds off, 8 rounds per exercise (20 minutes total)
2-Hand Swings
Right Hand Snatch
Left Hand Snatch
Bottoms-Up Squats
Kettlebell Thrusters

FINISH WITH 3 SETS OF THIS CIRCUIT:
Bite Belt: 10 reps to the front, and both sides
6 Position Concave Abs, 10 second hold in each variation:
1) Knees and elbows together
2) Legs straight
3) Legs and arms out straight
4) Right arm to left knee, other limbs extended
5) Left arm to right knee, other limbs extended
6) Knees and elbows together

INSTRUCTIONS: This routine has many varied components. The first section uses dynamic tension, once it is done, move on to the next circuit and then perform the two sets of the get-ups. We'll get some good power work in with the complex circuit and then it's on to the Tabata! Give yourself one or two minutes to recover and finish the three circuits.

FREQUENCY: Mix this routine into your regimen once every other week.

DURATION: This routine, including the warm-up, should take 55 to 60 minutes.

SCRAMBLED EGGS INTERMEDIATE #3

Our Scrambled Eggs circuit requires anywhere from 6 to 8 minutes to complete prior to the 1 minute of rest between sets. A high school wrestling match is 6 minutes, an MMA round is 5 minutes, and these circuits enable you to prepare yourself for constant movement for those time periods. You may find yourself in a grinding contest; conditioning and the will to win is what determines victory. This type of training prepares the body to deal with lactic acid produced during combat.

CIRCUIT: 2 sets
2 Hand Swings: 50 reps
Armbars: 10 each side
Side Press: 10 each side
Dual Kettlebell Rows (feet close): 10 reps

SCRAMBLED EGGS: 1 Kettlebell, 2 rotations

2 Hand Swings: 20 reps
Hand to Hand Swings: 10 reps each side
Snatches: 10 each side
High Pulls: 10 each side
Swing Squats: 10 reps
Waiter Press: 5 each side
Single-Leg Deadlift: 5 reps each side
Bottoms-Up Press: 5 reps each side

One Minute of Rest

ADDITIONAL MOVEMENTS:
Double Kettlebell Swings: 10 reps, 3 sets
Ladder Snatches: 8 increments
Bite Belt neck exercises

INSTRUCTIONS: Do the circuit for two rotations and then proceed on to the Scrambled Eggs circuit for two rounds. Once you have completed the circuit, hit the additional movements. For the ladder snatches, start at one rep each side and go all the way up to 8 reps on each arm without rest. Finish the routine with your neck work.

FREQUENCY: Mix this routine into your regimen once a week.

DURATION: This routine, including the warm-up, should take 55 minutes.

These training routines are based on an 8- to 10-week fight camp. If you have less time, make the necessary adjustments in accordance with the time you have allotted to prepare.

THE NEXT 3 WEEKS OF FIGHT CAMP

SCRAMBLED EGGS ADVANCED #1

Another routine from our Scrambled Eggs library, except more challenging movements are employed with both kettlebells and bodyweight.

BODYWEIGHT CIRCUIT:
Dips: 20 reps
1/2 Squats: 30 reps
Air Lunges: 5 reps each side
Dual Kettlebell Push-ups: 20 reps
Deep Squats: 20 reps
Pull-ups: 8 reps
Leap-ups: 20 reps

KETTLEBELL CIRCUIT:
Armbars, Lying Side Press, Kettlebell Pull-over
2 sets, 10 reps each side (where applicable)

SCRAMBLED EGGS CIRCUIT: 2 or 3 Rotations
Hand to Hand Swings: 10 reps
Snatches: 10 reps each side
Bottoms-Up Single Kettlebell Push-ups: 10 reps
Two-Hand Swings: (20 reps) or Single Hand Swing Flips: (10 reps)
Goblet Squat & Curl: 10 reps
Lunatic Lunge: 5 reps each side
Dual Alternating Kettlebell Rows: 8 reps each side
Get-ups: 3 reps each side
Around the Worlds: 5 reps each direction

COOL DOWN:
10 reps of Cat and Cow
Brettzles, 20 seconds each side.

INSTRUCTIONS: Do the bodyweight circuit for one rotation and then do two circuits of the armbar, lying side press and kettlebell pull-overs. Perform the Scrambled Eggs circuit for two or three rounds, depending upon your fatigue level. Finish the routine with a good cool down.

FREQUENCY: Mix this routine into your regimen once every other week.

DURATION: This routine, including the warm-up, should take 48-55 minutes.

5 ROUNDS OF PAIN #2

It's now time to "See the Devil" in our session. Generally, we do not advocate going to complete failure during your training for very good reasons, but there are times you need to push yourself to go beyond what you could do before. I call this "Seeing the Devil". What's going to happen when you "See the Devil?" Will you falter and collapse, or will you look him in the eye and spit in his face? You can't do these workouts too often or in succession, but you'll need to test yourself and prepare yourself for the inevitable devil you will face in combat.

Begin with 3 minutes on the jump rope.

MOBILITY DRILLS:
Zombie Rolls, Cross Lunge, Thoracic Bridge.

FIVE ROUNDS OF PAIN CIRCUIT:
45 second rounds, non-stop for 37 1/2 minutes. I list the recommended repetitions next to the exercise when applicable. Repeat the series 5 times.

1) Jump Rope (60 to 90 skips)
2) Get-ups (1 each side)
3) Push-ups (25-40 reps)
4) Hand to Hand Swings (20-26 or 10-13 each side)
5) Bodyweight Squats (25-40 reps)
6) Jump Rope (60 to 90 skips)
7) Dual Kettlebell Rows (15-20 reps)
8) Flat Press (20-25 reps)
9) Hanging Abdominals or Wheel of Death
10) Alternating Double Kettlebell Lunges

INSTRUCTIONS: Jump rope and perform your warm-ups with fervor, preparing your mind to put your body through a hard core, nonstop 37 1/2 minutes of pure hell. The challenge is to hit your rep numbers and keep your technique consistent.

FREQUENCY: Mix this routine into your regimen once every 10 days.

DURATION: This routine, including the warm-up, should take 48-50 minutes.

THE LAST 2 WEEKS OF FIGHT CAMP

MMA TRAINING: CONDITIONING CIRCUITS

These routines are used during the last few weeks of your fight camp, or if you're not a fighter to break up your fitness routine and hone your fighting skills. You've put in your time, you feel good and you're ready to FIGHT! You are antsy about the upcoming contest and you want to stay sharp, but not burn out. During this period, we heal up and prepare ourselves for the task ahead. We want to be loose, quick, flexible and ready to unleash hellish power on our adversary. Don't leave anything on the gym floor, save it for the cage, mat or ring. During this time, we make last minute tweaks and slight adjustments if necessary. But on the whole, you're ready to roll!

HOW OFTEN SHOULD WE DO THESE ROUTINES?

Alternate these routines every other strength and conditioning workout. You should be doing these workouts 3 to 4 times during your week. This also depends on how much you are sparring, doing your roadwork, and your drilling sessions as well as your individual striking, grappling and training. Make sure that your energy level is high and that you warm-up completely prior to every one of your workouts.

CIRCUIT # 1: 30 MINUTES

Warm-up:
Jump Rope for 6 minutes
Bo Staff: 6 Back Stretches & Shoulders
Freehand Stretches

Set the timer for two ten minute rounds of 30 Second Intervals. Move from one station to another, with no rest except for the 30 second break between rounds. Do 30 seconds of each exercise:

Heavy Bag (Punching and Kicking)
Shadow Kick Boxing (with Sprawls)
Skip Rope
Push-ups
Abs

There will be 4 rounds of each exercise for each 10-minute round.

CIRCUIT # 2: 30 MINUTES

Warm-up:
Jump Rope for 6 minutes
Bo Staff: 6 Back Stretches & Shoulders
Freehand Stretches

Set timer for two ten-minute rounds of 30 second intervals. Move from one station to another, with no rest except for the 30 second break between rounds. Do 30 seconds of each exercise:

Heavy Bag
Shadow Kick Boxing (with Sprawls)
Skipping Rope
Push-ups
Abdominals
Two-Hand Swings
Bottoms-Up Squats
Snatches (one side per round)
Double Kettlebell Rows
Jump Shrugs

There will be 2 rounds of each exercise for each 10 minute round.

1 Round may be added for additional work.

FINAL SHOT

To be a successful fighter requires a great deal of training and attributes—natural or enhanced—and a great deal of work. There are also circumstances that will dictate the feasibility of success, mediocrity or failure. The overarching factor is: what are you willing to sacrifice to become great?

How much work are you willing to put into your craft to increase your chances of being successful? Are you willing to listen to others? Are you able to recognize the proper advice? Are you willing to move outside of your comfort zone to improve your game? It's not simply working out and sparring. There are a great number of components, both physical and mental that go into forging the *Iron Will of a Champion*!

Good luck with your training and I wish you the best in your martial arts career!

Coach Phil Ross

Strength and Honor!

Fighters fight: Phil with one of his BJJ Coaches, Jay Hayes, after winning the NAGA 2010 Battle at the Beach Submission Fighting Tournament. Five Fights, Five Wins, no points scored against.

"The Kettlebell-Lover's One-Stop-Shop for Quick, Safe Gains and Fundamental Athletic Excellence..."

The kettlebell, this almost magical "gym-in-the-palm-of-your-hand", can deliver spectacular results—be it in strength, conditioning, power or movement quality. Warrior-athletes revere the kettlebell for the added resilience and hitting-power it gives them. Endurance athletes value the extreme conditioning challenge. Kyphotic desk-jockeys see salvation in the end to their back-pain and a renewed vitality. Both genders appreciate the dramatic toning and firming of butt, thighs and abs. Physical culturists embrace the total-body impact of the kettlebell's explosive moves.

The health-strength benefits of vigorous, dedicated, skilled exercise with kettlebells can indeed be off-the-charts. But note the all-important word "skill". Because without the proper know-how, the kettlebell reverts to just an iron ball with a handle—or to a misused, misunderstood tool that heaps abuse and perhaps injury on its unskilled user. Which is the reason for **Master RKC, Max Shank's** *Master the Kettlebell*…

Max Shank champions an approach to kettlebell training that emphasizes safe, sustainable gains for a long, strong and above-all healthy life. *Master the Kettlebell* accordingly presents straightforward, practical programs that allow a beginner to make steady yet dramatic progress—while providing strategies and methods for even the most accomplished athlete to up their game.

You will see immediately from the photographs illustrating the book, that Max is indeed a magnificent athletic specimen—combining a great physique with impressive strength and terrific form. Study Max—either in this book or in person—and if you replicate what you see, athletic gold awaits you. As importantly, you'll be rewarded in *Master the Kettlebell* with an absolutely fluff-free blueprint on how to develop your own high-level skills in movement, power generation and strength—using the world's single best tool for the job.

Master The Kettlebell
How to Develop High-Level Skills in Movement Power Generation and Strength—Using the World's Single Best Tool for the Job
By Max Shank, Master RKC

Book #B78 $29.95
eBook #EB78 $19.95
Paperback 8.5 x 11 • 178 pages, 216 photos

Wish I had had this book as a beginner!
"Simply put, I wish this was the book I had had when first starting out with kettlebells. So many useful photos, and seeing both Max and Beth demonstrate the exercises makes them so much easier to understand--for men and women. This book is a must-have for current or aspiring RKC or HKC instructors, or anyone who needs real, practical, and POWERFUL advice for kettlebell use.

The exercise descriptions, mobility information, and solid program design strategies are incredibly worthwhile. My advanced clients will love having a resource to reference when practicing new intermediate/advanced moves at home too. A great all around approach and one that I will be very proud to regularly reference and share."— **ADRIENNE HARVEY, Senior PCC, Winter Park, FL**

My New Go-to Book in the Gym!
"This kettlebell book is a must-have for the personal trainer, strength coach or fitness buff who is learning to use kettlebells or who has been using them for awhile and wants to refine their technique. The format is easy-to-use and the layout, design and photographs are spectacular with both Max Shank and Beth Andrews demonstrating the movements. What I found most useful is that Max has included lots of cues, tips and coaching points on the movements/lifts, mobility and programming based on his vast experience as an athlete and a coach. He gets to the point on all of the key kettlebell movements without getting bogged down in too much detail. His real-world perspective on how to assess, teach, correct and regress/progress students with the kettlebell movements is fresh and inspiring."—**LORI CROCK, RKC Team Leader, Dublin, OH**

Next Generation
"This is the kettlebell book I have been waiting on... we have seen several titles on kettlebell training that, for the most part, have been very similar in content... regardless of title, the information has been basically rehashed over and over... Max has done something very special with *Master the Kettlebell*... he's taken the information and moved it forward... not only is he bringing, in my mind, a fresh approach to our beloved system but he's also giving us so many other tools to use when developing our programs... Mobility, assessments, program design, he hits it all... the book itself is visually beautiful... the framing of the pages is such a clever way of making each page its own masterpiece... and Beth and Max are in such beautiful shape that they really convey the "potential" of Max's message... so well done..."—**DR. CHRIS HOLDER, Senior RKC, San Luis Obispo, CA**

Add a Dragon Door Kettlebell to Your Arsenal—Durable, Resilient and Perfectly Designed to Give You Years of Explosive Gains in Strength, Endurance and Power

Even a man of average initial strength can immediately start using the 16kg/35lb kettlebell for two-handed swings and quickly gravitate to one-handed swings, followed by jerks, cleans and snatches. Within a few weeks you can expect to see spectacular gains in overall strength and conditioning—and for many—significant fat loss.

Dragon Door re-introduced kettlebells to the US with the uniquely designed 35lb cast iron kettlebell—and it has remained our most popular kettlebell. Why? Let Dragon Door's own satisfied customers tell the story:

MONEY BACK GUARANTEE ONE YEAR

Our most popular kettlebell weighs 35lb (16kg)—and is the ideal size for most men to jumpstart their new cardio, conditioning and strength programs.

Excellent Quality

"Unlike other kettlebells I have used, Dragon Door is of far superior quality. You name it, Dragon Door has got it! Where other bells lack, Dragon Door kettlebells easily meet, if not exceed, what a bell is supposed to have in quality! Great balance, nice thick handle for grip strength, and a finish that won't destroy your hands when doing kettlebell exercises."
—BARRY ADAMSON, Frederick, MD

Continually Impressed

"Dragon Door never fails to impress with their quality service and products. I bought the 16kg last month and since adding it to my kettlebell 'arsenal', I am seeing huge improvement from the heavier weight. I have larger hands for a woman so the handle on the 16kg fits my hands perfectly and it feels great...This is my fifth month using kettlebells and I cannot imagine NOT using them. They have changed my life." –TRACY ANN Mangold, Combined Locks, WI

Dragon Door bells just feel better

"I purchased this 35lb bell for a friend, and as I was carrying it to him I was thinking of ways I could keep it for myself. Everything about this bell is superior to other brands. The finish is the perfect balance of smooth and rough. The handle is ample in both girth and width even for a 35 lb bell, and the shape/ dimensions make overhead work so much more comfortable. There is a clear and noticeable difference between Dragon Door bells and others. Now I am looking to replace my cheap bells with Dragon Door's. On a related note, my friend is thrilled with his bell."–RAPHAEL SYDNOR, Woodberry Forest, VA

Made for Heavy-Duty Use!

"These kettlebells are definitely made for heavy-duty use! They are heftier than they appear, and the centrifugal force generated while swinging single or two-handed requires correct form. I have read numerous online reviews of different companies who manufacture kettlebells, and it I have yet to read a negative review of the kettlebells sold by Dragon Door. I have both the 35 and 44 lbs KBs, and I expect to receive a 53 lbs KB from Dragon Door by next week. And as I gain in strength and proficiency, I will likely order the 72 lbs KB. If you like to be challenged physically and enjoy pushing yourself, then buy a Russian Kettlebell and start swinging!"
—MIKE DAVIS, Newman, CA

New Dragon Door Bells—Best Ever!

"Just received a new e-coat 16 yesterday. Perfect balance, perfect texturing, non-slip paint, and absolutely seamless."
—DANIEL FAZZARI, Carson City, NV

Dragon Door Kettlebells: The Real Deal!

"The differences between Dragon Door's authentic Russian kettlebell and the inferior one which I had purchased earlier at a local big box sports store are astounding! The Dragon Door design and quality are clearly superior, and your kettlebell just 'feels' right in my hand. There is absolutely no comparison (and yes, I returned the substandard hunk of iron to the big box store for a credit as soon as I received your kettlebell). I look forward to purchasing a heavier kettlebell from dragondoor.com as soon as I master the 16kg weight!"—STEPHEN WILLIAMS, Arlington, VA

Are You Serious About Your Training?—Then Insist On Dragon Door's Premium RKC Kettlebells

Size		Product #	Price	
4 kg	(approx. 10 lbs.) Kettlebell	#P10N	$41.75	(plus s/h)
6 kg	(approx. 14 lbs.) Kettlebell	#P10P	$54.95	(plus s/h)
8 kg	(approx. 18 lbs.) Kettlebell	#P10M	$65.95	(plus s/h)
10 kg	(approx. 22 lbs.) Kettlebell	#P10T	$71.45	(plus s/h)
12 kg	(approx. 26 lbs.) Kettlebell	#P10G	$76.95	(plus s/h)
14 kg	(approx. 31 lbs.) Kettlebell	#P10U	$87.95	(plus s/h)
16 kg	(approx. 35 lbs.) Kettlebell Narrow Handle	#P10S	$96.95	(plus s/h)
16 kg	(approx. 35 lbs.) Kettlebell	#P10A	$96.75	(plus s/h)
18 kg	(approx. 40 lbs.) Kettlebell	#P10W	$102.75	(plus s/h)
20 kg	(approx. 44 lbs.) Kettlebell	#P10H	$107.75	(plus s/h)
22 kg	(approx. 48 lbs.) Kettlebell	#P10X	$112.75	(plus s/h)
24 kg	(approx. 53 lbs.) Kettlebell	#P10B	$118.75	(plus s/h)
26 kg	(approx. 57 lbs.) Kettlebell	#P10Y	$129.99	(plus s/h)
28 kg	(approx. 62 lbs.) Kettlebell	#P10J	$142.95	(plus s/h)
30 kg	(approx. 66 lbs.) Kettlebell	#P10Z	$149.99	(plus s/h)
32 kg	(approx. 70 lbs.) Kettlebell	#P10C	$153.95	(plus s/h)
36 kg	(approx. 79 lbs.) Kettlebell	#P10Q	$179.95	(plus s/h)
40 kg	(approx. 88 lbs.) Kettlebell	#P10F	$197.95	(plus s/h)
44 kg	(approx. 97 lbs.) Kettlebell	#P10R	$241.95	(plus s/h)
48 kg	(approx. 106 lbs.) Kettlebell	#P10L	$263.95	(plus s/h)
60 kg	(approx. 132 lbs.) Kettlebell	#P10I	$329.99	(plus s/h)

US ORDERING
- Kettlebells are shipped via UPS ground service, unless otherwise requested.
- Kettlebells ranging in size from 4kg To 24kg can be shipped to P.O. boxes or military addresses via the U.S.. Postal Service, but we require physical addresses for UPS deliveries for all sizes 32kg and heavier.

Check on website or by phone for shipping charges.

ALASKA/HAWAII KETTLEBELL ORDERING
Dragon Door now ships to all 50 states, including Alaska and Hawaii, via UPS Ground. 32kg and above available for RUSH (2-day air) shipment only.

CANADIAN KETTLEBELL ORDERING
Dragon Door now accepts online, phone and mail orders for Kettlebells to Canada, using UPS Standard service. UPS Standard to Canada service is guaranteed, fully tracked ground delivery, available to every address in all of Canada's 10 provinces. Delivery time can vary between 3 to 10 business days.

24 HOURS A DAY
ORDER NOW
1·800·899·5111
www.dragondoor.com

Order Dragon Door Kettlebells online:
www.dragondoor.com/shop-by-department/kettlebells/

Customer Acclaim for Dragon Door's Bestselling 12kg/26lb Kettlebell

Converted Gym Rat....

"I have seen DRASTIC changes in EVERYWHERE on my body within a very short time. I have been working out religiously in the gym for the past 15 years. I have seen more change in JUST 1 month of kettlebell training. KB's build bridges to each muscle so your body flows together instead of having all of these great individual body parts. The WHOLE is GREAT, TIGHT and HARD. Just what every woman wants."

—Terri Campbell, Houston, TX

Best Kettlebells Available

"Okay, they cost a lot and, with the shipping costs, it's up there. However, the local kettlebells were far inferior in quality—do you want rough handles when you're swinging? And, if you order a cheaper product online, you won't even KNOW the quality until you have them. Dragon Door kettlebells are well formed, well-balanced and have no rough edges. Sometimes you just have to go with the best and these are the best!"

—Judy Taylor/ Denver, CO

Awesome tool for the toolbox!!!

"I took some time off from grappling to focus on strength using my new kettlebells... Needless to say my training partners knew something was up. My 'real' total body strength had increased dramatically and I had lost about 5 pounds of bodyfat weight. We are getting more!!!!"

—Jason Cavanaugh, Marietta, PA

More Fun Than a Dumbbell or Barbell

"Very satisfied. A lot of fun. Indestructable. Delivered quickly. Much more fun to use than dumbbells or barbells. Everytime I see the bells I pick them up and do something with them. Great!"—Sonny Ritscher, Los Angeles, CA

Beautiful Cast Iron

"The casting was so well done that the kettlebell doesn't look like a piece of exercise equipment."—Robert Collins, Cambridge, MA

Changing a 64 year old's life!

"After being very fit all my life with everything from Tae Kwon Do to rock climbing and mountain biking, I hit 60 ... had a heart valve repair and got horribly out of condition, It was difficult for me just to get up off the floor when I sat to put wood in the wood burning fireplace. In just 6 weeks with a 12 kilo kettlebell I've improved dramatically. The 'real life' strength that you develop is amazing. The difference to your 'core' is dramatic. Wish I'd discovered kbells years ago!"—Lowell Kile, Betchworth, United Kingdom

I Love My Kettlebell!

"I am really enjoying my kettlebell. When I received mine, I was so pleased with the finish and the handle. It is definitely a high quality product and when I work my strength up, I will order my next kettlebell from DragonDoor as well."—Diana Kerkis, Bentonville, AR

GREAT Piece of Equipment

"Excellent quality and finish. I'm a runner who doesn't do heavy weights; this 26 lb. KB is a great addition to my training and has made a meaningful difference, even in the first few weeks. Something about the shape INVITES you to work with it!

Highly recommended."—Matthew Cross, Stamford, CT

Maximum Results

"There is not a product around that compares to the 26 lb kettlebell. It is a health club, of its own. In my opinion anybody of any age or fitness level can achieve results. "—Jim Thoma, Shoreline, WA

The Handler

"The Kettlebell is the authority of weights. I'm 50 years old and have been working out since I was 12. I purchased the 12kg kettlebell, and at the present time used it for six different exercises. Its shape makes such a big difference; you can be creative using it to strengthen areas of your body simultaneously in one motion. In the future I will purchase the 35 kg."

—Ronald Bradley, Alpharetta, GA

Excellent Product

"I have bought two other (competitor's) kettlebells since the purchase of this product, and there's an obvious difference in quality. I am very pleased with the purchase from Dragondoor. Thanks."

—Steve Crocker, Coupeville, WA

Russian Kettlebell - 12kg (26 lbs.)

Authentic Russian kettlebell, w/rust resistant e-coat #P10G $76.95

How to Get Stronger Than Almost Anyone— And The Proven Plan to Make It Real

"Strength Rules is one of the finest books on strength I've ever read. No ifs, ands or buts. Not just 'bodyweight strength'—*strength*, period. There are a million and one strength books out there about hoisting heavy iron and screwing up your joints...usually written by coaches and athletes using steroids and other drugs. But if you want to learn how to unleash *ferocious* strength and power while also improving your health and ridding yourself of extra fat and joint pain, THIS is the book you need to own.

If you are a bodyweight master, this is the bible you will want to go back to again and again, to keep you on the straight and narrow. If you are raw beginner—Jeez, then get this book right now, *follow the rules*, and save yourself years of wasted effort! Strength Rules is as good as it gets!"
—**PAUL WADE**, author of *Convict Conditioning*

How to Be Tough as Nails— Whatever You Do, Wherever You Go, Whenever You Need it...

Want to get classically strong—in every dimension of your life— gut, heart and mind...?

In other words, do you want to be:

- **More than** just gym-strong?
- **More than** just functionally strong?
- **More than** just sport-specifically strong?
- **More than** just butt-kicker strong?
- And—certainly—**more than** just look-pretty-in-a-bodybuilding-contest strong?

Do you demand—instead—to be:

- Tensile **Strong?**
- Versatile **Strong?**
- Pound-for-Pound **Strong?**
- The Ultimate Physical **Dynamo?**
- A Mental **Powerhouse?**
- A Spiritual **Force?**
- An Emotional **Rock?**

Then welcome to **Danny's World**... the world of *Strength Rules*— where you can stand tall on a rock-solid foundation of classic strength principles...Arm-in-arm with a world leader in the modern calisthenics movement...

Then... with Danny as your constant guide, grow taller and ever-stronger—in all aspects of your life and being—with a Master Blueprint of progressive calisthenic training where the sky's the limit on your possible progress...

Do Danny's classical **Strength Rules**—and, for sure, you can own the keys to the strength kingdom...

Ignore Danny's classical **Strength Rules**—break them, twist them, lame-ass them, screw with them—then doom yourself to staying stuck in idle as a perpetual strength mediocrity...

The choice is yours!

"I have been waiting for a book to be written on strength training that I can recommend to all of my patients, and **Danny Kavadlo** has delivered with *Strength Rules*. Danny has written a stripped down approach to strength that is accessible to everyone.

He has distilled his wealth of knowledge and experience in coaching and bodyweight strength training into a program that is cohesive, scalable, and instantly applicable to all comers. He has also added a rock solid approach to nutrition and ample doses of inspirational story telling and philosophy, resulting in the gem that is *Strength Rules*.

I dare anyone to read this book and still give me an excuse why they can't strengthen their body and improve their health. No excuses. Get the book and get to work!"
—**DR. CHRISTOPHER HARDY**, author of *Strong Medicine*

However brilliant most strength books might be, 99% of them have a fatal flaw...

99% of otherwise excellent strength books focus on only one aspect of strength: how to get physically stronger through physical exercise. Health and multi-dimensional well-being is given at best a cursory nod... Nutritional advice is most often a thinly disguised pitch for a supplement line...

If you want a book that gives you the goods on full-body training, full-body health and full-body strength, then there's precious little out there... So, thank God for the advent of *Strength Rules*!

Strength Rules embodies all elements of strength—even how they work into our day-to-day existence, the highs and lows of our being, for better or for worse...

Strength Rules is dedicated to those who are down with the cause. Those who want to work hard to get strong. Who insist they deserve to build their own muscle, release their own endorphins and synthesize *their own* hormones.

Strength Rules has no interest in fly-by-night fitness fads. Classic exercises have stood the test of time for a reason. *Strength Rules* shouts a loud "just say no!" to cumbersome, complicated workout equipment. *Strength Rules* walks a path free from trendy diets, gratuitous chemical concoctions and useless gear...

Almost every strength exercise comes down to the basics. Essentially, Squat, Push and Pull. These three broad, essential movements are the granddaddies of 'em all. Throw in some Flexion, Transverse Bends and Extension, and you've got yourself the tools for a lifetime of full body strength training... That's why the exercises contained in *Strength Rules* are divided into these few, broad categories. Everything else is a variation. There is no reason to overcomplicate it.

The *Strength Rules* mission is to help anybody and everybody get in the best shape of their lives Strength Rules lays out the truth clearly and succinctly, giving you the tools you need to grow stronger and persevere in this mad world—with your head held high and your body lean and powerful...

The exercise portion of *Strength Rules* (titled ACTIONS) is split into three levels: Basic Training (Starting Out), Beast Mode (Classic Strength) and Like A Boss (Advanced Moves). Naturally, not everyone will fall 100% into one of these groups for all exercises in all categories and that's fine. In fact, it's likely that even the same individual's level will vary from move to move. That's cool; we all progress at different rates. Respect and acknowledge it. Trust your instincts.

Speaking of instincts, we are wired with them for a reason. If our instincts are wrong then that's millions of years of evolution lying to us. A large part of *Strength Rules* embraces empowerment, faith in oneself and emotional awareness. Danny believes that being honest with yourself, physically, mentally and spiritually is a magnificent (and necessary) component of true, overall strength. Yes, sometimes the truth hurts, but it must be embraced if we are ever to be fit and free. We all have the power within ourselves. Use it.

Strength Rules cries out to all body types, age groups, backgrounds and disciplines. It talks to the beginning student. It calls on the advanced practitioner, looking for new challenges. It speaks to the calisthenics enthusiast and all the hard-working personal trainers... *Strength Rules* is for *everyone* who wants to get strong—and then some...

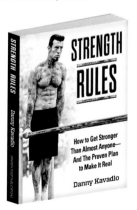

Strength Rules
How to Get Stronger Than Almost Anyone— And The Proven Plan to Make It Real
By Danny Kavadlo

Book #B84 $39.99
eBook #EB84 $9.99
Paperback 8.5 x 11
264 pages, 305 photos

C-MASS

How To Maximize Muscle Growth Using Bodyweight-Only

I s it really possible to add significant extra muscle-bulk to your frame using bodyweight exercise only? The answer, according to calisthenics guru and bestselling *Convict Conditioning* author Paul Wade, is a resounding Yes. Legendary strongmen and savvy modern bodyweight bodybuilders both, have added stacks of righteous beef to their physiques—using just the secrets Paul Wade reveals in this bible-like guide to getting as strong AND as big as you could possibly want, using nothing but your own body.

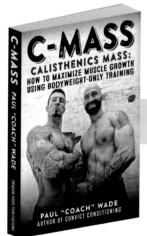

Paul Wade's trenchant, visceral style blazes with hard-won body culture insight, tactics, strategies and tips for the ultimate blueprint for getting huge naturally without free weights, machine supplements or—God forbid—steroids. With *C-Mass*, Paul Wade further cements his position as the preeminent modern authority on how to build extraordinary power and strength with bodyweight exercise only.

⬇ Get All of This When You Invest in Paul Wade's *C-Mass* Today: ⬇

C-MASS
Calisthenics Mass: How To Maximize Muscle Growth Using Bodyweight-Only Training
By Paul "Coach" Wade

Book #B75 $24.95
eBook #EB75 $9.95
Paperback 8.5 x 11 • 136 pages, 130 photos

1. Bodyweight Muscle? No Problem!

Build *phenomenal* amounts of natural muscle mass and discover how to:

- Add 20-30+ pounds of solid muscle—with perfect proportions
- Reshape your arms with 2-3 inches of gnarly beef
- Triple the size of your pecs and lats
- Thicken and harden your abdominal wall into a classic six-pack
- Throw a thick, healthy vein onto your biceps
- Generate hard, sculpted quads and hamstrin gs that would be the envy of an Olympic sprinter
- Build true "diamond" calves
- Stand head and shoulders above the next 99% of natural bodybuilders in looks, strength and power
- Boost your testosterone naturally to bull-like levels

Understand the radically different advantages you'll get from the two major types of resistance work, *nervous system* training and *muscular system* training.

If you really want to explode your muscle growth—if SIZE is your goal—you should train THIS way...

2. The Ten Commandments of Calisthenics Mass

Truly effective muscular training boils down into THESE Ten Commandments.

COMMANDMENT I: Embrace reps!

Why reps are key when you want to build massive stacks of jacked up muscle.

Understanding the biochemistry of building bigger muscles through reps...

COMMANDMENT II: Work Hard!

Want to turn from a twig into an ok tree? Why working demonically hard and employing brutal physical effort is essential to getting nasty big...

2

THE TEN COMMANDMENTS OF CALISTHENICS MASS

COMMANDMENT I: EMBRACE REPS!

MAXIMUM CHEST

C-MASS

40 C-MASS – CALISTHENICS MASS

C-MASS – CALISTHENICS MASS 41

COMMANDMENT III: Use Simple, Compound Exercises!

Why—if you want to get swole—you need to toss out complex, high-skill exercises.

Why *dynamic* exercises are generally far better than *static holds* for massive muscle building.

These are the very best dynamic exercises—for bigger bang for your muscle buck.

How to ratchet up the heat with THIS kick-ass strategy and sprout new muscle at an eye-popping rate.

COMMANDMENT IV: Limit Sets!

What it takes to trigger explosive muscle growth—and why most folk foolishly and wastefully pull their "survival trigger" way too many futile times...

Why you need to void "volume creep" at all costs when size is what you're all about.

COMMANDMENT V: Focus on Progress—and Utilize a Training Journal!

Why so few wannabe athletes ever achieve a good level of strength and muscle—let alone a *great* level—and what it really takes to succeed.

Golden tip: how to take advantage of the *windows of opportunity* your training presents you.

How to transform miniscule, incremental gains into long-range massive outcomes.

Forgot those expensive supplements! Why keeping a training log can be the missing key to success or failure in the muscle-gain biz.

COMMANDMENT VI: You Grow When You Rest. So Rest!

If you *really* wanted to improve on your last workout—add that rep, tighten up your form—how would you want to approach that workout? The answer is right here...

Ignore THIS simple, ancient, muscle-building fact—and be prepared to go on spinning your muscle-building wheels for a VERY long time...

10 secrets to optimizing the magic rest-muscle growth formula...

Why you may never even come close to your full physical potential—but how to change that....

COMMANDMENT VII: Quit Eating "Clean" the Whole Time!

Warning—Politically incorrect statement: Why, if you are trying to pack on more muscle, eating junk now and again is not only okay, it can be positively *anabolic*.

COMMANDMENT VIII: Sleep More!

How is it that prison athletes seem to gain and maintain so much dense muscle, when guys on the outside—who are taking supplements and working out in super-equipped gyms—can rarely gain muscle at all?

Discover the 3 main reasons why, sleep, the natural alternative to steroids, helps prison athletes grow so big...

COMMANDMENT IX: Train the Mind Along With the Body!

Why your mind is your most powerful supplement...

How 6 major training demons can destroy your bodybuilding dreams—and where to find the antidote...

COMMANDMENT X: Get Strong!

Understanding the relationship between the nervous system and the muscular system—and how to take full advantage of that relationship.

Why, if you wish to gain as much muscle as your genetic potential will allow, just training your *muscles* won't cut it—and what more you need to do...

The secret to mixing and matching for both growth AND strength...

3. "Coach" Wade's Bodypart Tactics

Get the best bodyweight bodybuilding techniques for 11 major body areas.

1. Quadzilla! (...and Quadzookie.)

Why the Gold Standard quad developer is squatting—and why you absolutely need to master the Big Daddy, the *one-legged squat*...

How to perform the Shrimp Squat, a wonderful quad and glute builder, which is comparable to the one-leg squat in terms of body-challenge.

Why you should employ THESE 7 jumping methods to put your quad gains through the roof...

How to perform the hyper-tough, man-making Sissy Squat—favorite of the Iron Guru, Vince Gironda—great bodybuilding ideologist of the Golden Era, and trainer of a young Mr. Schwarzenegger. He wouldn't let anyone perform barbell squats in his gym!

2. Hamstrings: Stand Sideways With Pride

Enter *Lombard's Paradox*: how and why you can successfully brutalize your hammies with calisthenics.

Why bridging is a perfect exercise for strengthening the hamstrings.

How to correctly work your hamstrings and activate your entire posterior chain.

Why THIS workout of straight bridges and hill sprints could put muscle on a pencil.

How to employ the little-known secret of the *bridge curl* to develop awesome strength and power in the your hammies.

Why explosive work is essential for fully developed hamstrings—and the best explosive exercise to make your own...

3. Softball Biceps

THIS is the best biceps exercise in the world *bar none*. But most bodybuilders never use it to build their biceps! Discover what you are missing out on and learn to do it right...

And then you can make dumbbell curls look like a redheaded stepchild with THIS superior bicep blower-upper...

Another great compound move for the biceps (and forearms) is *rope climbing*. As with all bodyweight, this can be performed progressively. Get the details here on why and how...

Despite what some trainers may ignorantly tell you, you can also perform bodyweight biceps *isolation* exercises—such as the classic (but-rarely-seen-in-gyms) *curl-up*. Pure power! If you can build one, THIS old school piece of kit will give you biceps straight from Hades.

4. Titanic Triceps

Paul Wade has *never* met a gym-trained bodybuilder who understands how the triceps work. Not one. Learn how the triceps REALLY work. This stuff is gold—pay attention. And discover the drills that are going to CRUCIFY those tris!

4. Farmer Forearms

Paul Wade wrote the definitive mini-manual of calisthenics forearm and grip training in *Convict Conditioning 2*. But HERE'S a reminder on the take-home message that the forearms are best built through THESE exercises, and you can build superhuman grip by utilizing intelligent THESE progressions.

Why crush-style grippers are a mistake and the better, safer alternative for a hand-pulping grip...

5. It's Not "Abs", It's "Midsection"

As a bodybuilder, your method should be to pick a big, tough midsection movement and work at it hard and progressively to thicken your six-pack. This work should be a cornerstone of your training, no different from pullups or squats. It's a requirement. Which movements to pick? Discover the best drills here...

And the single greatest exercise for scorching your abs in the most effective manner possible is THIS...

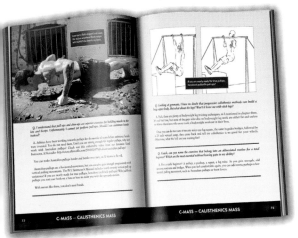

How to best train your obliques and lateral chain...

The simplest and most effective way to train your transversus...

6. Maximum Chest

The roll call of classical bodyweight chest exercises is dynamic and impressive. It's an ancient, effective, tactical buffet of super-moves. Get the list here...

THE best chest routine is THIS one...

If super-sturdy arms and shoulders mean your pecs barely get a look in when you press, then focus on THESE progressions instead—and your pecs will be burning with a welcome new pain...

Why Al Kavadlo has a lean, athletic physique, but his pecs are as thick as a bodybuilder's...

THIS could be the ultimate bodyweight drill to get thick, imposing pectoral muscles...

And here's the single finest exercise for enlarging your pec minor—yet hardly anyone has figured it out...

Why you need to master the art of deep breathing, strongman style, to truly develop a massive chest—and where to find unbeatable advice from proven champions...

7. Powerful, Healthy Shoulders

All die-hard bodybuilders need to know is that the deltoids have three heads. Here's how they work...

If you want to give any of your shoulder heads an enhanced, specialist workout, a great tactic is THIS.

How to make your lateral deltoids scream for mercy—and thank you later when you ignore their pleas...

If you *really* want to build your rear delts, THIS drill should be your number one exercise...

THESE kinds of drills can result in shoulder injury, rotator cuff tears, frozen shoulder and chronic pain—what to stick with instead...

THIS is a fantastic deltoid movement which

will swell up those cannonballs fast...

Why old school hand balancing is so great for strength, size and coordination, while surprisingly easy on the shoulders, especially as you get a bit older...

The number one go-to guy in the whole world for hand-balancing is THIS calisthenics master...

8. Ah'll be Back

THIS exercise is the finest lat-widener in the bodybuilding world and should be the absolute mainstay of your back training. This one's a no-brainer—if adding maximum torso beef as fast and efficiently as possible appeals to you...

Are you an advanced bodyweight bodybuilder? Then you may wish to add THIS to your upper-back routine. Why? Well—THIS will blitz your rear delts, scapular muscles and the lower heads of the trapezius. These are the "detail" muscles of the back, so loved by bodybuilders when they grow and thicken, resembling serpents swirling around the shoulder-blades.

Paul Wade demands that all his students begin their personal training with a brutal regime of THIS punishing drill. Why? Find out here...

Real strength monsters can try THIS. But you gotta be real powerful to survive the attempt...

Many bodybuilders think only in terms of "low back" when working the spinal muscles, but this is a mistake: find out why...

How bridging fully works all the deep tissues of the spine and bulletproofs the discs.

The single most effective bridge technique for building massive back muscle...

Why back levers performed THIS way are particularly effective in building *huge* spinal strength and thickness.

Why *inverse hyperextensions* are a superb lower-back and spine exercise which requires zero equipment.

9. Calving Season

THIS squat method will make your calves larger, way more supple, more powerful, and your ankles/Achilles' tendon will be bulletproofed like a steel cable...

Whether you are an athlete, a strength trainer or a pure bodyweight bodybuilder, your first mission should be to gradually build to THIS. Until you get there, you don't need to waste time on any specialist calf exercises.

If you DO want to add specific calf exercises to your program, then THESE are a good choice.

The calves are naturally explosive muscles, and explosive bodyweight work is very good for calf-building. So add THESE six explosive drills into your mix...

Methods like THIS are so brutal (and effective) that they can put an inch or more on stubborn calves in just weeks. If you can train like this just once a week for a few months, you better get ready to outgrow your socks...

10. TNT: Total Neck and Traps

Do bodybuilders even need to do neck work? Here's the answer...

The best neck exercises for beginners.

HERE is an elite-level technique for developing the upper trapezius muscles between the neck and shoulders..

THIS is another wonderful exercise for the traps, developing them from all angles.

By the time you can perform two sets of twenty deep, slow reps of THIS move, your traps will look like hardcore cans of beans.

If you want more neck, and filling out your collar is something you want to explore, forget those decapitation machines in the gym, or those headache-inducing head straps. The safest, most natural and most productive techniques for building a bull-nape are THESE.

4. Okay.
Now Gimme a Program

If you want to pack on muscle using bodyweight, it's no good training like a *gymnast* or a *martial artist* or a dancer or a *yoga expert*, no matter how impressive those *skill-based* practitioners might be at performing advanced calisthenics. You need a different mindset. You need to train like a bodybuilder!

Learn the essential *C-Mass* principles behind programming, so you can master your own programming...

The most important thing to understand about bodybuilding routines...

Simple programs with **minimum** complexity have THESE features

By contrast, programs with **maximum** complexity have THESE features

Why Simple Beats Complex, For THESE 3 Very Important Reasons...

When to Move up the Programming Line

If simpler, more basic routines are always the best, why do advanced bodybuilders tend to follow more complex routines? Programs with different sessions for different bodyparts, with dozens of exercises? Several points to consider...

The best reason is to move up the programming line is THIS

Fundamental Program Templates
- Total Body 1, Total Body 2
- Upper/Lower-Body Split 1, Upper/Lower-Body Split 2
- 3-Way Split 1, 3-Way Split 2
- 4-Way Split 1, 4-Way Split 1

5. Troubleshooting Muscle-Growth: The FAQ

Q. *Why bodyweight? Why can't I use weights and machines to build muscle?*

Q. *I understand that pull-ups and chin-ups are superior exercises for building muscle in the lats and biceps. Unfortunately I cannot yet perform pull-ups. Should I use assistance bands instead?*

Q. *Looking at gymnasts, I have no doubt that progressive calisthenics methods can build a huge upper body. But what about the legs? Won't it leave me with stick legs?*

Q. *Coach, can you name the exercises that belong into an abbreviated routine for a total beginner? Which are the most essential without leaving gaps in my ability?*

Q. *Big" bodyweight exercises such as push-ups and pull-ups may target the larger muscles of the body (pecs, lats, biceps, etc.), but what about the smaller muscles which are still so important to the bodybuilder? Things like forearms, the calves, the neck?*

Q. *I have been told I need to use a weighted vest on my push-ups and pull-ups if I want to get stronger and gain muscle. Is this true?*

Q. *Is bodyweight training suitable for women? Do you know of any women who achieved the "Master Steps" laid out in Convict Conditioning?*

Q. *I am very interested in gaining size—not just muscle mass, but also height. Is it possible that calisthenics can increase my height?*

Q. *You have said that moving exercises are superior to isometrics when it comes to mass gain. I am interested in getting huge shoulders, but Convict Conditioning gives several static (isometric) exercises early on in the handstand pushup chain. Can you give me any moving exercises I can use instead, to work up to handstand pushups?*

Q. *I have heard that the teenage years are the ideal age for building muscle. Is there any point in trying to build muscle after the age of forty?*

Q. *I have had some knee problems in the past; any tips for keeping my knee joints healthy so I can build more leg mass?*

Q. *I'm pretty skinny and I have always had a huge amount of trouble putting on weight—any weight, even fat. Building muscle is virtually impossible for me. What program should I be on?*

Q. *I've read in several bodybuilding magazines that I need to change my exercises frequently in order to "confuse" my muscles into growth. Is that true?*

Q. *I read in several bodybuilding magazines that I need to eat protein every 2-3 hours to have a hope in hell of growing. They also say that I need a huge amount of protein, like two grams per pound of bodyweight. Why don't your Commandments mention the need for protein?*

Q. *I have heard that whey is the "perfect" food for building muscle. Is this true?*

6. The Democratic Alternative…how to get as powerful as possible without gaining a pound

There is a whole bunch of folks who either want (or need) massive strength and power, but without the attendant muscle bulk. Competitive athletes who compete in weight limits are one example; wrestlers, MMA athletes, boxers, etc. Females are another group who, as a rule, want to get stronger when they train, but without adding much (or any) size. Some men desire steely, whip-like power but see the sheer weight of mass as non-functional—many martial artists fall into this category; perhaps Bruce Lee was the archetype.

But bodybuilders should also fall under this banner. All athletes who want to become as huge as possible need to spend some portion of their time focusing on *pure strength*. Without a high (and increasing) level of strength, it's impossible to use enough load to stress your muscles into getting bigger. This is even truer once you get past a certain basic point.

So: You want to build power like a Humvee, with the sleek lines of a classic Porsche? The following Ten Commandments have got you covered. Follow them, and we promise you *cannot* fail, even if you had trouble getting stronger in the past. Your days of weakness are done, my friend.

Enter the "Bullzelle"

There are guys who train for pure mass and want to look like bulls, and guys who only train for athleticism without mass, and are more like gazelles. Al Kavadlo has been described as a "bullzelle"—someone who trains mainly for strength, and has some muscle too, but without looking like a bulked-

up bodybuilder. And guess what? It seems like many of the new generation of athletes want to be bullzelles! With Paul Wade's C-Mass program, you'll have what you need to achieve bullzelle looks and functionality should you want it...

COMMANDMENT I: Use low reps while keeping "fresh"!

If you want to generate huge strength without building muscle, here is the precise formula...

COMMANDMENT II: Utilize Hebb's Law—drill movements as often as possible!

How pure strength training works, in a nutshell...

Why frequency—how often you train—is often so radically different for *pure strength* trainers and for bodybuilders...

Training recipe for the perfect bodybuilder—and for the perfect strength trainer...

Why training for pure strength and training to *master a skill* are virtually identical methods.

COMMANDMENT III: Master muscle synergy!

If there is a "trick" to being supremely strong, THIS is it...

As a bodybuilder, are you making this huge mistake? If you want to get super-powerful, unlearn these ideas and employ THIS strategy instead...

Another great way to learn muscular coordination and control is to explore THESE drills...

COMMANDMENT IV: Brace Yourself!

If there is a single tactic that's *guaranteed* to maximize your body-power in short order, it's bracing. *Bracing* is both an art-form and a science. Here's how to do it and why it works so well.

COMMANDMENT V: Learn old-school breath control!

If there is an instant "trick" to increasing your strength, it's *learning the art of the breath*. Learn the details here...

Why inhalation is so important for strength and how to make it work most efficiently while lifting...

How the correctly-employed, controlled, forceful exhalation activates the muscles of the trunk, core and ribcage...

COMMANDMENT VI: Train your tendons!

When the old-time strongmen talked about strength, they rarely talked about muscle power—they typically focused on the integrity of the tendons. THIS is why...

The concept of "supple strength" and how to really train the *tendons* for optimal resilience and steely, real-life strength...

Why focusing on "peak contraction" can be devastating to your long-term strength-health goals...

COMMANDMENT VII: Focus on weak links!

THIS is the essential difference between a mere *bodybuilder* and a *truly powerful human being*...

Why focusing all your attention on the biggest, strongest muscle groups is counterproductive for developing your true strength potential...

Pay extra attention to your weakest areas by including THESE 4 sets of drills as a mandatory part of your monster strength program...

COMMANDMENT VIII: Exploit Neural Facilitation!

The nervous system—like most sophisticated biological systems—possesses different sets of *gears*. Learn how to safely and effectively shift to high gear in a hurry using THESE strategies...

COMMANDMENT IX: Apply Plyometric Patterns to Hack Neural Inhibition

Why it is fatal for a bodyweight master to focus only on tension-generating techniques and what to do instead...

How very fast movements can hugely increase your strength—the light bulb analogy.

The difference between "voluntary" and "involuntary" strength—and how to work on both for greater gains...

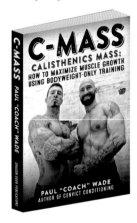

COMMANDMENT X: Master the power of the mind!

How to train the mind to make the body achieve incredible levels of strength and ferocity—as if it was tweaking on PCP...

5 fundamental ways to harness mental power and optimize your strength...

BONUS CHAPTER: 7. Supercharging Your Hormonal Profile

Why you should never, ever, ever take steroids to enhance your strength...

Hormones and muscle growth

Your *hormones* are what build your muscle. All your training is pretty secondary. You can work out hard as possible as often as possible, but if your hormonal levels aren't good, your gains will be close to nil. Learn what it takes to naturally optimize a cascade of powerful strength-generating hormones and to minimize the strength-sappers from sabotaging your gains...

Studies and simple experience have demonstrated that, far from being some esoteric practice, some men have increased their diminished total testosterone levels by *over a thousand percent*! How? Just by following a few basic rules.

What rules? Listen up. THIS is the most important bodybuilding advice anyone will ever give you.

The 6 Rules of Testosterone Building

THESE rules are the most powerful and long-lasting, for massive testosterone generation. Follow them if you want to get diesel.

The iron-clad case against steroid use and exogenous testosterone in general.

C-MASS

Calisthenics Mass: How To Maximize Muscle Growth Using Bodyweight-Only Training
By Paul "Coach" Wade

Book #B75 $24.95
eBook #EB75 $9.95
Paperback 8.5 x 11 • 136 pages, 130 photos

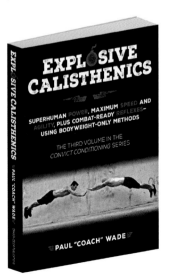

Teach your body to be the lightning-fast, explosive, acrobatic super-hunter your DNA is coded to make you…

With *Explosive Calisthenics*, **Paul Wade** challenges you to separate yourself from the herd of also-ran followers—to become a leader, survivor and winner in the physical game of life. But he doesn't just challenge and inspire you. He gives you the direct means, the secrets, the science, the wisdom, the blueprints, the proven methods and the progressions—that make success inevitable, when you supply your end in consistent, diligent, skillful application.

Now a legendary international bestseller, *Convict Conditioning* can lay claim to be the Great Instigator when it comes to the resurgence of interest in bodyweight exercise mastery.

And—while *Convict Conditioning 2* cemented Wade's position as the preeminent authority on bodyweight exercise—there is no doubt that his magisterial new accomplishment, *Explosive Calisthenics* is going to blow the doors off, all over again.

What makes *Explosive Calisthenics* so exciting—and so profound in its implications?

See, it goes back to the laws of brute survival. It's not "Only the strongest shall survive". No, it's more like: "Only the strongest, quickest, most agile, most powerful and most explosive shall survive." To be a leader and dominator and survivor in the pack, you need to be the complete package…

A vanishing percent of people who workout even attempt to unlock their body's inherent power and speed—choose to be different: reclaim your pride and dignity as a fully-realized human being by fully unleashing your true athletic capacity…

Now—for those who have the balls and the will and the fortitude to take it on—comes the next stage: *Explosive Calisthenics*. The chance not only to be strong and healthy but to ascend to the Complete Package. If you want it, then here it is…

PART I: POWER, SPEED, AGILITY
1: POWER UP! *THE NEED FOR SPEED*
Power defined—understanding the difference between strength and power…P 3

Functional speed—and the golden mean for power in athletics…P 6

Discover how to move your entire body with lightning speed… P 6

Agility defined…P 7

Discover how to efficiently alter your movement at high velocity…P 7

The difference between complex power and simple power—and what it means for athletic success…P 7

Discover how to enhance your reflexes to generate higher levels of power speed and agility…P 9

Why most gym-trained athletes lack THESE qualities—and will therefore NEVER attain true athleticism…P 10

2: EXPLOSIVE TRAINING: *FIVE KEY PRINCIPLES*…P 11

How modern Americans have become the slowest, least agile members of our species in all history—and what we can do about it…P 11

How you CAN teach your body to be the lightning-fast, explosive, acrobatic super-hunter your DNA is coded to make you…P 12

The 5 key principles for developing speed, power and agility… P 12

How to be the COMPLETE explosive machine…P 13

Why traditional box work, core training and Olympic lifting simply won't cut it—when your goal is high-level explosiveness…P 14

If you really want to build monstrous power, speed and agility in the shortest possible time—HERE is what you absolutely MUST stick with…P 18

The 6 movements you must master—for the ultimate in hardcore explosiveness…P 19

The true essence of calisthenics mastery lies here—and only here…P 19

3: HOW TO USE THIS BOOK: *CORE CONCEPTS AND ANSWERS*…P 23

Do you need to learn the Explosive 6 in any particular order?…P 26

Do you have to start with Step 1?…P 27

How to train short-distance speed…P 32

Mastery of progressive calisthenics is like

building an arsenal-full of weapons for your physical transformation. The Power Jump and Power Pushup will set up your foundation by supercharging your nervous system, ramping up your reflexes and amping your speed and power.

Expect to be remarkably and resiliently strengthened in your bones, joints, tissues and muscles—over the entire body.

In other words: hard, dedicated work on just the Power Jump and the Power Pushup alone can turn a slow, clumsy Joe Average into a lightning-powered cyborg…

PART II: THE EXPLOSIVE SIX
4: POWER JUMPS: *ADVANCED LEG SPRING*… P 37

If you really want to become explosive, then the legs are the source of it all—and the best way to train the legs is with progressive power jumps. Here is the 10-step blueprint for achieving ultimate leg power…

Understanding the importance of developing springy legs…P 37

Deconstructing the power jumps…P 38

How to develop the crucial skills of launching, tucking and landing…P 38—40

How to take advantage of *Myotatic* Rebound—to correctly absorb and redirect force…

How to correctly block when you jump…P 41

Do you need Plyo boxes?…P 43

Step One: Straight Hop—Performance, X-Ray, Regressions, Progressions…P 44

Step Two: Squat Jump—Performance,

X-Ray, Regressions, Progressions…P 46

Step Three: Vertical Leap—Performance, X-Ray, Regressions, Progressions…P 48

Step Four: Block Jump—Performance, X-Ray, Regressions, Progressions…P 50

How to develop the ability to transfer force in dramatic fashion…P 50

Step Five: Butt-Kick Jump—Performance, X-Ray, Regressions, Progressions…P 52

Step Six: Slap Tuck Jump—Performance, X-Ray, Regressions, Progressions…P 54

Step Seven: Tuck Jump—Performance, X-Ray, Regressions, Progressions…P 56

Confers some serious explosive power to the lower body—and is a perquisite for becoming really fast…P 56

Step Eight: Catch Tuck Jump—Performance, X-Ray, Regressions, Progressions…P 58

Step Nine: Thread Jump—Performance, X-Ray, Regressions, Progressions…P 60

Master Step: Suicide Jump—Performance, X-Ray…P 62

The ultimate tucking drill—once you master this drill, kip ups, front flips and back flips will come much easier than you ever imagined…P 62

Going Beyond…P 64

Reverse Suicide Jump…P64

Small Space Drills—3 useful speed and power techniques…P 69

Cossacks—for great supple strength and balance…P 69

Wide-to-Close Pop-Ups…P 70

— EXPLOSIVE CALISTHENICS —

5: POWER PUSHUPS: *STRENGTH BECOMES POWER*…P 73

To round out a basic power training regime, you need to pair jumps with a movement chain which performs a similar job for the upper-body and arms. The best drills for these are power push ups. Here is the 10-step blueprint for becoming an upper-body cyborg…

How to get arms like freaking jackhammers…P 73

How to skyrocket pour power levels, maximize your speed and add slabs of righteous beef to you torso and guns…P 73

How to develop upper-body survival-power—for more effective punching, blocking, throwing and pushing…P 73

How speed-power training trains the nervous system and joints to handle greater loads…P 73

The more power you have in your arms, chest and shoulders, the stronger they become. And the stronger they become, the harder you can work them and the bigger they get…P 73

Gives you an extra edge in strength AND size…P 73

Why the best way is the natural way…P 74

Deconstructing Power Pushups…P 74

Correct elbow positioning and where to place your hands (crucial)—to spring back with optimal power…P 74

Why cheating with the Earthworm will only rob you—if freakish strength gains are your goal…P 76

How to apply the Myotatic Rebound effect to maximal advantage in your power pushups…P 78

The Power Pushup Chain…P 79

Step One: Incline Pop-Up—Performance, X-Ray, Regressions, Progressions…P 80

A perfect way to gently condition the shoulders, elbows and wrists for the harder work to come

Step Two: Kneeling Push-Off—Performance, X-Ray, Regressions, Progressions…P 82

How to turn your strength into power—and an exceptional way to build your punching force…P 82

Step Three: Pop-Up—Performance, X-Ray, Regressions, Progressions…P 84

A nearly magical preliminary exercise to get better at clap pushups.

Step Four: Clap Pushup—Performance, X-Ray, Regressions, Progressions…P 86

How the clap pushup builds exceptional levels of torso power and quick hands, whilst toughening the arms and shoulders—invaluable for boxers, martial artists and football players.

Step Five: Chest-Strike Pushup—Performance, X-Ray, Regressions, Progressions…P 88

Step Six: Hip-Strike Pushup—Performance, X-Ray, Regressions, Progressions…P 90

A killer bridging exercise between clapping in front of the body and clapping behind.

Step Seven: Convict Pushup—Performance, X-Ray, Regressions, Progressions…P 92

Step Eight: Half-Super—Performance, X-Ray, Regressions, Progressions…P 94

Builds high levels of pure shoulder speed—excellent for all martial artists.

Step Nine: Full Body Pop-Up—Performance, X-Ray, Regressions, Progressions…P 96

Master Step: The Superman—Performance, X-Ray…P 98

A wicked, wicked move that works the whole body—both anterior and posterior chains.

Get upper-body pushing muscles that are king-fu powerful and robust as a gorilla's…P 98

If God had handed us a "perfect" explosive upper-body exercise, it might be this…P 98

Going Beyond…P 100

The Aztec Pushup…P 101

The Crossing Aztec Pushup… P 102

The One-Arm Clapping Pushup…P 103

Small Space Drills…P104

The Push Get-Up…P 104

Round-the-Clock Pushups…P 105

360 Jump…P 106

Fast feet and hands go together like biscuits and gravy—here's how to make it happen.

6: THE KIP-UP: *KUNG FU BODY SPEED*…P 109

The mesmerizing Kip-Up is the most explosive way of getting up off your back—and is a surprisingly useful skill to possess. Learn how here…P 109

Deconstructing Kip-Ups…P 110

The Roll-Up, Hand Positioning, the Kick and the Rotation…P 112

Step One: Rolling Sit-Up—Performance, X-Ray, Regressions, Progressions…P 114

A fantastic conditioning exercise, which strengthens the midsection, hips and back…P 114

Step Two: Rolling Squat—Performance, X-Ray, Regressions, Progressions…P 116

How to generate forward momentum.

Step Three: Shoulder Pop—Performance, X-Ray, Regressions, Progressions…P 118

Strengthens and conditions the wrists and shoulders for the task of explosively pushing the body up.

Step Four: Bridge Kip—Performance, X-Ray, Regressions, Progressions…P 120

Learn how to generate enough lower body power to throw the head, shoulders and upper back off the floor.

Step Five: Butt Kip—Performance, X-Ray, Regressions, Progressions…P 122

Step Six: Half Kip—Performance, X-Ray, Regressions, Progressions…P 124

Step Seven: Kip-Up—Performance, X-Ray, Regressions, Progressions…P 126

Impossible without an explosive waist, super-fast legs and the total-body ability of a panther—which you will OWN when you master step seven…

Step Eight: Straight Leg Kip-Up—Performance, X-Ray, Regressions, Progressions…P 128

Step Nine: Wushu Kip-Up—Performance, X-Ray, Regressions, Progressions…P 130

Master Step: No-Hands Kip-Up—Performance, X-Ray, Regressions, Progressions…P 132

If there is a more impressive—or explosive—way to power up off the floor, then humans haven't invented it yet…

Master this advanced drill and your total-body speed and agility will start to bust off the charts…P 132

Going Beyond—Roll Kip, Head Kip and Ditang Breakfall…P 134—136

Small Space Drills…P 137

Bridge Push-Offs, Sitting Kips and prone Kips…P 137—139

7: THE FRONT FLIP: *LIGHTNING MOVEMENT SKILLS*…P 141

The Front Flip is THE explosive exercise par excellence—it is the "super-drill" for any athlete wanting more speed, agility and power.

Discover how to attain this iconic test of power and agility—requiring your entire body, from toes to neck, to be whip-like explosive…P 141

— EXPLOSIVE CALISTHENICS —

"Coach Wade saved the best for last! *Explosive Calisthenics* is the book all diehard **Convict Conditioning** fans have been waiting for. There has never been anything like it until now!

With his trademark blend of old-school philosophy, hard-earned wisdom and in-your-face humor, Coach expands his infamous system of progressive bodyweight programming to break down the most coveted explosive moves, including the back flip, kip-up and muscle-up. If you want to know how far you can go training with just your own bodyweight, you owe it to yourself to get this book!"**–Al Kavadlo**, author, *Stretching Your Boundaries*

Deconstructing Front Flips…P 142

Run-Up, Take-Off, Unfurl, landing…P 142—143

The Front Flip Chain…P 144

Step One: Shoulder Roll—Performance, X-Ray, Regressions, Progressions…P 146

Step Two: Press Roll—Performance, X-Ray, Regressions, Progressions…P 148

Step Three: Jump Roll—Performance, X-Ray, Regressions, Progressions…P 150

Step Four: Handstand Roll—Performance, X-Ray, Regressions, Progressions…P 152

Step Five: Backdrop Handspring—Performance, X-Ray, Regressions, Progressions…P 154

Step Six: Front Handspring—Performance, X-Ray, Regressions, Progressions…P 156

A phenomenal explosive drill in its own right…

Step Seven: Flyspring—Performance, X-Ray, Regressions, Progressions…P 158

Step Eight: Back Drop Flip—Performance, X-Ray, Regressions, Progressions…P 160

Step Nine: Running Front Flip—Performance, X-Ray, Regressions, Progressions…P 162

Master Step: Front Flip—Performance, X-Ray…P 164

Going Beyond…P 166

The Round-Off and the Cartwheel…P 166—167

Small Space Drills…P 170

Kojaks, Thruster and Unilateral Jump…P 170—172

8: THE BACK FLIP: ULTIMATE AGILITY…P 175

The Back Flip is the most archetypal acrobatic feat—displaying integrated mastery of some of the most fundamental traits required for total explosive strength.

If you want to be a contender for the power crown, then you have to get to own the Back Flip—which defines true agility…

Discover how to develop a super-quick jump, a massive hip snap, a powerful, agile waist and spine—and an upper body that can generate higher levels of responsive force like lightning…

Simply put, this is the single greatest test of explosive power, true speed and agility found in nature. Here is how to pass the test…

Deconstructing the Back Flip…P 176

General tips for the many skills needed to master the Back Flip…P 176

5 key exercises to strengthen you arms and shoulders…P 178

How to achieve a powerful Tuck…P 179

How to use the Depth Jump to further condition your joints…P 179

The Back Flip Chain…P 180

THIS is the most important consideration to have in place for finally achieving the Back Flip…P 180

Step One: Rear Shoulder Roll—Performance, X-Ray, Regressions, Progressions…P 182

Step Two: Rear Press Roll—Performance, X-Ray, Regressions, Progressions…P 184

Step Three: Bridge Kick Over—Performance, X-Ray, Regressions, Progressions…P 186

A great antidote to fear of the Back Handspring

Step Four: Side Macaco—Performance, X-Ray, Regressions, Progressions…P 188

Step Five: Back Macaco—Performance, X-Ray, Regressions, Progressions…P 190

Step Six: Monkey Flip—Performance, X-Ray, Regressions, Progressions…P 192

Step Seven: Back Handspring—Performance, X-Ray, Regressions, Progressions…P 194

Step Eight: One-Arm Back Handspring—Performance, X-Ray, Regressions, Progressions…P 196

Step Nine: Four Point Back Flip—Performance, X-Ray, Regressions, Progressions…P 198

Master Step: Back Flip—Performance, X-Ray…P 200

Going Beyond…P 202

Small Space Drills…P 205

One-Arm Wall Push-Aways (great exercise for powerful, bulletproof elbows)…P 205

Donkey Kick and Scissors Jump…P 206

9: THE MUSCLE-UP: OPTIMAL EXPLOSIVE STRENGTH…P 209

If ever one popular strength exercise qualified as a "complete" feat, it would probably be the mighty Muscle-Up—one of the most jealously-admired skills in all of bodyweight training…

The Muscle-Up requires a very explosive pull, plus a push—so works almost the entire upper-body; the back and biceps pull, while the chest, triceps and shoulders push. Your grip needs to be insanely strong, your stomach crafted out of steel and you require a highly athletic posterior chain.

Discover the complete blueprint for achieving the planet's hottest bodyweight move…

Learn how to achieve the elusive, total-body-sync, X factor the Muscle-Up requires—and build insane explosive power in a highly compressed time frame…

Deconstructing the Muscle-Up…P 211—214

The Muscle-Up Chain…P 217

Step One: Swing Kip—Performance, X-Ray, Regressions, Progres-

"*Explosive Calisthenics* by Paul 'Coach' Wade is a masterfully constructed roadmap for the attainment of power, functional speed, and agility. The book is extreme in that only a small percentage of the population would be able or willing to fully take the challenge, but at the same time, brilliant in that the path proceeds methodically and progressively from relatively simple to extremely advanced, allowing a discretionary endpoint for each individual.

The book is also refreshingly raw. The exercises are all done using only bodyweight and little in the way of equipment. There are only five moves to master and yet each is a proverbial double-edge sword—at the same time dangerous yet potentially transformative.

Take this on and I doubt you will ever again be satisfied with the mundane bench press or the other exercise machines found in the typical gym."**–Patrick Roth, M.D.**, author of *The End of Back Pain: Access Your Hidden Core to Heal Your Body*, Chairman of Neurosurgery at Hackensack University Medical Center and the director of its neurosurgical residency training program.

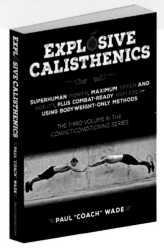

Explosive Calisthenics
Superhuman Power, Maximum Speed and Agility, Plus Combat-Ready Reflexes— Using Bodyweight-Only Methods
By Paul "Coach" Wade

Book #B80 $39.95
eBook #EB80 $19.95
Paperback 8.5 x 11 • 392 pages, 775 photos

Al Kavadlo's Progressive Plan for Primal Body Power

How to Build Explosive Strength and a Magnificent Physique—Using Bodyweight Exercise Only

What is more satisfying than owning a primally powerful, functionally forceful and brute-strong body? A body that packs a punch. A body that commands attention with its etched physique, coiled muscle and proud confidence...A body that can PERFORM at the highest levels of physical accomplishment...

Well, both Al Kavadlo—the author of *Pushing the Limits!*—and his brother Danny, are supreme testaments to the primal power of body culture done the old-school, ancient way—bare-handed, with your body only.

The brothers Kavadlo walk the bodyweight talk—and then some. The proof is evident on every page of *Pushing the Limits!*

Your body is your temple. Protect and strengthen your temple by modeling the methods of the exercise masters. Al Kavadlo has modeled the masters and has the "temple" to show for it. Follow Al's progressive plan for primal body power within the pages of *Pushing the Limits!*—follow in the footsteps of the great bodyweight exercise masters—and you too can build the explosive strength and possess the magnificent physique you deserve.

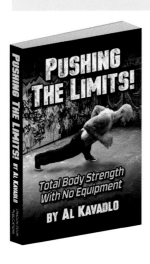

Pushing the Limits!
Total Body Strength With No Equipment
By Al Kavadlo

Book #B69 $39.95
eBook # EB69 $19.95
Paperback 8.5 x 11
224 pages • 240 photos

Reader Reviews of Pushing the Limits submitted on DragonDoor.

Time to work smart hard!

"I'm a physical therapist in orthopedics with all the frame wear and tear of a lifter. I use Al's stuff for myself and for patients and always get good outcomes. On my field there are those that make it happen, those that watch it happen, and those that dash in afterwards and ask "Hey, what just happened?" Grab a copy of Al's book. Make it happen."
—GARRETT MCELFRESH, PT, Milwaukee, WI

Al you did it again!

"I'm a doctor that uses functional rehab to get my patients better. This book has helped so much with all the great pics and showing and explaining what and why they are doing these exercises. Also when I get down and show them myself they can see that it is totally achievable! If you are wavering on getting this book, get it! I promise you won't regret it!

From a functional stand point Al, Danny, and Paul are spot on! I've seen and experienced "miracles" from doing these workouts! I have had a bad shoulder, low back, and hyperextended both knees in college football and was told I needed multiple surgeries and was always going to have pain..... WRONG! I am completely pain free and thank these hard working guys for everything they do! I can't wait to see what's next!" —DR. ROB BALZA, Cincinnati, OH

One of the best fitness books I have purchased!

"I recommend this book to anyone who enjoys being active. No matter what sport or training regimen you are currently following, Al's book has something for everyone. Novices and advanced practitioners alike, will find detailed movements that help increase their strength, mobility, and flexibility. Great read with beautiful photography." —LANCE PARVIN, Las Vegas, NV

"I LOVE this freaking Book!!! Every time you put out a new book it becomes my NEW favorite and my inspiration! I love the blend of strength, power, health and overall athleticism in this book! This book covers the BIG picture of training for ALL aspects of human performance.

I will use it with my athletes, with the adults I train, in my own training and absolutely these books will be the books I share with my kids. This stuff reminds me of the old school *Strength & Health Magazine*, I'm fired UP!"—ZACH EVEN-ESH, author of *The Encyclopedia of Underground Strength and Conditioning*

"This is the book I wish I had when I first started working out. Knowing Al's secrets and various progressions would have saved me years of wasted time, frustration and injuries. The variations of The Big Three and progressions Al lays out will keep you busy for years."—JASON FERRUGGIA

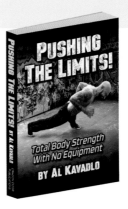

Pushing the Limits!
Total Body Strength With No Equipment
By Al Kavadlo

Book #B69 $39.95
eBook # EB69 $19.95
Paperback 8.5 x 11
224 pages • 240 photos

Sample Spreads From The Interior of *Stretching Your Boundaries*

—TABLE OF CONTENTS —

Foreword by Elliott Hulse

PART ONE- Stretch Manifesto
- ➡ Stretching For Strength 1
- ➡ Taking Your Medicine. 9
- ➡ Kid Stuff 15
- ➡ Mobility Matters. 21
- ➡ Breath is Life 29

PART TWO - The Stretches
- ➡ Preface. 39
- ➡ Dynamics. 41
- ➡ Standing Statics. 49
- ➡ Grounded Statics. 95

PART THREE - Programming and Sample Routines
- ➡ Standards of Practice 153
- ➡ On Mats 161
- ➡ Symmetry 163
- ➡ Hypothetical Training Splits 171
- ➡ Sample Routines 177

Stretching and Flexibility Secrets To Help Unlock Your Body—Be More Mobile, More Athletic, More Resilient And Far Stronger...

"The ultimate bodyweight mobility manual is here! Al Kavadlo's previous two Dragon Door books, *Raising the Bar* and *Pushing the Limits,* are the most valuable bodyweight strength training manuals in the world. But strength without mobility is meaningless. Al has used his many years of training and coaching to fuse bodyweight disciplines such as yoga, martial arts, rehabilitative therapy and bar athletics into the ultimate calisthenics stretching compendium. *Stretching your Boundaries* belongs on the shelf of any serious athlete—it's bodyweight mobility dynamite!"

—"COACH" PAUL WADE, author of *Convict Conditioning*

"In this book, Al invites you to take a deeper look at the often overlooked, and sometimes demonized, ancient practice of static stretching. He wrestles with many of the questions, dogmas and flat out lies about stretching that have plagued the fitness practitioner for at least the last decade. And finally he gives you a practical guide to static stretching that will improve your movement, performance, breathing and life. In *Stretching Your Boundaries,* you'll sense Al's deep understanding and love for the human body. Thank you Al, for helping to bring awareness to perhaps the most important aspect of physical education and fitness."

—ELLIOTT HULSE, creator of the *Grow Stronger* method

"An absolutely masterful follow up to *Raising The Bar* and *Pushing The Limits,* Stretching Your Boundaries really completes the picture. Both easy to understand and fully applicable, Al's integration of traditional flexibility techniques with his own unique spin makes this a must have. The explanation of how each stretch will benefit your calisthenics practice is brilliant. Not only stunning in its color and design, this book also gives you the true feeling of New York City, both gritty and euphoric, much like Al's personality."

—MIKE FITCH, creator of Global Bodyweight Training

"Stretching Your Boundaries is a terrific resource that will unlock your joints so you can build more muscle, strength and athleticism. Al's passion for human performance radiates in this beautifully constructed book. Whether you're stiff as a board, or an elite gymnast, this book outlines the progressions to take your body and performance to a new level."

—CHAD WATERBURY, M.S., author of *Huge in a Hurry*

"Al Kavadlo has done it again! He's created yet another incredible resource that I wish I had twenty years ago. Finding great material on flexibility training that actually enhances your strength is like trying to find a needle in a haystack. But look no further, because *Stretching Your Boundaries* is exactly what you need."

—JASON FERRUGGIA, Strength Coach

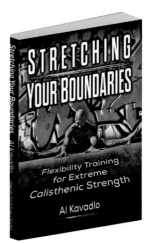

Stretching Your Boundaries
Flexibility Training for Extreme Calisthenic Strength
By Al Kavadlo

Book #B73 $39.95
eBook # EB73 $19.95
Paperback 8.5 x 11
214 pages • 235 photos

How Do YOU Stack Up Against These 6 Signs of a TRUE Physical Specimen?

According to Paul Wade's Convict Conditioning you earn the right to call yourself a 'true physical specimen' if you can perform the following:

1. **AT LEAST one set of 5 one-arm pushups each side—** with the ELITE goal of 100 sets each side

2. **AT LEAST one set of 5 one-leg squats each side—** with the ELITE goal of 2 sets of 50 each side

3. **AT LEAST a single one-arm pullup each side—** with the ELITE goal of 2 sets of 6 each side

4. **AT LEAST one set of 5 hanging straight leg raises—** with the ELITE goal of 2 sets of 30

5. **AT LEAST one stand-to-stand bridge—** with the ELITE goal of 2 sets of 30

Well, how DO you stack up?

Chances are that whatever athletic level you have achieved, there are some serious gaps in your OVERALL strength program. Gaps that stop you short of being able to claim status as a truly accomplished strength athlete.

The good news is that—in *Convict Conditioning*—Paul Wade has laid out a brilliant 6-set system of 10 progressions which allows you to master these elite levels.

And you could be starting at almost any age and in almost in any condition...

Paul Wade has given you the keys—ALL the keys you'll ever need— that will open door, after door, after door for you in your quest for supreme physical excellence. Yes, it will be the hardest work you'll ever have to do. And yes, 97% of those who pick up *Convict Conditioning*, frankly, won't have the guts and the fortitude to make it. But if you make it even half-way through **Paul's Progressions**, you'll be stronger than almost anyone you encounter. Ever.

Here's just a small taste of what you'll get with *Convict Conditioning*:

Can you meet these 5 benchmarks of the *truly* powerful?... Page 1

The nature and the art of real strength... Page 2

Why mastery of *progressive calisthenics* is the ultimate secret for building maximum raw strength... Page 2

A dozen one-arm handstand pushups without support—anyone? Anyone?... Page 3

How to rank in a powerlifting championship—*without ever training with weights*... Page 4

———

Calisthenics as a hardcore strength training technology... Page 9

Spartan "300" calisthenics at the Battle of Thermopolylae... Page 10

How to cultivate the perfect body—the Greek and Roman way... Page 10

———

The difference between "old school" and "new school" calisthenics... Page 15

The role of prisons in preserving the older systems... Page 16

Strength training as a primary survival strategy... Page 16

———

The 6 basic benefits of bodyweight training... Pages 22–27

Why calisthenics are the *ultimate* in functional training... Page 23

The value of cultivating *self-movement*—rather than *object-movement*... Page 23

The *real* source of strength—it's not your *muscles*... Page 24

One crucial reason why a lot of convicts deliberately avoid weight-training... Page 24

How to progressively strengthen your joints over a lifetime—and even heal old joint injuries... Page 25

Why "authentic" exercises like pullups are so perfect for strength and power development... Page 25

Bodyweight training for quick physique perfection... Page 26

———

How to normalize and regulate your body fat levels—with bodyweight training only... Page 27

Why weight-training and the psychology of overeating go hand in hand... Page 27

———

The best approach for rapidly strengthening your whole body is this... Page 30

This is the most important and revolutionary feature of *Convict Conditioning*.... Page 33

A jealously-guarded system for going from puny to powerful—when your life may depend on the speed of your results... Page 33

———

The 6 "Ultimate" Master Steps—only a handful of athletes in the whole world can correctly perform them all. Can you?... Page 33

How to Forge Armor-Plated Pecs and Steel Triceps... Page 41

Why the pushup is the *ultimate* upper body exercise—and better than the bench press... Page 41

How to effectively bulletproof the vulnerable rotator cuff muscles... Page 42

Observe these 6 important rules for power-packed pushups... Page 42

How basketballs, baseballs and *kissing-the-baby* all translate into greater strength gains... Page 44

How to guarantee steel rod fingers... Page 45

Do you make this stupid mistake with your push ups? This is wrong, wrong, wrong!... Page 45

How to achieve 100 consecutive one-arm pushups each side... Page 64

Going Beyond the One-Arm Pushup... Pages 68–74

Going up!— how to build elevator-cable thighs... Page 75

Where the *real* strength of an athlete lies... Page 75

Most athletic movements rely largely on this attribute... Page 76

The first thing to go as an athlete begins to age—and what you MUST protect... Page 76

THE best way to develop truly powerful, athletic legs... Page 77

The phenomenon of *Lombard's Paradox*—and it contributes to power-er-packed thighs... Page 78

Why bodyweight squats blow barbell squats away... Page 79

The enormous benefits of mastering the one-leg squat... Page 80

15 secrets to impeccable squatting—for greater power and strength... Pages 81–82

Transform skinny legs into pillars of power, complete with steel cord quads, rock-hard glutes and thick, shapely calves... Page 102

How to achieve one hundred perfect consecutive one-leg squats on each leg... Page 102

Going Beyond the One-Leg Squat... Pages 106–112

How to add conditioning, speed, agility and endurance to legs that are already awesome.... Page 107

How to construct a barn door back—and walk with loaded guns... Page 113

Why our culture has failed to give the pullup the respect and attention it deserves... Page 113

Benefits of the pullup—king of back exercises... Page 114

The dormant superpower for muscle growth waiting to be released if you only do this... Page 114

Why pullups are the single best exer-

cise for building melon-sized biceps... Page 115

Why the pullup is THE safest upper back exercise... Page 115

The single most important factor to consider for your grip choice... Page 118

How to earn lats that look like wings and an upper back sprouting muscles like coiled pythons... Page 138

How to be strong enough to rip a body-builder's arm off in an arm wrestling match... Page 138

How to take a trip to hell—and steal a Satanic six-pack... Page 149

The 5 absolute truths that define a genuine six-pack from hell... Page 150

This is the REAL way to gain a six-pack from hell... Page 152

3 big reasons why—in prisons—leg raises have always been much more popular than sit-ups... Page 152

Why the hanging leg raise is the greatest single abdominal exercise known to man... Page 153

10 waist training secrets to help you master the hanging leg raise... Pages 154–155

How to correctly perform the greatest all-round midsection exercise in existence... Page 174

Going beyond the hanging straight leg raise... Page 178

Setting your sights on the most powerful midsection exercise possible—the V raise.... Page 178

How to develop abdominal muscles with enormous contractile power—and iron hip strength... Page 178

How to combat-proof your spine... Page 185

Why the bridge is the most important strength-building exercise in the world... Page 185

How to train your spine—as if your life depended on it... Page 185

Why you should sell your barbell set and buy a cushioned mat instead... Page 188

How to absorb punitive strikes against your spine—and bounce back smiling... Page 188

Why lower back pain is the foremost plague of athletes the world over... Page 189

Why bridging is the *ultimate* exercise for the spinal muscles... Page 189

The 4 signs of the perfect bridge... Page 191

How to master the bridge... Page 192

How to own a spine that feels like a steel whip... Page 193

How the bridging series will grant you an incredible combination of strength paired with flexibility... Page 216

Why bridging stands alone as a *total* training method that facilitates development in practically every area of fitness and health... Page 216

How to look exceptionally masculine—with broad, etched, and powerful shoulders... Page 219

Those vulnerable shoulders—why they ache and the best way to avoid or fix the pain... Page 220

How to choose authentic over *artificial* shoulder movements... Page 223

Why an understanding of *instinctive* human movement can help solve the shoulder pain problem... Page 224

Remove these two elements of pressing—and you will remove virtually all chronic shoulder problems... Page 225

The ultimate solution for safe, pain-free, powerful shoulders... Page 225

The mighty handstand pushup... Page 226

Using the handstand pushup to build *incredibly* powerful, muscularized shoulders in a short span of time... Page 225

How to strengthen the *vestibular system*—using handstand pushups... Page 225

8 secrets to help you perfect your all-important handstand pushup technique... Pages 228–229

Discover the ultimate shoulder and arm exercise... Page 248

Going beyond the one-arm handstand pushup... Page 252

The master of this old technique will have elbows strong as titanium axles... Page 255

The cast iron principles of Convict Conditioning success... Page 259

The missing "x factor" of training success... Page 259

The best ways to warm up... Page 260

How to create training momentum... Page 262

How to put strength in the bank... Page 263

This is the real way to get genuine, lasting strength and power gains... Page 265

Intensity—what it is and what it isn't... Page 265

Why "cycling" or "periodization" is unnecessary with bodyweight training... Page 266

How to make consistent progress... Page 266

5 powerful secrets for busting through your plateaus... Page 267

The nifty little secret of *consolidation* training... Page 268

Living by the buzzer—and the importance of regime... Page 275

5 major *Convict Conditioning* training programs... Page 276

The *New Blood* training program... Page 278

The *Good Behavior* training program... Page 279

The *Veterano* training program... Page 280

The *Solitary Confinement* training program... Page 281

The *Supermax* training program... Page 282

Convict Conditioning

How to Bust Free of All Weakness— Using the Lost Secrets of Supreme Survival Strength

By Paul "Coach" Wade

Book #B41 $39.95

eBook #EB41 $19.95

Paperback 8.5 x 11
320 pages • 191 photos

Dragon Door Customer Acclaim for Paul Wade's Convict Conditioning

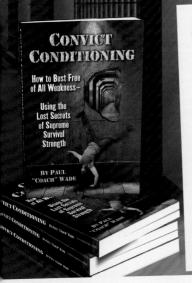

A Strength Training Guide That Will Never Be Duplicated!

"I knew within the first chapter of reading this book that I was in for something special and unique. The last time I felt this same feeling was when reading *Power to the People!* To me this is the Body Weight equivalent to Pavel's masterpiece.

Books like this can never be duplicated. Paul Wade went through a unique set of circumstances of doing time in prison with an 'old time' master of calisthenics. Paul took these lessons from this 70 year old strong man and mastered them over a period of 20 years while 'doing time'. He then taught these methods to countless prisoners and honed his teaching to perfection.

I believe that extreme circumstances like this are what it takes to create a true masterpiece. I know that 'masterpiece' is a strong word, but this is as close as it gets. No other body weight book I have read (and I have a huge fitness library)...comes close to this as far as gaining incredible strength from body weight exercise.

Just like Power to the People, I am sure I will read this over and over again...mastering the principles that Paul Wade took 20 years to master.

Outstanding Book!"—*Rusty Moore - Fitness Black Book - Seattle, WA*

must for all martial artists

a dedicated martial artist for more than seven years, this k is exactly what I've been looking for.

a while now I have trained with machines at my local gym to rove my muscle strength and power and get to the next level in my ning. I always felt that the modern health club, technology based rcise jarred with my martial art though, which only required body vement.

ally this book has come along. At last I can combine perfect body vement for martial skill with perfect body exercise for ultimate ength.

fighting arts are based on body movement. This book is a complete tbook on how to max out your musclepower using only body move- nt, as different from dumbbells, machines or gadgets. For this rea- it belongs on the bookshelf of every serious martial artist, male d female, young and old."—*Gino Cartier - Washington DC*

e packed all of my other training books away!

read CC in one go. I couldn't put it down. I have purchased a lot bodyweight training books in the past, and have always been etty disappointed. They all seem to just have pictures of different ercises, and no plan whatsoever on how to implement them and ogress with them. But not with this one. The information in this ook is AWESOME! I like to have a clear, logical plan of progression follow, and that is what this book gives. I have put all of my other aining books away. CC is the only system I am going to follow. This now my favorite training book ever!"—*Lyndan - Australia*

Brutal Elegance.

"I have been training and reading about training since I first joined the US Navy in the 1960s. I thought I'd seen everything the fitness world had to offer. Sometimes twice. But I was wrong. This book is utterly iconoclastic.

The author breaks down all conceivable body weight exercises into six basic movements, each designed to stimulate different vectors of the muscular system. These six are then elegantly and very intelligently broken into ten progressive techniques. You master one technique, and move on to the next.

The simplicity of this method belies a very powerful and complex training paradigm, reduced into an abstraction that obviously took many years of sweat and toil to develop. Trust me. Nobody else worked this out. This approach is completely unique and fresh.

I have read virtually every calisthenics book printed in America over the last 40 years, and instruction like this can't be found anywhere, in any one of them. *Convict Conditioning* is head and shoulders above them all. In years to come, trainers and coaches will all be talking about 'progressions' and 'progressive calisthenics' and claim they've been doing it all along. But the truth is that Dragon Door bought it to you first. As with kettlebells, they were the trail blazers.

Who should purchase this volume? Everyone who craves fitness and strength should. Even if you don't plan to follow the routines, the book will make you think about your physical prowess, and will give even world class experts food for thought. At the very least if you find yourself on vacation or away on business without your barbells, this book will turn your hotel into a fully equipped gym.

I'd advise any athlete to obtain this work as soon as possible."
—*Bill Oliver - Albany, NY, United States*

More Dragon Door Customer Acclaim for Convict Conditioning

Fascinating Reading and Real Strength

"Coach Wade's system is a real eye opener if you've been a lifetime iron junkie. Wanna find out how really strong (or weak) you are? Get this book and begin working through the 10 levels of the 6 power exercises. I was pleasantly surprised by my ability on a few of the exercises...but some are downright humbling. If I were on a desert island with only one book on strength and conditioning this would be it. (Could I staple Pavel's "Naked Warrior" to the back and count them as one???!) Thanks Dragon Door for this innovative new author."—*Jon Schultheis*, RKC (2005) - Keansburg, NJ

Single best strength training book ever!

"I just turned 50 this year and I have tried a little bit of everything over the years: martial arts, swimming, soccer, cycling, free weights, weight machines, even yoga and Pilates. I started using *Convict Conditioning* right after it came out. I started from the beginning, like Coach Wade says, doing mostly step one or two for five out of the six exercises. I work out 3 to 5 times a week, usually for 30 to 45 minutes.

Long story short, my weight went up 14 pounds (I was not trying to gain weight) but my body fat percentage dropped two percent. That translates into approximately 19 pounds of lean muscle gained in two months! I've never gotten this kind of results with anything else I've ever done. Now I have pretty much stopped lifting weights for strength training. Instead, I lift once a week as a test to see how much stronger I'm getting without weight training. There are a lot of great strength training books in the world (most of them published by Dragon Door), but if I had to choose just one, this is the single best strength training book ever. BUY THIS BOOK. FOLLOW THE PLAN. GET AS STRONG AS YOU WANT. "—*Wayne - Decatur, GA*

Best bodyweight training book so far!

"I'm a martial artist and I've been training for years with a combination of weights and bodyweight training and had good results from both (but had the usual injuries from weight training). I prefer the bodyweight stuff though as it trains me to use my whole body as a unit, much more than weights do, and I notice the difference on the mat and in the ring. Since reading this book I have given the weights a break and focused purely on the bodyweight exercise progressions as described by 'Coach' Wade and my strength had increased more than ever before. So far I've built up to 12 strict one-leg squats each leg and 5 uneven pull ups each arm.

I've never achieved this kind of strength before - and this stuff builds solid muscle mass as well. It's very intense training. I am so confident in and happy with the results I'm getting that I've decided to train for a fitness/bodybuilding comp just using his techniques, no weights, just to show for real what kind of a physique these exercises can build. In sum, I cannot recommend 'Coach' Wade's book highly enough - it is by far the best of its kind ever!"—*Mark Robinson - Australia, currently living in South Korea*

A lifetime of lifting...and continued learning.

"I have been working out diligently since 1988 and played sports in high school and college before that. My stint in the Army saw me doing calisthenics, running, conditioning courses, forced marches, etc. There are many levels of strength and fitness. I have been as big as 240 in my powerlifting/strongman days and as low as 185-190 while in the Army. I think I have tried everything under the sun: the high intensity of Arthur Jones and Dr. Ken, the Super Slow of El Darden, and the brutality of Dinosaur Training Brooks Kubic made famous.

This is one of the BEST books I've ever read on real strength training which also covers other just as important aspects of health; like staying injury free, feeling healthy and becoming flexible. It's an excellent book. He tells you the why and the how with his progressive plan. This book is a GOLD MINE and worth 100 times what I paid for it!"
—*Horst - Woburn, MA*

This book sets the standard, ladies and gentlemen

"It's difficult to describe just how much this book means to me. I've been training hard since I was in the RAF nearly ten years ago, and to say this book is a breakthrough is an understatement. How often do you really read something so new, so fresh? This book contains a complete new system of calisthenics drawn from American prison training methods. When I say 'system' I mean it. It's complete (rank beginner to expert), it's comprehensive (all the exercises and photos are here), it's graded (progressions from exercise to exercise are smooth and pre-determined) and it's totally original. Whether you love or hate the author, you have to listen to him. And you will learn something. This book just makes SENSE. In twenty years people will still be buying it."—Andy McMann - Ponty, Wales, GB

Convict Conditioning
How to Bust Free of All Weakness—Using the Lost Secrets of Supreme Survival Strength
By Paul "Coach" Wade

Book #B41 $39.95
eBook #EB41 $19.95
Paperback 8.5 x 11
320 pages • 191 photos

The Experts Give High Praise to Convict Conditioning 2

"Coach Paul Wade has outdone himself. His first book *Convict Conditioning* is to my mind THE BEST book ever written on bodyweight conditioning. Hands down. Now, with the sequel *Convict Conditioning 2*, Coach Wade takes us even deeper into the subtle nuances of training with the ultimate resistance tool: our bodies.

In plain English, but with an amazing understanding of anatomy, physiology, kinesiology and, go figure, psychology, Coach Wade explains very simply how to work the smaller but just as important areas of the body such as the hands and forearms, neck and calves and obliques in serious functional ways.

His minimalist approach to exercise belies the complexity of his system and the deep insight into exactly how the body works and the best way to get from A to Z in the shortest time possible.

I got the best advice on how to strengthen the hard-to-reach extensors of the hand right away from this exercise Master I have ever seen. It's so simple but so completely functional I can't believe no one else has thought of it yet. Just glad he figured it out for me.

Paul teaches us how to strengthen our bodies with the simplest of movements while at the same time balancing our structures in the same way: simple exercises that work the whole body.

And just as simply as he did with his first book. His novel approach to stretching and mobility training is brilliant and fresh as well as his take on recovery and healing from injury. Sprinkled throughout the entire book are too-many-to-count insights and advice from a man who has come to his knowledge the hard way and knows exactly what he speaks.

This book is, as was his first, an amazing journey into the history of physical culture disguised as a book on calisthenics. But the thing that Coach Wade does better than any before him is his unbelievable progressions on EVERY EXERCISE and stretch! He breaks things down and tells us EXACTLY how to proceed to get to whatever level of strength and development we want. AND gives us the exact metrics we need to know when to go to the next level.

Adding in completely practical and immediately useful insights into nutrition and the mindset necessary to deal not only with training but with life, makes this book a classic that will stand the test of time.

Bravo Coach Wade, Bravo." —**Mark Reifkind**, Master RKC, author of *Mastering the HardStyle Kettlebell Swing*

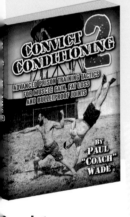

Convict Conditioning 2

Advanced Prison Training Tactics for Muscle Gain, Fat Loss and Bulletproof Joints
By Paul "Coach" Wade

Book #B59 $39.95
eBook #EB59 $19.95
Paperback 8.5 x 11
354 pages • 261 photos

"The overriding principle of *Convict Conditioning* 2 is 'little equipment-big rewards'. For the athlete in the throwing and fighting arts, the section on Lateral Chain Training, Capturing the Flag, is a unique and perhaps singular approach to training the obliques and the whole family of side muscles. This section stood out to me as ground breaking and well worth the time and energy by anyone to review and attempt to complete. Literally, this is a new approach to lateral chain training that is well beyond sidebends and suitcase deadlifts.

The author's review of passive stretching reflects the experience of many of us in the field. But, his solution might be the reason I am going to recommend this work for everyone: The Trifecta. This section covers what the author calls The Functional Triad and gives a series of simple progressions to three holds that promise to oil your joints. It's yoga for the strength athlete and supports the material one would find, for example, in Pavel's *Loaded Stretching*.

I didn't expect to like this book, but I come away from it practically insisting that everyone read it. It is a strongman book mixed with yoga mixed with street smarts. I wanted to hate it, but I love it."
—**Dan John**, author of *Don't Let Go* and co-author of *Easy Strength*

"I've been lifting weights for over 50 years and have trained in the martial arts since 1965. I've read voraciously on both subjects, and written dozens of magazine articles and many books on the subjects. This book and Wade's first, *Convict Conditioning*, are by far the most commonsense, information-packed, and result producing I've read. These books will truly change your life.

Paul Wade is a new and powerful voice in the strength and fitness arena, one that is commonsense, inspiring, and in your face. His approach to maximizing your body's potential is not the same old hackneyed material you find in every book and magazine piece that pictures steroid-bloated models screaming as they curl weights. Wade's stuff has been proven effective by hard men who don't tolerate fluff. It will work for you, too—guaranteed.

As an ex-cop, I've gone mano-y-mano with ex-cons that had clearly trained as Paul Wade suggests in his two *Convict Conditioning* books. While these guys didn't look like steroid-fueled bodybuilders (actually, there were a couple who did), all were incredibly lean, hard and powerful. Wade blows many commonly held beliefs about conditioning, strengthening, and eating out of the water and replaces them with result-producing information that won't cost you a dime." —**Loren W. Christensen**, author of *Fighting the Pain Resistant Attacker*, and many other titles

"*Convict Conditioning* is one of the most influential books I ever got my hands on. *Convict Conditioning 2* took my training and outlook on the power of bodyweight training to the 10th degree—from strengthening the smallest muscles in a maximal manner, all the way to using bodyweight training as a means of healing injuries that pile up from over 22 years of aggressive lifting.

I've used both *Convict Conditioning* and *Convict Conditioning 2* on myself and with my athletes. Without either of these books I can easily say that these boys would not be the BEASTS they are today. Without a doubt *Convict Conditioning 2* will blow you away and inspire and educate you to take bodyweight training to a whole NEW level."
—**Zach Even-Esh**, Underground Strength Coach

Online Praise for Convict Conditioning 2

Best Sequel Since The Godfather 2!

"Hands down the best addition to the material on *Convict Conditioning* that could possibly be put out. I already implemented the neck bridges, calf and hand training to my weekly schedule, and as soon as my handstand pushups and leg raises are fully loaded I'll start the flags. Thank you, Coach!"

— Daniel Runkel, Rio de Janeiro, Brazil

Just as brilliant as its predecessor!

"Just as brilliant as its predecessor! The new exercises add to the Big 6 in a keep-it-simple kind of way. Anyone who will put in the time with both of these masterpieces will be as strong as humanly possible. I especially liked the parts on grip work. To me, that alone was worth the price of the entire book."

—Timothy Stovall / Evansville, Indiana

The progressions were again sublime

"Never have I heard such in depth and yet easy to understand description of training and physical culture. A perfect complement to the first book although it has its own style keeping the best attributes of style from the first but developing it to something unique. The progressions were again sublime and designed for people at all levels of ability. The two books together can forge what will closely resemble superhuman strength and an incredible physique and yet the steps to get there are so simple and easy to understand."

—Ryan O., Nottingham, United Kingdom

If you liked CC1, you'll love CC2

"*CC2* picks up where *CC1* left off with great information about the human flag (including a version called the clutch flag, that I can actually do now), neck and forearms. I couldn't be happier with this book."

—Justin B., Atlanta, Georgia

Well worth the wait

"Another very interesting, and as before, opinionated book by Paul Wade. As I work through the CC1 progressions, I find it's paying off at a steady if unspectacular rate, which suits me just fine. No training injuries worth the name, convincing gains in strength. I expect the same with *CC2* which rounds off CC1 with just the kind of material I was looking for. Wade and Dragon Door deserve to be highly commended for publishing these techniques. A tremendous way to train outside of the gym ecosystem."

—V. R., Bangalore, India

From the almost laughably-simple to realm-of-the-gods

"*Convict Conditioning 2* is a great companion piece to the original Convict Conditioning. It helps to further build up the athlete and does deliver on phenomenal improvement with minimal equipment and space.

The grip work is probably the superstar of the book. Second, maybe, is the attention devoted to the lateral muscles with the development of the clutch- and press-flag.

Convict Conditioning 2 is more of the same - more of the systematic and methodical improvement in exercises that travel smoothly from the almost laughably-simple to realm-of-the-gods. It is a solid addition to any fitness library."

—Robert Aldrich, Chapel Hill, GA

Very Informative

"*Convict Conditioning 2* is more subversive training information in the same style as its original. It's such a great complement to the original, but also solid enough on its own. The information in this book is fantastic-- a great buy! Follow this program, and you will get stronger."

—Chris B., Thunder Bay, Canada

Brilliant

"Convict Conditioning books are all the books you need in life. As Bruce Lee used to say, it's not a daily increase but a daily decrease. Same with life. Too many things can lead you down many paths, but to have Simplicity is perfect."

—Brandon Lynch, London, England

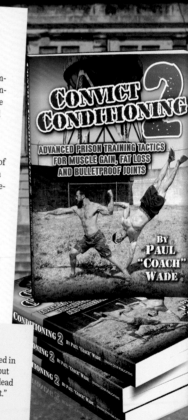

Convict Conditioning 2

Advanced Prison Training Tactics for Muscle Gain, Fat Los[s] and Bulletproof Join[ts]

By Paul "Coach" Wad[e]

Book #B59 $39.95
eBook #EB59 $19.95
Paperback 8.5 x 11
354 pages • 261 photos

–TABLE OF CONTENTS –

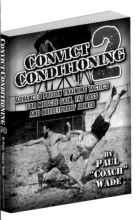

Foreword
The Many Roads to Strength by Brooks Kubik

Opening Salvo: *Chewing Bubblegum and Kicking Ass*

1. Introduction: *Put Yourself Behind Bars*

Convict Conditioning 2
Advanced Prison Training Tac-ics for Muscle Gain, Fat Loss nd Bulletproof Joints
By Paul "Coach" Wade

Book #B59 $39.95
Book #EB59 $19.95
aperback 8.5 x 11
54 pages • 261 photos

PART I: SHOTGUN MUSCLE

Hands and Forearms

2: Iron Hands and Forearms: *Ultimate Strength –with Just Two Techniques*

3: The Hang Progressions: *A Vice-Like Bodyweight Grip Course*

4: Advanced Grip Torture: *Explosive Power + Titanium Fingers*

5: Fingertip Pushups: *Keeping Hand Strength Balanced*

6: Forearms into Firearms: *Hand Strength: A Summary and a Challenge*

Lateral Chain

7: Lateral Chain Training: *Capturing the Flag*

8: The Clutch Flag: *In Eight Easy Steps*

9: The Press Flag: *In Eight Not-So-Easy Steps*

Neck and Calves

10. Bulldog Neck: *Bulletproof Your Weakest Link*

11. Calf Training: *Ultimate Lower Legs–No Machines Necessary*

PART II: BULLETPROOF JOINTS

12. Tension-Flexibility: *The Lost Art of Joint Training*

13: Stretching–the Prison Take: *Flexibility, Mobility, Control*

14. The Trifecta: *Your "Secret Weapon" for Mobilizing Stiff, Battle-Scarred Physiques–for Life*

15: The Bridge Hold Progressions: *The Ultimate Prehab/Rehab Technique*

16: The L-Hold Progressions: *Cure Bad Hips and Low Back–Inside-Out*

17: Twist Progressions: *Unleash Your Functional Triad*

PART III: WISDOM FROM CELLBLOCK G

18. Doing Time Right: *Living the Straight Edge*

19. The Prison Diet: *Nutrition and Fat Loss Behind Bars*

20. Mendin' Up: *The 8 Laws of*

Healing

21. The Mind: *Escaping the True Prison*

!BONUS CHAPTER!

Are You Dissatisfied With Your Abs?

"Diamond-Cut Abs condenses decades of agonizing lessons and insight into the best book on ab-training ever written. Hands down." —**PAUL WADE**, author of *Convict Conditioning*

A re you dissatisfied with your abs? Does it seem a distant dream for you to own a rock-solid center? Can you only hanker in vain for the chiseled magnificence of a Greek statue? Have you given up on owning the tensile functionality and explosive power of a cage-fighter's core?

According to Danny Kavadlo, training your abs is a whole-life endeavor. It's about right eating, right drinking, right rest, right practice, right exercise at the right time, right motivation, right inspiration, right attitude and right lifestyle. If you don't have that righteous set of abs in place, it's because you have failed in one or more of these areas.

With his 25-plus years of rugged research and extreme physical dedication into every dimension of what it takes to earn world-class abs, Danny Kavadlo is a modern-day master of the art. It's all here: over 50 of the best-ever exercises to develop the abs—from beginner to superman level—inspirational photos, no BS straight talk on nutrition and lifestyle factors and clear-

cut instructions on what to do, when. Supply the grit, follow the program and you simply cannot fail but to build a monstrous mid-section.

In our culture, Abs are the Measure of a Man. To quit on your abs is to quit on your masculinity—like it or not. *Diamond-Cut Abs* gives you the complete, whole-life program you need to reassert yourself and reestablish your respect as a true physical specimen—with a thunderous six-pack to prove it.

Are You Dissatisfied With Your Abs?

In the Abs Gospel According to Danny, training your abs is a whole-life endeavor. It's about right eating, right drinking, right rest, right practice, right exercise at the right time, right motivation, right inspiration, right attitude and right lifestyle.

So, yes, all of this Rightness gets covered in *Diamond-Cut Abs*. But let's not confuse Right with Rigid. Apprentice in the Danny School of Abs and it's like apprenticing with a world-class Chef—a mix of incredible discipline, inspired creativity and a passionate love-affair with your art.

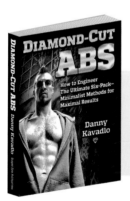

"Danny has done it again! *Diamond-Cut Abs* is a no-nonsense, results driven approach that delivers all the goods on abs. Nutrition, training and progression are all included, tattoos optional!"— ROBB WOLF, author of *The Paleo Solution*

"There are a lot of abs books and products promising a six-pack. What sets Danny's book apart is the realistic and reasonable first section of the book... His insights into nutrition are so simple and sound, there is a moment you wish this book was a stand alone dieting book."—DAN JOHN, author of *Never Let Go*

Diamond-Cut Abs
How to Engineer the Ultimate Six-Pack— Minimalist Methods for Maximum Results
By Danny Kavadlo

Book #B77 $39.95
eBook #EB77 $19.95
Paperback 8.5 x 11
230 pages, 305 photos

⬇ Here's a Taste of What You'll Get When You Invest in *Diamond-Cut Abs* ⬇

Part I An Abs Odyssey
Chapter 1 Cultural Obsession

- Why there is no one-size-fits-all program for training your abs...3
- Danny's big promise: why you will get everything you need to know about sculpting and maintaining amazingly defined and beautiful abs...4

Chapter 2 Abs Defined

- You cannot fake the funk—getting clear about what it'll take to Man up and earn that six-pack of your dreams...11
- The What of the What: basic anatomy and function: know your abs-tech details so you know what you are working on...12—15
- What the core really consists of...it's more than most people think...15

Chapter 3 Personal Obsession

- The extreme value of push-ups and pull-ups for Danny-like abs...18
- Danny Obsessed: 300 reps, 5 days a week for 10 years = close on 8 million reps!— yet Danny's functionally stronger and aesthetically more appealing NOW with WAY less reps. Discover why...19
- Danny's personal mission for you: distinguish the fitness BS from the hype...21
- Why protein supplements are a waste of money...21

Part II Nutritional Musings
Chapter 4 Primordial Soup

- How to bring back the joy to your fitness-nutrition program...28
- Why you need to develop and maintain a love affair with food—if you want that manly six-pack...

Chapter 5 Common Sense Versus Over-compartmentalization

- Why what we eat is single most important decision we can make about our abs...31
- Why Danny's Dietary Advice has proved 100% effective for those who have followed it...33
- The 3 golden keys you must consider when choosing the right foods to feed your abs...35
- Why you should eat THESE fats every day for great abs...36
- Why sugar is the #1 nutritional enemy of defined abs...37
- Why Danny's abs were at an all-time best after 90 days without THESE two nutrients...39
- Why you should eat organ meat, for an extra edge in your abs training...42
- Why you need FAR less protein in your diet...44

Chapter 6 Weighing in on Weight Loss

- The 3 major keys to successful fat reduction...48
- How to shed body fat now...48
- Why a food's fat content has no bearing on whether it will fatten you...49
- Why you should ignore the BMI...50
- The role of sacrifice in obtaining ripped abs...50

Chapter 7 What I Eat

- The secret of "mostly"...54
- For the love and care of food...54
- Danny's 3-Day sample food log...56—57

Chapter 8 The Fat and the Curious

- The 4 Steps of the Beginner's Cleanse...60
- Fruit n Veggie Cleanse—optimal duration of...61
- Juice Fast...62
- The 7-Day Plan—Fruit n Veggie/Juice fast...62
- Danny's 4 favorite juices...63
- The True Fast...63
- The Absolute Fast...64
- 4 big tips for safe and successful fasting...64

Chapter 9 More Food for Thought

- The perils of genetically and chemically compromised foods...67—69
- How to avoid toxins in your food...69
- Food's most powerful secret ingredient...69

Chapter 10 Top Tips for Tip Top Abs

- Why water is SO important for your abs...72

Part III Training Your Abs
Chapter 11 Make an Executive Decision

- Why and how your abs training should be like a martial art ...79

Chapter 12 Fundamentals of Abdominal Strength Training

- The 10 Principles you must follow for every rep of every exercise...83—89
- THIS principle makes you stronger, more shredded and more anatomically aware...83
- THE #1 Principle you'll need to employ for spectacular abs...91

Chapter 13 On Cardio

- The limitations of cardio for abs training—and what you should do instead...93—97

Part IV The Exercises

- Each drill comes with explanatory text, recommended set/rep range plus a specialized Trainer Tip

Chapter 14 Danny, What Do You Do?

- Danny's 50+ best abs and abs-related training exercises...101

Chapter 15 Core Curriculum

- Crucial exercises for overall gains...105
- How to perform the perfect squat—the most functional exercise on the planet...105
- How to perform the perfect push-up—the ultimate upper-body exercise...108
- How to perform the perfect pull-up...111—112

Chapter 16 Beginner Abs

- Full Body Tension Drill...116
- How to have complete body awareness through progressive, isometric tensing...116
- The Plank...117
- The Side Plank—to emphasize the obliques and lateral chain...119
- Lying Bent Knee leg Raise...120
- Lying Knee Tuck...121
- Sit-Up...122
- Modified Side Jackknife—to help beginners target their obliques...123
- Crossover...124
- Bicycle...125
- Straight Arm/Straight Leg Crossover...126
- V-Leg Toe Touch...127
- Why No Crunches?—And the #1 reason not to bother with them...127

Chapter 17 Intermediate Abs

- Unstable Plank—a fun way to add an extra challenge to the traditional isometric standard... 130
- Seated Knee Raise—the missing link between floor-based and bar-based abs training...131

"As soon as I received *Diamond-Cut Abs*, I flipped to the table of contents. Amazingly I found what I have been fruitlessly looking for in ab books for decades: 66 pages dedicated to NUTRITION. Kavadlo passed his second Marty audition by not echoing all the bankrupt politically-correct, lock-step, mainstream nutritional commandments. When Dan starts riffing about eating like a horse, eating ample amounts of red meat, shellfish and the divine pig meat (along with all kinds any types of nutrient-dense food), I knew I had to give my first ever ab book endorsement. When he noted that he drank whiskey while getting his abs into his all time best shape, it sealed the deal for me. Oh, and the ab exercises are excellent."
—**MARTY GALLAGHER**, 3-Time Powerlifting Champion, Author of *The Purposeful Primitive*

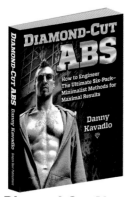

- The N-Sit—an iso that helps set you up for the L-Sit...132
- Jackknife—a fighter's favorite and a most excellent motha for firing up those deeper abs muscles, building better full body co-ordination—and progressing to the Dragon Flag and Hanging Straight Leg Raise...133
- Side Jackknife—masochists will welcome intensifying their abdominal agony when they flip the great classic on its side...134
- Advanced Sit-Up—Bad Boy Danny's tweaks will up the ante here in a pleasantly nasty way (curses optional)...135
- Lying Straight Leg Raise—and how to make it even harder...136
- Grounded Wiper...137
- Danny adores the classic Windshield Wiper—but it's a helluva challenge. The GW helps you rehearse the movement pattern before taking on the full-on manliness of the WW...137
- Throwdown...138
- Here's another old school classic that should be part of any serious practitioner's arsenal. The explosivity will have your whole body screaming in indignation—fortunately...138
- Side Plank Hip Raise—notorious for being deceptively challenging, includes leverage tips to progress the hardness...139
- How to Hang...140
- How to grip the bar to really squeeze the most out of every rep...140
- Why you should avoid Assistance Straps—and the better alternatives...140
- How to employ a flex hang to add a unique neurological twist and increase your upper body muscle activation—Highly Recommended by da Abs Bossman!...140
- Hanging Contest...141
- A fun competitive spin on hanging—but here's some important tips on how to keep it real...141
- One Arm Hang...142
- Did someone shout Man Maker? The OAH is a total body drill that will make the boys cry and the men grin with pain—plus bonus tips for optimal vengeance on that brutalized six-pack...142
- Ab Wheel Roll Out (Bent Knee)...143
- An old time classic—incorporates stability, strength and focus in a truly unique way...143
- Hanging Bicycle—last step before conquering the Hanging Knee Raise, plus common mistakes and how to fix them...144
- Hanging Knee Raise—one of the most important of all abdominal exercises. Master it here...145

Chapter 18 Advanced Abs
- SERIOUS training now! These moves are all full-on, full-body. Emphasis is on every cell in your bod. No mercy. Tremendous demand on the abs—requires heavy-duty injection of Will, complete harmony of mind and muscle, steely strength. Think you are a Man? Measure your Manliness here and report back...
- The L-Sit—you will feel it everywhere. How to do it and how to extract the ultimate mechanical advantage...147–148
- Gecko Hold—a "limited contact" plank that poses a unique strength challenge. A ripped six-pack is meaningless without the strength to back it up—get that strength with the GH...149
- Ab Wheel Roll Out (Straight Leg)—incredibly challenging for all levels, full body tension is key, regressions included for ramping up to complete studliness...150
- Hanging Leg Raise—one of Danny's favorites, for good reason, 6 controlled reps and you're doin' good...151
- Washing Machine—this infamous move is a key step to mastering the mighty Windshield Wiper, regressions and progressions to full MANitude provided...152
- Windshield Wiper—brace yourself buddy, the going just got a whole lot harder. Builds and requires tremendous upper body strength...153
- V-Leg Wiper—ho! This is a true brutalizer of the core plus a helluva glute-banger, to boot...154
- Perfect Circle—an exaggerated WW for the MEN who can hack it ...155
- Skinning the Cat—a precursor to many extreme bar calisthenics moves and a phenomenal abs exercise in its own right, with some optional grip strategies...156
- One Arm Flex Hang—this just about breaks the mercury on the Achievometer, hyper-challenging, requires an incredibly strong upper body ...157
- Dragon Flag—one of the all-time sexiest moves on the planet and a Bruce Lee trademark, you gotta get this one down if you want to truly strut your Man Stuff. Bad Boy Danny likes to hold it for an iso. Can you?...158
- Tuck Front Lever—this regressed version of the Front Lever still requires a brutal level of upper body power. Have at it!...159
- V-Leg Front Lever—another extremely difficult move, with some favorable leverage variations to help progress it...160
- Front Lever—this one tops the Manometer for sure. A masterful and utterly unforgiving move that will simultaneously tortu[...] your abs, lats, glutes, arms, shoulders an[...] everything in between. No mercy here a[...] hopefully, none asked for...161

Chapter 19 Supplemental Stretches
- Why stretching IS important—and the 9 surefire benefits you'll gain from right stretching...173
- The Hands Up—the 4 main benefits to t[...] Danny's first stretch before a workout...[...]
- Forward, back and Side-to-Side Bend...[...]
- Hands Down—another fantastic stretch the entire front of the body...176

Chapter 20 Workouts
- 9 sample combinations for different levels—a beginning guideline...181–185
- On the importance of mixing it up and shocking the system...181

Part V Abs and Lifestyle
Chapter 21 Viva La Vida
- Abs and the quality of your life...190
- A life-oriented approach to training...191

Chapter 22 The Mud and the Blood and the Beer
- Coffee, alcohol and other beverages—ho[...] to handle in regard to your training...193–195

Chapter 23 Seasons
- How to adopt and adapt your training to the changing seasons...198

Diamond-Cut Abs
How to Engineer the Ultimate Six-Pack—Minimalist Methods for Maximum Results
By Danny Kavadlo

Book #B77 $39.95
eBook #EB77 $19.95
Paperback 8.5 x 11
230 pages, 305 photos

Reader Praise for Convict Conditioning Ultimate Bodyweight Training Log

Above and Beyond!

"Not JUST a log book. TONS of great and actually useful info. I really like to over complicate programming and data entries at times. And honestly, All one has to do is fill in the blanks... Well that and DO THE WORK. Great product."
—**NOEL PRICE, Chicagoland, IL**

A unique training log

"This log book is one of a kind in the world. It is the only published body weight exclusive training log I have personally seen. It is well structured and provides everything for a log book in a primarily body weight oriented routine. The book is best integrated with the other books in the convict conditioning series however has enough information to act as a stand alone unit. It is a must have for anyone who is a fan of the convict conditioning series or is entering into calisthenics."
—**CARTER D., Cambridge, Canada**

Excellent Companion to
Convict Conditioning 1 & 2

"This is an amazing book! If you are a fan of Convict Conditioning (1 & 2) you need to get this training log. If you are preparing for the Progressive Calisthenics Certification then it's a must-have!!! The spiral bound format is a huge improvement over the regular binding and it makes it that much more functional for use in the gym. Great design, amazing pictures and additional content! Once again - Great job Dragon Door!"
—**MICHAEL KRIVKA, RKC Team Leader, Gaithersburg, MD**

Excellent latest addition to the CC Program!

"A terrific book to keep you on track and beyond. Thank you again for this incredible series!"
—**JOSHUA HATCHER, Holyoke, MA**

Calling this a Log Book is Selling it Short

"I thought, what is the big deal about a logbook! Seriously mistaken. It is a work of art and with tips on each page that would be a great book all by itself. Get it. It goes way beyond a log book...the logging part of this book is just a bonus. You must have this!"—**JON ENGUM, Brainerd, MN**

The Ultimate Bodyweight Conditioning

"I have started to incorporate bodyweight training into my strength building when I am not going to the gym. At the age of 68, after 30 years in the gym the 'Convict Conditioning Log' is going to be a welcome new training challenge."
—**WILLIAM HAYDEN, Winter Park, FL**

Convict Conditioning Ultimate Bodyweight Training Log
By Paul "Coach" Wade

Book #B67 $29.95
eBook #EB67 $19.95
Paperback (spiral bound) 6 x 9
290 pages • 175 photos

1•800•899•5111 • 24HOURS
FAX YOUR ORDER (866) 280-7619
ORDERING INFORMATION

Telephone Orders For faster service you may place your orders by calling Toll Free 24 hours a day, 7 days a week, 365 days per year. When you call, please have your credit card ready.

Customer Service Questions? Please call us between 9:00am– 11:00pm EST Monday to Friday at 1-800-899-5111. Local and foreign customers call 513-346-4160 for orders and customer service

100% One-Year Risk-Free Guarantee. If you are not completely satisfied with any product—we'll be happy to give you a prompt exchange, credit, or refund, as you wish. Simply return your purchase to us, and please let us know why you were dissatisfied--it will help us to provide better products and services in the future. Shipping and handling fees are non-refundable.

COMPLETE AND MAIL WITH FULL PAYMENT TO: DRAGON
DOOR PUBLICATIONS, 5 COUNTY ROAD B EAST, SUITE 3, LITTLE CANADA, MN 55117

Please print clearly
Sold To:
A

Name_____

Street_____

City_____

State _____ Zip _____

Please print clearly
Sold To: (Street address for delivery) **B**

Name_____

Street _____

City _____

State _____ Zip _____

Email_____

WARNING TO FOREIGN CUSTOMERS:

The Customs in your country may or may not tax or otherwise charge you an additional fee for goods you receive. Dragon Door Publications is charging you only for U.S. handling and international shipping. Dragon Door Publications is in no way responsible for any additional fees levied by Customs, the carrier or any other entity.

Item #	Qty.	Item Description	Item Price	A or B	Total

HANDLING AND SHIPPING CHARGES • NO CODS
Total Amount of Order Add (Excludes kettlebells and kettlebell kits):

$00.00 to 29.99	Add $7.00	$100.00 to 129.99	Add $14.00
$30.00 to 49.99	Add $6.00	$130.00 to 169.99	Add $16.00
$50.00 to 69.99	Add $8.00	$170.00 to 199.99	Add $18.00
$70.00 to 99.99	Add $11.00	$200.00 to 299.99	Add $20.00
		$300.00 and up	Add $24.00

Canada and Mexico add $6.00 to US charges. All other countries, flat rate, double US Charges. See Kettlebell section for Kettlebell Shipping and handling charges.

Total of Goods	
Shipping Charges	
Rush Charges	
Kettlebell Shipping Charges	
OH residents add 6.5%	
sales tax	
MN residents add 6.5% sales	

METHOD OF PAYMENT ___CHECK ___M.O. ___MASTERCARD ___VISA ___DISCOVER ___AMEX

Account No. (Please indicate all the numbers on your credit card)   EXPIRATION DATE

☐☐☐☐ ☐☐☐☐ ☐☐☐☐ ☐☐☐☐   ☐☐/☐☐

Day Phone: _____

Signature: _____ Date: _____

NOTE: We ship best method available for your delivery address. Foreign orders are sent by air. Credit card or International M.O. only. **For RUSH processing** of your order, add an additional $10.00 per address. Available on money order & charge card orders only.

Errors and omissions excepted. Prices subject to change without notice.

1•800•899•5111 • 24HOURS

FAX YOUR ORDER (866) 280-7619

ORDERING INFORMATION

Telephone Orders For faster service you may place your orders by calling Toll Free 24 hours a day, 7 days a week, 365 days per year. When you call, please have your credit card ready.

Customer Service Questions? Please call us between 9:00am– 11:00pm EST Monday to Friday at 1-800-899-5111. Local and foreign customers call 513-346-4160 for orders and customer service

100% One-Year Risk-Free Guarantee. If you are not completely satisfied with any product—we'll be happy to give you a prompt exchange, credit, or refund, as you wish. Simply return your purchase to us, and please let us know why you were dissatisfied--it will help us to provide better products and services in the future. Shipping and handling fees are non-refundable.

COMPLETE AND MAIL WITH FULL PAYMENT TO: DRAGON DOOR PUBLICATIONS, 5 COUNTY ROAD B EAST, SUITE 3, LITTLE CANADA, MN 55117

Please print clearly
Sold To:
A

Name_____

Street_____

City_____

State _____ Zip _____

Please print clearly
Sold To: (Street address for delivery) **B**

Name_____

Street_____

City_____

State _____ Zip _____

Email_____

WARNING TO FOREIGN CUSTOMERS:

The Customs in your country may or may not tax or otherwise charge you an additional fee for goods you receive. Dragon Door Publications is charging you only for U.S. handling and international shipping. Dragon Door Publications is in no way responsible for any additional fees levied by Customs, the carrier or any other entity.

ITEM #	QTY.	ITEM DESCRIPTION	ITEM PRICE	A OR B	TOTAL

HANDLING AND SHIPPING CHARGES • NO CODS

Total Amount of Order Add (Excludes kettlebells and kettlebell kits):

$00.00 to 29.99	Add $7.00	$100.00 to 129.99	Add $14.00
$30.00 to 49.99	Add $6.00	$130.00 to 169.99	Add $16.00
$50.00 to 69.99	Add $8.00	$170.00 to 199.99	Add $18.00
$70.00 to 99.99	Add $11.00	$200.00 to 299.99	Add $20.00
		$300.00 and up	Add $24.00

Canada and Mexico add $6.00 to US charges. All other countries, flat rate, double US Charges. See Kettlebell section for Kettlebell Shipping and handling charges.

Total of Goods	
Shipping Charges	
Rush Charges	
Kettlebell Shipping Charges	
OH residents add 6.5%	
sales tax	
MN residents add 6.5% sales	

METHOD OF PAYMENT ___CHECK ___M.O. ___MASTERCARD ___VISA ___DISCOVER ___AMEX

Account No. (Please indicate all the numbers on your credit card)   EXPIRATION DATE

☐☐☐☐ ☐☐☐☐ ☐☐☐☐ ☐☐☐☐ ☐☐☐☐   ☐☐/☐☐

Day Phone: _____

Signature: _____ Date: _____

NOTE: We ship best method available for your delivery address. Foreign orders are sent by air. Credit card or International M.O. only. **For RUSH processing** of your order, add an additional $10.00 per address. Available on money order & charge card orders only.

Errors and omissions excepted. Prices subject to change without notice.